THE ECONOMIC HISTORY
OF ENGLAND
(1760–1860)

The Economic History of England
1760-1860

ARTHUR REDFORD, M.A., Ph.D.
*Formerly Professor of Economic History
in the University of Manchester*

GREENWOOD PRESS, PUBLISHERS
WESTPORT, CONNECTICUT

Library of Congress Cataloging in Publication Data

Redford, Arthur.
    The economic history of England, 1760-1860.

    Reprint of the 2d ed. published by Longmans, London,
in series: The economic history of Great Britain.
    Bibliography: p.
    1. Great Britain--Economic conditions--1760-1860.
2. Great Britain--Social conditions. 3. Great Britain
--Industries--History. I. Title. II. Series: The
economic history of Great Britain.
HC254.5.R37 1974   330.9'42   73-15244
ISBN 0-8371-7166-0

Second edition © *Arthur Redford 1960*

This edition originally published in 1960 by Longmans, London

Reprinted with the permission of Longman Group Limited

Reprinted in 1974 by Greenwood Press,
a division of Williamhouse-Regency Inc.

Library of Congress Catalog Card Number 73-15244

ISBN 0-8371-7166-0

Printed in the United States of America

PREFACE TO THE SECOND EDITION, 1960

IT IS NOW nearly thirty years since the first edition of this book appeared, and in the meantime economic historians have been extremely active in both research and publication. A few minor changes have been made in successive impressions of the first edition; the text of this new edition has been more radically revised in an attempt to incorporate major advances in our knowledge of the period without altering the established framework of the book. Particular reference has been made to recent books and articles on controversial points, and the list of works for further reading and reference, with which the book ends, has been revised and enlarged. While the new edition has been in preparation, the following relevant books have been published:

T. S. Ashton, *Economic Fluctuations in England, 1700–1800* (1959).

L. S. Pressnell (ed.) *Studies in the Industrial Revolution: presented to T. S. Ashton* (1960).

N. J. Smelser, *Social Change in the Industrial Revolution: an application of theory to the Lancashire Cotton Industry, 1770–1840* (1959).

By the time that the new edition is published, many other relevant works will doubtless have appeared; from this point the reader must collaborate in the endless task of revision.

The main burden of preparing the new edition has been shouldered by my colleague Dr. W. H. Chaloner. His emendations (together with my own) will be found dispersed throughout the book; but he has given especially important help in re-shaping the first chapter, in expanding the bibliography, and in revising the index. As originally planned, the book was to follow a companion volume dealing with the century 1660–1760; I was therefore constrained not to say much about the earlier eighteenth century, lest I should encroach on another writer's preserve. The earlier volume has never appeared, however, and it is therefore now justifiable (and even necessary) to give a more adequate account of the forces which were already changing the economic structure of the country before 1760.

I am very grateful to Dr. Chaloner for using his abounding energy to give a longer life to my book. I have worked with him at every stage in the work of revision, and where we have disagreed he has allowed me to have the last word; nevertheless, I could not have carried through the task under my own steam. I accept full responsibility for any errors which remain in the book, and for its many shortcomings. It still remains impossible, as it was thirty years ago, to pour a quart of ale into a pint pot. Dissatisfied aleconners may shy their brickbats at me; all bouquets should be presented to Dr. Chaloner. About the help given by my other friends and colleagues I can only repeat what I have already said in another place: I wish that I could do as much for them as they have done for me.

ARTHUR REDFORD

PREFACE TO THE FIRST EDITION

A SHORT BOOK does not need a long preface. In seventy thousand words I have tried to tell the plain truth about the most controversial century in the economic history of England; and in doing this I have tried to avoid controversy. In its main outlines the book is based on monographs and other authoritative works published within the last ten years; but on many points of detail I have ventured to supplement (and in some cases to correct) my secondary authorities by independent reference to original sources. To acknowledge all my debts to other writers by means of footnotes would be impracticable, and is perhaps not called for in a work of this size; I hope that the list of books at the end will be accepted as a partial compensation for the lack of more detailed references.

Several of my academic colleagues have assisted me by reading the book during its progress through the press. Professor G. W. Daniels read the proofs, and gave me sympathetic encouragement mingled with kindly criticism. Mr. T. S. Ashton corrected some serious errors in the chapters on financial subjects. Mr. H. L. Beales, of the London School of Economics, pointed out several weak points in my treatment of social questions. Principal J. F. Rees has not only given skilful editorial help at every stage of my work, but has shown a keen personal interest in discussing the economic problems of the period. My wife has shown unwearying patience in detecting ambiguities and verbal errors. Finally, I must thank the University of Birmingham for inviting me to examine an early draft of Mr. E. Roll's important book on the history of the firm of Boulton and Watt; and I am especially grateful to Mr. A. P. Wadsworth and Miss Julia Mann for allowing me to read in typescript their monumental work on the early development of the Lancashire textile industries.

ARTHUR REDFORD

MANCHESTER, *August* 1931

CONTENTS

Part One

THE GROWTH OF INDUSTRIALISM
(1760–1815)

Part Two

THE AGE OF REFORMS
(1815–1860)

PART I
THE GROWTH OF INDUSTRIALISM
(1760–1815)

CHAPTER ONE

The Birth of the Modern Industrial Economy

THE CAUSES OF the movement known as "the Industrial Revolution"[1] have now been sought by scholars for nearly three generations, and as yet there seems to be little agreement as to why the rapid increase in the rate of economic development which marked the period 1760–1830 in England should occur when it did. Some historians, following Adam Smith, have tried to explain it as the fruit of widening markets, both external and internal, others as the result of changes in the rate of capital accumulation, and yet others, ignoring parallel developments in other countries of Western Europe, have seen it mainly in terms of the rapid growth of population in England during the eighteenth and early nineteenth centuries. If these discussions have as yet led to little agreement on the part of scholars, at least they have revealed the inadequacy of the once widely held belief that England in 1760 possessed an undeveloped and immature economy. On the other hand, the only available index of industrial production suggests that the steep upward turn in the curve of industrial output came in the 1780s rather than around 1760.[2]

The fundamental stimulus to industrial change and technological innovation in England during the seventeenth and

[1] This phrase appears to have been first used in its modern meaning in 1837 by the French economist J. A. Blanqui (Sir George Clark, *The Idea of the Industrial Revolution*, 1953, p. 10).
[2] W. Hoffmann, *British Industry, 1700–1950*, 1955, pp. 30–32: for a discussion of Hoffmann's conclusions, see W. A. Cole, 'The measurement of industrial growth', *Economic History Review*, December 1958, pp. 312–13.

eighteenth centuries arose almost certainly from the effects of that progressive widening of the world's markets which followed the geographical discoveries of the fifteenth and sixteenth centuries, acting upon the highly specialised economy of a country rich in coal and metallic ores, and endowed with an enterprising and adaptable people.

By 1713 England had become the dominating sea-power of the western world, and had established an overseas empire of great economic importance. The population and total wealth of this overseas empire increased rapidly between 1660 and 1760, aided, as far as the North American and West Indian plantations were concerned, by free immigration, the importation of indentured labour, and the operation of the slave trade. From 1650–63, thanks to the Navigation and Staple Acts, this expanding market became, legally at any rate, the exclusive preserve of English merchants and shipowners and a growing outlet for the products of enterprising English manufacturers. The century after 1660 witnessed the phenomenal growth of Liverpool, a steady increase in the trade of Bristol, and a general stimulus to the trade of other ports which faced the Americas.[1] London, the home of rapidly growing banking and insurance services, still retained its unquestioned primacy among the country's ports, and continued to hold the profitable monopoly of the East India Company's trade. Growing imports of colonial sugar, tobacco and cotton, both for internal consumption and for re-export to Western Europe, widened the basis of England's economy and raised the standard of comfort of her people. Between 1696 and 1760 the volume of English imports and exports more than doubled, and the same was true of shipping cleared outwards from English ports.[2] As regards the

[1] C. N. Parkinson, *The Rise of the Port of Liverpool*, 1952; E. Williams, *Capitalism and Slavery*, 1944. Williams's views are criticised by G. R. Mellor, *British Imperial Trusteeship, 1783–1850*, 1951, pp. 11–80.
[2] W. Schlote, *British Overseas Trade from 1700 to the 1930's*, English trans., 1952, p. 8.

home market, the political and economic union of 1707 between England and Scotland had created the largest area free from internal tolls in Western Europe.

The essential features of modern industrialism have been considered to be "the aggregation of a body of workpeople in one workplace, drawn together by the necessity of attendance upon power-machinery and directed by capitalist employers";[1] but none of these factors was a novelty in the eighteenth century. Capitalism, aggregation of workpeople, machinery, water power, and even some knowledge of steam power can all be traced to the ancient world. In a narrower sense it can be shown that all these factors had appeared in English industry, in a more or less distinct form, before the beginning of the eighteenth century. The developments which took place in the reign of George III must therefore be regarded as the quickening of an age-long evolutionary process, rather than as a violent break with the past and a fresh beginning. In the period 1660–1760, however, the signs which heralded the steam-driven textile factories and iron-works of the 1780s and 1790s began to multiply.

Remarkable developments in large-scale production took place in English mining and manufacturing industries during the late seventeenth and eighteenth centuries, and often owed much to the demands of war.[2] In naval shipbuilding, the demands of the State played a dominating part. The intermittent wars against France from 1689 to 1763 witnessed the growth not only of the Royal Navy, but also of the public and private dockyards which built and serviced its vessels.[3] Indirectly, too, naval demands stimulated economic expansion. The most important figure in the iron

[1] Sir William Ashley, *Economic Organisation of England*, 3rd ed., 1949, pp. 141, 154.
[2] A. H. John, 'War and the English economy, 1700–1763', *Economic History Review*, April 1955, pp. 329–44.
[3] D. C. Coleman, 'Naval dockyards under the later Stuarts', *Economic History Review*, December 1953, pp. 134–55.

trade during the Wars of the League of Augsburg (1689–1697) and of the Spanish Succession (1702–13) was Sir Ambrose Crowley, who founded three large ironworks at Winlaton and Swalwell, not far from Newcastle-upon-Tyne, between 1691 and 1707. Winlaton was probably the largest ironworks in Europe. Profitable contracts for the supply of nails, anchors and other articles of ironware to the Navy, as well as extensive private sales both at home and abroad, enabled Crowley to organise these establishments by post in minute and paternal detail from successive offices in London and Greenwich. The large numbers of workmen he employed, the minute subdivision of labour in his works and the continuous check by the master manufacturer on the quality of the products foreshadowed the modern factory. Only the rotary steam engine and the machine tools of the Industrial Revolution were lacking. Human power was supplemented merely by horses and water-wheels.[1]

On the other hand, the copper and brass industries expanded from the 1690s onwards not only by reason of the application of technical improvements brought about partly by the demands of war, but also because of the abolition of the monopolistic rights of the Mines Royal Company in 1689–93 and the discovery of new veins of copper ore in Cornwall. The sales of copper ore in that county rose from about 2000 tons in 1729 to over 16,000 tons by 1760.[2]

The origins of some important discoveries which quickened the pace of economic change in the last four decades of the eighteenth century can now be followed back in some detail into the century before 1760, although it is still extremely difficult to trace direct connections between the much-dis-

[1] M. W. Flinn, 'Sir Ambrose Crowley, ironmonger, 1658–1713', *Explorations in Entrepreneurial History*, Vol. V, no. 3 (1952–3), pp. 162–80.

[2] R. O. Roberts, 'Copper and economic growth in Britain, 1729–1784', *National Library of Wales Journal*, Summer 1957, pp. 2–4; A. H. John, *loc. cit.*, pp. 330–1.

cussed 'flowering of Restoration science', symbolised by the foundation of the Royal Society of London in 1660-2, and the technological innovations which characterised the following century. For example, the two most important of these innovations, Abraham Darby I's successful introduction of a process for smelting iron ore with coke at Coalbrookdale between 1709 and 1712, and the erection of Thomas Newcomen's first engine to be supplied to a customer at a coal mine near Dudley Castle in Warwickshire during 1712, appear to have been undertaken by men with little direct knowledge of contemporary scientific work. It will be noted that while both these inventions date from about fifty years before 1760, their fortunes up to the middle of the eighteenth century were divergent. Whereas the coke-smelting process did not spread much beyond the Coalbrookdale area before the late 1750s, by the same period the steam engine was well-established at the Tyneside coal pits and there were dozens at work in other parts of the kingdom, although one informed observer hesitated about placing the number as high as a hundred.[1]

Similarly, it is now known that John Kay's fly shuttle of 1733, generally presented in isolation as the first of the important innovations in the textile industries, was actually the last of a series of improvements in weaving and cloth finishing which had begun during the reign of Charles II. This enables the alternating pattern of improvements in spinning and weaving to be traced back into the sixteenth century.[2] Studies of the tinplate and paper industries have shown that the successful introduction of new machines and processes in those industries took place in the first decades of the eighteenth century, although full advantage of the innovations

[1] Josiah Tucker in 1752, quoted in Ashton, *The Eighteenth Century*, p. 96; R. A. Raistrick, 'The steam engine on Tyneside', *Trans. Newcomen Soc.*, Vol. XVII, 1936-7, pp. 131-64.

[2] Sir George Clark, *Science and Social Welfare in the Age of Newton* (revised ed., 1949), pp. 42-5.

was not taken until after 1760.[1] Tinplate was apparently first made successfully on a commercial scale in this country by John Hanbury during the early years of the eighteenth century. Imports of German tinplate reached a peak of two million plates in 1710 and amounted to well over a million plates in most years up to 1738. After this year they declined sharply, probably because of the War of the Austrian Succession. During the war (1739-48) English ironmasters seized their opportunity and succeeded in filling the gap with home-produced tinplate on a permanent basis, since German imports had declined almost to vanishing point by 1760.

In the English paper-making industry, the large-scale introduction of the "hollander", a Dutch rag-pulping device invented about 1670-80, took place between the 1730s and 1760. It proved to be the major cause of increased productivity in the industry during the eighteenth century, although it was not affected by steam power until after 1800.[2] Furthermore, a recent study of the large-scale production of beer, which in the eighteenth century probably absorbed a higher proportion of the income of the English people than any other food except bread, has shown that brewing necessitated capital investment on a scale which rivalled that of the ironmasters and cotton magnates of the later eighteenth century.[3]

By the middle of the eighteenth century many branches of English manufacturing industry had become dependent on overseas trade, both for their raw materials and for their main markets. In some industries the source of raw material had from the beginning been foreign; among these exotic industries were the cotton and silk manufactures. In some other industries the home supply of raw material was be-

[1] W. E. Minchinton, *The British Tinplate Industry* (1957), esp. pp. 10-16; D. C. Coleman, *The British Paper Industry, 1495-1860* (1958).
[2] Coleman, *op. cit.*, pp. 110-112.
[3] P. Mathias, *The Brewing Industry in England, 1700-1830* (1959).

coming inadequate to supply the expanding demands of the manufacturers, or was actually shrinking in amount. Thus the English production of fine wool is said to have been decreased during the eighteenth century by the breeding of sheep primarily for mutton; as a result, English manufacturers of the finer kinds of cloth became dependent on the importation of wool from such regions as Spain and Saxony. In all industries to which technical improvements were applied the effect was to increase the size of the business unit and the scale of production; and this inevitably aggravated the difficulty of finding raw materials and securing markets. In industries which had thus become dependent on overseas trade, capitalist organisation was increasingly necessary.

The extent to which capitalist organisation and control had already penetrated manufacturing industry, before the middle of the eighteenth century, can be seen very clearly in the history of the woollen industry, which had been the only important export industry in the later Middle Ages, and remained the great staple trade of the kingdom right up to the nineteenth century. In the 1760s the woollen manufacture had very few of the technical characteristics of modern industry. It was widely dispersed throughout the country, and even within the main clothing districts the bulk of industrial workers lived scattered among the small villages rather than aggregated in the large towns. The cloth manufacture was still a handicraft, carried on in domestic workshops without power-driven machinery, except in the finishing processes, where water-driven mills were used for fulling the cloth. Yet already the industry was subject to a considerable degree of capitalist control.

The independence of the woollen weavers was greatest in the Yorkshire clothing district, where they commonly owned their house and land, as well as their looms and working materials. But even in the West Riding the supply of raw material and the disposal of the finished product were already

9

under capitalist organisation. In the older clothing district of the West Country the capitalist control was much more definite. There the organisation of the industy was dominated by the merchant clothier, who purchased the raw wool and arranged for it to be carded, spun, woven, fulled and dressed by domestic workers. These domestic workers might be nominally independent craftsmen, but in reality they were not far removed from the status of wage earners. As yet the majority of the weavers worked in their own loomshops; but here and there, as had already happened in the sixteenth century, clothiers employed ten or twelve weavers under one roof in a rudimentary manufactory. In the East Anglian worsted district the master clothiers are said to have been a veritable aristocracy, with the manners of gentlemen and with trading connections which extended to South America, India, and China. These master clothiers had control over the later stages of manufacture and marketing. The preparatory stages of combing and spinning were, in that district, under the control of a special class of middlemen, the master combers, who employed "putters out" to distribute the wool among the country workers.

A similar growth of capitalist organisation had already occurred also in the Lancashire textile districts. By the middle of the eighteenth century, and probably earlier, the majority of the workers in the woollen, linen, fustian and cotton manufactures of Lancashire were organised under a capitalist system, though they remained domestic workers. No detailed proof is needed to show that capitalism had already penetrated most of the other main industries of the country. The framework knitters of the London and Nottingham districts were necessarily under capitalist control from the beginning; for their trade was based on the operation of comparatively elaborate and expensive machinery. This was much more strongly the case in the silk-throwing industry, where power-driven machinery and a factory system had already been introduced during the first quarter of the century.[1] The heavy metal industries had been organised on a capitalist basis since the Middle Ages. Staffordshire pottery is said to have been still the product of a "peasant industry" in 1760, when Josiah Wedgwood was just beginning his independent career as a master potter; but there were at that time in Burslem and neighbourhood about a hundred and fifty separate pottery works, employing between forty and fifty workers each.[2]

If there were capitalist employers and industrial wage-earners, there were also the symptoms of that cleavage between capital and labour which has sometimes been regarded as a special characteristic of modern industrialism. By 1760 there were already established rudimentary trade clubs in all the main textile trades. It is clear also that there were similar organisations in the mining industries and the metal manufacturing trades; though no convincing evidence has yet been found of such activity among the smelters, founders and forgemen of the primary iron industry. Special Acts of Parliament prohibiting workmen's combinations in particular trades were frequent throughout the eighteenth century, and related quite as often to those branches of manufacture which were still organised on a domestic basis as to those branches in which power-driven machinery and the factory system had been introduced. Prohibition does not necessarily imply suppression, however, and there can be no doubt that many of the prohibited combinations persisted throughout the period, sometimes in the guise of benefit clubs and friendly societies, sometimes in the more dangerous form of secret brotherhoods with pseudo-mediaeval ritual.

The expansion of overseas trade during the earlier eighteenth century was accompanied by equally striking

---

[1] See below, p. 18.
[2] V. W. Bladen, 'The Potteries in the Industrial Revolution', in *Economic Journal*, Economic History Supplement, January 1926, p. 125.

changes in the organisation and scope of the home trade. The internal trade of the seventeenth century had still retained many mediaeval characteristics. The marketing of manufactured goods in the home market was still very largely carried on at periodical fairs, such as those of Stourbridge, Winchester, Boston and Beverley. Travelling merchants, with their caravans of pack animals, were still the chief wholesale link between the fairs and the retail trade. The retail trade itself was for the most part carried on by pedlars or chapmen. This persistence of primitive trading conditions was due mainly to the tardy development of banking and transport. Outside London commercial credit was still at an immature stage of development, even in the middle of the eighteenth century; the number of banking firms increased only slowly until the last two decades of the century, and provincial banking was especially backward before 1760.

Improvements in transport and communications were as necessary as improvements in financial organisation if the trade and industry of the country was to be efficiently linked together. The rising demand for goods, which expressed itself not only in the growth of imports and exports, but also in the expansion of the coastal and inland trades, stimulated transport improvements on a considerable scale long before 1760. For example, during the later stages of the expansion of joint-stock investment which began in the late 1680s and collapsed with the bursting of the South Sea Bubble in 1720, plans were set afoot in Lancashire and Cheshire for the improvement of navigation on the River Weaver, the Mersey and the Irwell, and the River Douglas, plans which received parliamentary approval in 1720–21. One cause of this development of inland transport was the increasing use of coal in industry and the home. The Weaver was improved in order to facilitate the carriage of coal into, and salt out of, Cheshire. Similarly the deepening of the Douglas promoted the growth of coal-mining in the Wigan area for the supply of

Liverpool and Dublin. Coal, being a heavy and bulky commodity, could not bear the high cost of road transport over any considerable distance: it was this fact which had given Tyneside coal, shipped coastwise from Newcastle, a virtual monopoly of the London market. The capital investment undertaken during the 1720s and 1730s in Lancashire and Cheshire under the powers conferred by the legislation of 1720-21 undoubtedly helped to expand local economic activity during these decades, which are known to have been marked by stagnation and depression in other parts of the country. In Yorkshire the Rivers Aire and Calder were improved for navigation from 1699 onwards in the interests of the West Riding woollen districts. Parallel but less successful activities leading to some improvement in local transport facilities by road and river in the Derwent–Trent river system between 1664 and 1759 helped on the industrialisation of the districts round Nottingham and Derby.[1]

On the map the English roads at the accession of George III might seem to form an adequate system, crossing the country in all directions in a fairly close network; but while the roads certainly existed, they were mostly in wretched condition. Many of them were too narrow even to allow pack animals to pass one another; and in wet weather the roads were liable to become streams, to be avoided rather than followed. Under such conditions, wheeled transport could develop only slowly. Some attempts at the improvement of the roads had already been made in the sixteenth and seventeenth centuries by the passing of Highway Acts and by the creation of the first turnpike trusts. In 1725, for example, an Act of Parliament was secured to turnpike the road from Manchester via Stockport to Buxton—the first road in Lancashire to be so treated. Between 1726 and 1735 six further

[1] J. D. Chambers, *The Vale of Trent, 1670–1800: a regional study of economic change* (*Economic History Review* Supplement No. 3, 1957), pp. 10–13.

Acts were passed setting up turnpike trusts for the improvement of roads in South Lancashire.[1] But it was not until the middle of the eighteenth century that the road-making movement became really active. Then for twenty years or so there was a veritable "road fever", in which the system of turnpike roads spread over the whole country. Between 1748 and 1760 the number of turnpike trusts increased from 160 to 530; and during the next fourteen years no fewer than 452 Acts of Parliament were passed dealing with the construction and maintenance of roads. The connection between such transport developments and contemporary changes in trade, industry and finance will be sufficiently clear; but it may not be out of place to note that the agricultural changes of the period may also have had some influence on the changes in transport. Progressive farming, as well as progressive industry, required better roads for the marketing of produce; the time when the land was being redivided and enclosed was an especially favourable time for the laying-out of new roads, and some Enclosure Acts of the period expressly stipulated that sufficient space should be left for a public highway.

Improvement in the condition of the roads was naturally followed by changes in the organisation of road transport. Coach services were greatly quickened and extended; after 1766 the Warrington "flyer", which ran twice a week, brought Liverpool and Manchester within three days of London. Carriers' waggons began to supersede pack transport for the carriage of goods; commercial travellers with samples and order books took the place of the travelling merchants with their strings of pack horses. Charges for the carriage of goods still, however, remained very high.

This movement for improved communications, which owed something to the cheap rates at which money could be

[1] G. H. Tupling, 'The turnpike trusts of Lancashire' (*Mem. and Proc. Manchester Lit. and Phil. Soc.*, vol. 94, 1952-3, pp. 1-23).

borrowed for long-term capital investment in the period between the 1720s and the 1750s, achieved its two major successes between 1755 and 1776. The first was the construction, financed by Liverpool merchants, of the Sankey Navigation from the coalfield of St. Helens down to the River Mersey at Warrington. Although originally planned as a river improvement this enterprise was completed in 1757 as a canal or "deadwater navigation" and can claim to be the first English canal of the eighteenth century.[1] The cutting of the Duke of Bridgewater's canal from Worsley by way of Salford and Manchester across the North Cheshire plain to Runcorn, between 1759 and 1776, constituted the second great achievement. It was opened to Cornbrook by 1761 and to its Manchester terminus by 1764. This was the first English navigation of the eighteenth century to be planned as a canal from its inception. It is said to have halved the price of coal at Manchester, and its completion in 1776 reduced the charge for goods traffic between Liverpool and Manchester from twelve shillings a ton to six shillings. Its immediate success led quickly to still bolder plans for the improvement of inland navigation. James Brindley, the engineer of the Worsley canal, remained the chief worker in the movement, with financial backing from the Duke of Bridgewater and other magnates. By 1765–6 Brindley was already engaged in a much bigger undertaking, the Grand Trunk Canal; this was to connect the Trent and the Mersey, thus opening up communication between the Irish Sea and the North Sea, and incidentally linking up Liverpool with the Staffordshire potteries. The Grand Trunk Canal was successfully completed in 1777, though Brindley had died, from overwork, in 1772. Before his death, however, he had sketched out schemes for the construction of a network of canals throughout England. By the end of the eighteenth century the whole

---

[1] T. C. Barker and J. R. Harris, *A Merseyside Town in the Industrial Revolution: St. Helens 1750–1900*, 1954, Chap. II.

country was covered with a complex system of inter-connecting waterways; and this development was especially important in the mining and manufacturing districts, which depended on the canals for their extremely rapid growth in that generation. Adam Smith declared in 1776 that industrial development depended on facilities for water transport; before his death in 1790 this principle seemed to have been fulfilled in the relation between industry and the canals, though in the next generation canal transport itself was to be threatened by the iron railroad and the steam locomotive.

CHAPTER TWO

Changes in the Textile Industries

WHEN MODERN INDUSTRY is described as "machine industry", it is implied not merely that machinery is in use, but that the use of machinery is the central factor in industrial organisation, determining the quantity, quality, and cost of the industrial product. Until the eighteenth century, machinery remained a subordinate factor in industry; for this reason the "Industrial Revolution of the Eighteenth Century" is sometimes regarded as having displaced hand industry, organised under a domestic system, in favour of machine industry, organised under a factory system. Such a generalisation may be convenient and useful for analytical purposes, but it is likely to be historically misleading, in that it tends to oversimplify the historical factors involved, as well as to exaggerate the rapidity and completeness of the transition. It has also to be remembered that many of the relatively crude laboursaving devices of the eighteenth century economised poorly paid unskilled labour rather than highly paid skilled labour.[1] The transition appears most sudden and most complete if attention is concentrated on the history of the cotton industry, the classical type of modern large-scale industry. Yet as late as the end of the eighteenth century cottons could not rival woollens in the export trade; and even in the 1830s the female domestic servants of England formed a trade group "probably more than 50 per cent. more numerous than all the men and women, boys and girls, in the cotton industry

---

[1] Ashton, *Economic History of England: the Eighteenth Century*, 1955, pp. 108–10.

put together".[1] The history of the cotton trade during the reign of George III cannot properly be treated as typical of the changes then taking place in industry. This becomes especially clear if the textile changes are compared with changes in the heavy metal trades and in coal-mining. In these industries the gradual character of the transition to modern conditions has never been seriously questioned; and even in the cotton trade the changes were far less revolutionary than has often been supposed.

By 1760 the factory system and the use of power-driven machinery were already firmly established in the English silk-throwing industry. Sir Thomas Lombe is said to have made a fortune of £120,000 out of his silk-throwing factory at Derby before his patent expired in 1732. In that year the trade was thrown open, and thenceforward developed rapidly on the new model, particularly in such northern centres as Stockport, Macclesfield and Manchester; though one of the largest factories was actually in London. By the decade 1760–70 there were manufacturers in the silk trade employing as many as 1500 workers at a time, though some of these were probably weavers, who would work at home. At Macclesfield, in 1761, there were nearly 2500 workers employed in silk-throwing; in 1770 there were at Stockport four silk-throwing factories, employing among them 1000 workers.

This early development of the modern factory system in the silk-throwing industry is important, not only in itself, but also as leading up to the similar development in the cotton industry a generation later. Many of the new northern centres of the silk manufacture were homes also of the early factory movement in the cotton industry; and in many cases the early cotton factories were converted silk mills.[2] If the continuity of development needs to be further stressed, it may be pointed out that many of the early water-power factories,

---

[1] Clapham, *Economic History of Modern Britain*, Vol. I, 1926, p. 73.
[2] Cf. Unwin, *Samuel Oldknow and the Arkwrights*, 1924, p. 27.

in both the silk and the cotton industries, were the mediaeval corn mills newly converted to manufacturing purposes. At Ashton-under-Lyne, only six miles from Manchester, one of the manorial corn mills had, in 1848, "recently been appropriated to cotton spinning"; the other mill remained "in full operation as a soak mill, the tenants of the manor being still obliged to grind their corn there".[1] Most of the early spinning factories were very small, according to modern standards; yet some of them already employed as many as six hundred workers in the 1780s, and the *form* of the typical factory did not change much during the next generation, though there was a general tendency for the factories to increase in size. By 1816 the *average* number of workers employed in 43 Manchester textile factories was already as high as 300.[2]

The rapid and spectacular growth of the English cotton industry took place after 1760; but the industry was firmly established in Lancashire long before that time, and technical progress had already begun. By the middle of the eighteenth century Manchester was importing raw cotton through both London and Liverpool, from both Asia and America. In return, Manchester was exporting cotton goods to Italy, Germany, North America, Africa, Asia Minor and even to China. By that time John Kay's fly shuttle had quickened the speed of weaving; and Lewis Paul's roller-spinning machine had pointed the way to the more famous invention of Arkwright. Kay's fly shuttle, which was patented in 1733, was for use with the ordinary hand-loom, and consisted mainly of a picking-peg contrivance which enabled the weaver to jerk the shuttle to and fro through the warp, using only one hand. This simple device thus made it possible for the weaver, not only to work more quickly, but also to weave a wider cloth without assistance. Nor was this the only

---

[1] S. Lewis, *Topographical Dictionary of England*, 7th ed., 1848, Vol. I, p. 95.
[2] Clapham, *Economic Journal*, 1915, p. 477.

weaving invention of that generation: Kay himself made various other improvements in the loom, and in 1760 his son Robert invented the "drop box", which facilitated the weaving of three-colour patterns.

The acceleration of the weaving process, which was called for by the steady expansion of the market for textile goods, in its turn stimulated the improvement of the spinning and preparatory processes. Even so early as 1736, before Kay's fly shuttle had begun to affect the situation, it was said that four spinners were needed to supply one weaver with yarn. The cleaning and carding of the cotton were still performed by hand; spinning was as yet carried on by means of the spinning wheel. On the ordinary spinning wheel only one thread could be spun, and the spinning alternated with the winding of the spun thread. It is true that on the improved Saxony wheel there was a flyer spindle which allowed the processes of spinning and winding to be performed simultaneously. It was also possible to spin two threads at a time on the Saxony wheel, one thread with each hand; but this wheel was more suitable for flax or wool than for cotton. Hitherto the spinning had often been done by the weaver's wife and children, without much outside help; spinning and weaving could then be carried on as a purely domestic concern, the families of those days being normally larger than modern families. One effect of such weaving inventions as Kay's fly shuttle was to increase the weaver's capacity beyond the power of his family to keep him provided with yarn. The consequent scarcity of yarn tended to break down the family economy in the cotton industry, thus accelerating the introduction of improved machines and a factory system in spinning.

An early attempt to mechanise the spinning process was reflected in the roller-spinning machine patented by Lewis Paul in 1738. The main principle of Paul's machine was to draw out the cotton roving into a fine thread by passing it through successive pairs of cylinders, the later cylinders revolving more quickly than the earlier and thus giving "stretch" to the yarn. Additional "stretch", and possibly also a little "twist", was given to the yarn as it was finally wound on to the spindle. This invention was tried in a small experimental factory at Birmingham, where the machinery was worked by two donkeys and attended by ten women; but the experiment did not achieve any practical success. After the bankruptcy of the first partnership in 1742, the patent was taken over by Edward Cave, the editor of the *Gentleman's Magazine*, and exploited on a larger scale. Cave set up a water-power mill at Northampton, using the roller-spinning machinery in combination with Paul's cylindrical carding machines, and employed fifty workers of both sexes. This undertaking also proved unprofitable, and was ultimately bought up by Richard Arkwright; it may, nevertheless, be claimed that this was the first water-power cotton-spinning factory in England, and a significant prophecy of later developments.

Hargreaves' spinning jenny, which was patented in 1770, was a comparatively simple extension of the principle of the spinning wheel, and did not at first involve either the use of power or the introduction of a factory system. Whereas the spinning wheel turned only one spindle, and spun only one thread at a time, the jenny carried several spindles on a simple framework, and spun several threads. The number of spindles soon rose from eight to eighty, and ultimately to a hundred and twenty. Children could work the machine, and it was actually first used in cottages and domestic workshops. In the first instance, indeed, the jenny may have tended to revive the moribund family economy in the cotton industry; the introduction of the jenny made it easier for the weaver to supply himself with yarn by the labour of his wife and family. On the other hand, Arkwright's water frame was from the first designed to be used as a power machine, and necessarily implied the adoption of a factory economy. A further difference between the two machines arose from the fact that the yarn produced by the jenny was more suitable for use as the weft than as the warp; whereas one of the most important features of Arkwright's water frame was that it produced yarn suitable for the warp. The jenny and the water frame were thus in some degree complementary rather than competing machines.

Arkwright's water frame, which was patented in 1769, was planned on the same general lines as Paul's roller-spinning machine. The technical defect of Paul's machine seems to have been the inadequate "twist" which it gave; the yarn consequently tended to break, and at its best was too weak to be satisfactory for weaving. Arkwright's frame embodied the principle of spinning by rollers, but remedied the deficiency in twist by means of a special flyer spindle, which was already in use for hand-spinning and had been known since the time of Leonardo da Vinci. Arkwright's original patent provided for the machinery to be worked by horses; but his famous factory at Cromford, which was started in 1771, was driven by water power derived from the Derwent, which also worked Lombe's original silk factory. Both Hargreaves and Arkwright met great opposition in their native county of Lancashire, and sought kindlier treatment in Nottinghamshire. The opposition expressed, no doubt, the natural hostility to exclusive patent rights in a rapidly developing industry. There was, however, the further question whether the machines as patented were substantially different from machines invented by other men and already known to the trade. Both the patents were legally contested, and both were eventually broken down. There is still some doubt concerning the real authorship of the inventions, and the doubt is especially strong in the case of the water frame.

One reason for the bitter legal contest waged against Arkwright by other manufacturers, between 1781 and 1785, was that improved spinning machines were now available which might be held to infringe Arkwright's patents, especially as the specifications of the original patents had been deliberately left vague and obscure. Chief among the new machines was Samuel Crompton's "mule", which combined the most important features of the jenny and the water frame. Crompton's original machine was completed in 1779, and very quickly demonstrated its superiority for the spinning of fine yarns. It was the use of mule-spun yarns which enabled the English manufacturers of such finer stuffs as cambrics and muslins to compete favourably with the Indian manufacturers, who had hitherto supplied the English market. For some time the general introduction of the mule was retarded by the struggle against Arkwright's patents; but after these had been finally annulled in 1785 the new machine came rapidly into use. The mule was never patented, however, partly because it would have been difficult to establish its difference from the earlier patented machines, but mainly because Crompton's business capacity was not equal to his inventive talent.

Various improvements were made in the mule within a few years of its freer use. Henry Stones, of Horwich, replaced Crompton's wooden rollers with metal cylinders, and introduced an automatic device to stop them when they had given out the proper length of roving. As a result of his improvements longer mules were brought into operation, bearing as many as a hundred and thirty spindles. A further improvement arose from the invention of the slubbing billy, about the year 1782. The billy was a combination of the mule and the jenny, which made the carded cotton into rovings ready to be spun on the mule, the jenny, or the water frame; whereas before that time the rovings had been made less efficiently either on the spinning wheel or on Arkwright's machinery. The mule now began to supersede the jenny, with which it had come into direct competition in the spinning of fine yarns; in the spinning of coarse yarns, especially yarns intended to be used as warp, there was still scope for the water frame.

23

At first the mule was a hand machine, and was chiefly used in country cottages; in this respect it resembled the jenny and was unlike the water frame. It was in 1790 that William Kelly, the manager of David Dale's cotton mills at New Lanark, first applied water power to the mule; this at once led to its enlargement, and to a further extension of its use. A Manchester machine-maker named Wright soon constructed a double mule, carrying about four hundred spindles; but it was not until 1825 that the numerous attempts to give the mule an automatic action culminated in the invention of the self-actor mule by Richard Roberts, another Manchester machine-maker. Meanwhile, the application of power to the mule had led to its complete absorption into the factory system, which gained ground rapidly in the cotton industry after 1790.

The various inventions in spinning had been called forth by a scarcity of yarn aggravated by improvements in weaving. The situation was now reversed by the cheapening of the preparatory processes and the consequent increase in the demand for finished textile goods. Cotton yarn was now so plentiful that it was difficult for manufacturers to get it all woven. There was a great scarcity of weavers, a rapid rise in weavers' wages and a stimulus to inventions which aimed at improving or superseding the hand-loom. During the generation preceding the French wars, the weavers were earning higher wages than most other industrial workers, and far more than the agricultural labourers. In 1792 the weavers of fancy muslins were paid up to 3s. 6d. a yard at Bolton, and weavers of cotton velveteen might earn as much as 35s. a week. It is true that this "golden age" of the weavers soon faded away amidst the economic dislocation of the wars. It is equally true that the privileged position of the weavers could not have been maintained for long, even if there had been no war. High weaving wages tempted thousands of unskilled workers to enter the trade; and spinning firms exported yarn in increasing quantities, to be woven abroad at cheaper rates.

It was quite evident that the hand-loom must in time be supplanted by a more efficient power-loom.

For ribbon weaving, improved looms had been widely employed for a long time, both on the Continent and in England. There is some uncertainty concerning the origin of these improved looms. According to one tradition the original invention was made by a certain Anton Muller of Dantzig, about the end of the sixteenth century; but technical progress in weaving was more closely associated with Holland than with Germany, and it was from Holland that these "Dutch looms" or "engine looms" were introduced into England. An improved form of the Dutch loom, known as the "swivel loom", was introduced in the Manchester district about the middle of the eighteenth century; and by that time attempts were being made (notably by John Kay, the inventor of the fly shuttle) to apply water power to the new weaving machinery. These pioneer attempts at power-loom weaving did not, however, meet with any striking practical success. All the early engine looms and swivel looms were slow, complicated, and unsuitable for the weaving of wide fabrics. The power-loom which Edmund Cartwright patented in 1785 was an independent invention, and seems to have been as clumsy as any of its predecessors. "The reed fell with a force of at least half a hundredweight, and the springs which threw the shuttle were strong enough to have thrown a Congreve rocket." [1] Cartwright managed by successive improvements to produce a workable machine; but his efforts to make power-loom weaving commercially profitable were ill-fated. In 1787 he set up an experimental factory at Doncaster with twenty looms: eight for calicoes, ten for muslins, one for cotton checks, and one for coarse linen. At first the machinery was worked by horse gins, but in 1789 Cartwright bought a

[1] *Encyclopædia Britannica*, Supplement of 1824, Vol. III, p. 402, article 'Cotton'; *Memoirs of Dr. Cartwright*, pp. 63–64, quoted by Mantoux, *The Industrial Revolution in the Eighteenth Century*, 1928, p. 247.

steam engine. Two years later he entered into a contract with Manchester cotton spinners for the establishment of a large steam factory, which was to contain four hundred power-looms; but the factory was destroyed by incendiaries before its equipment was completed, and this deterred Cartwright from further enterprise. Nevertheless, various manufacturers established power-loom factories during the succeeding decade, in spite of the war; and in 1803 Horrocks of Stockport introduced metal power-looms which were brought into use in several Lancashire towns. By the end of the Napoleonic wars the power-loom was entering into effective rivalry with the hand-loom in the cotton industry, though another generation was to elapse before the battle was finally decided.

Technical change came later in the woollen industries than in the cotton. This may have been partly because the woollen industries were of longer standing, and had a stronger craft tradition making for conservatism. Moreover, wool has a softer fibre than cotton, and was therefore more difficult to spin on the crude machines of those days. The technical changes in the woollen industries were at first almost entirely confined to the West Riding of Yorkshire, where the example of the neighbouring cotton industry of Lancashire gave a special stimulus to the adoption of machinery. The spinning jenny was being tried in Yorkshire by 1773; but its use did not become common there until after 1785, by which time it was already becoming out of date in the cotton industry. The general introduction of such machines in the West Country clothing district was much later. It is true that riots against the introduction of the jenny occurred in the West Country as early as 1776; but both the fly shuttle and the jenny were still regarded as innovations there in 1794.

The introduction of the fly shuttle or the jenny did not, of course, necessitate the use of power-driven machinery or the building of factories; the transition to a factory system was, indeed, curiously tardy in the woollen industries. In worsted spinning, it is true, the factory system was already developing before the end of the eighteenth century. The first worsted mill was established in 1787 on the River Wharfe at Addingham, near Skipton. Bradford had no spinning mills until 1794; yet by 1800 there were no fewer than ten worsted spinning factories in the town, and the West Riding was already beginning to threaten the supremacy of the East Anglian worsted district. By that time almost all the Yorkshire clothiers were using the jenny or the mule for spinning, and the fly shuttle in weaving; carding, also, was being done by machinery. The invention of Cartwright's combing machinery, in 1789-92, had as its object the cheapening of production in the worsted industry, by weakening the monopolistic power of the master combers. Nevertheless, machinery for this purpose did not actually come into general use until the second quarter of the nineteenth century, although it was tried in several factories round Bradford and Nottingham within a few years of its appearance.

The introduction of the power-loom was surprisingly slow, even in the cotton industry; and in all the other textile trades it was slower still. In 1835 there were 116,801 power-looms at work in the United Kingdom; but of these all except 7175 were in the cotton industry. The 5127 power-looms operative in the woollen manufactures at that date were mostly employed in worsted weaving, to which they had been first applied about 1824. So late as 1840 power-loom weaving in the woollen industry proper was in its infancy. It was more difficult to introduce power-driven machinery in this industry, because it used wool of shorter staple than did the worsted manufacture. Not until the second half of the nineteenth century did the factory system become completely supreme in the woollen districts.

Bleaching, dyeing and printing shared in the general technical progress of the time. The traditional method of bleaching cotton or linen was to steep it in sour milk, and then leave it exposed to the air; bleaching by this process sometimes took as long as eight months. A pioneering step towards quicker methods was taken by John Roebuck, who afterwards became famous as the principal proprietor of the Carron Iron Works and patron of James Watt. Roebuck introduced oil of vitriol (concentrated sulphuric acid) into the bleaching process; he set up works at Manchester in 1746, and at Prestonpans in 1749. More striking changes followed Berthollet's experiments with chlorine as a bleaching agent in 1785. James Watt brought back details of the new process when he returned from France in 1786; it was tried in the bleach-field of Watt's father-in-law at Glasgow, and soon reduced bleaching to a matter of a few days.[1] Meanwhile, the other finishing branches of the textile industries were being improved with almost equal rapidity; new colours and dyes were continually appearing on the market during the later eighteenth century, and hand-block printing was being rapidly superseded by cylinder printing.

Calico printing was already well established in England by the later seventeenth century, and was at first carried on in the southern counties. Even at the close of the eighteenth century the industry still persisted in the neighbourhood of London; but by that time its main home was Lancashire, where it had been introduced in the middle of the century by Clayton of Bamber Bridge, and by the important firm of Haworth, Peel, and Yates. The printing was at first done by means of engraved blocks, applied to the cloth by hand. To print a piece of calico twenty-eight yards long in a single colour required 448 applications of the block; if a second colour was to be introduced the work would be doubled. This was necessarily a slow and expensive business, and many

---

[1] A. and N. L. Clow, *The Chemical Revolution*, 1952, Chaps. IX and X; see also R. A. Padley, 'The beginnings of the British alkali industry', in *University of Birmingham Historical Journal*, Vol. III, no. 1, 1951, pp. 64–78, also T. C. Barker and others, 'The origins of the synthetic alkali industry in Britain', *Economica*, May 1956, pp. 158–71.

attempts were made to mechanise the process. Patents for printing by cylinders were taken out in 1743, 1764, and 1767; but the pioneers met with little practical success. Finally, in 1783, Thomas Bell successfully devised copper cylinders to take the place of the hand blocks; the fabric was passed between engraved cylinders, two or more colours could be printed by the same operation, and the labour required was drastically reduced. Thenceforth, one revolving press could do as much work as had previously employed a hundred workers.[1]

[1] See A. and N. L. Clow, *op. cit.*, Chap. XI.

29

CHAPTER THREE

Changes in the Iron, Coal, and Engineering Industries

WHATEVER MAY BE thought about the textile changes of the eighteenth century, it may be safely asserted that there was nothing revolutionary about the changes which were then taking place in the metal and mining industries. The structure and organisation of these latter industries were not fundamentally altered; the technical inventions followed naturally along lines already laid down. Nevertheless, the iron and coal industries must inevitably occupy a central place in the economic history of the period. Progress in the iron industries depended on the use of coal; further progress in the textile trades, after the early epoch of water power and wooden machinery, depended on the increasing use of iron machinery driven by steam engines stoked with coal. The main groups of industries were thus closely interrelated in the process of transition.

The iron industry was divided into two main branches; it comprised the mining and smelting industries on the one hand, and the various metal manufacturing industries on the other. At the beginning of the eighteenth century these two main branches were reasonably prosperous; the metal manufacturing trades were in general flourishing, but in some areas the smelting industry was either stagnant or actually declining. Iron smelting was as yet dependent on the use of charcoal as fuel in the blast furnaces; the supply of charcoal depended on the supply of suitable timber, and suitable timber was becoming increasingly scarce, although it is easy to exaggerate the effect of this problem on the location of the smelting industry. The charcoal most suitable for iron making was obtained from trees of about twenty years' growth. Therefore the thinnings of woodlands could be used in charcoal-burning, leaving the remaining trees to provide timber for constructional purposes in the future. Difficulties arising from the high price of charcoal had been felt even so early as the sixteenth century, and many industries had begun to use either peat or pit coal instead of charcoal. In the seventeenth century various attempts to smelt iron with coal or coke had been made, but without practical success. In addition, irregularity of water power during the summer months, and dwindling or low-quality ore deposits in some of the older iron-smelting districts, tended to raise the cost of production above those of the Swedish and Russian iron-masters. The production of iron in England therefore dwindled between about 1620 and the end of the Civil War, and the industry tended to migrate from such old-established centres as the Sussex Weald to districts in the western Midlands, where fuel was cheaper. As time went on the iron-masters were forced to go still further afield, to South Wales, to the northern counties of England, and even to Scotland. By the beginning of the eighteenth century these migrations of the industry, a symptom of growth rather than of decline,[1] were already being determined by the presence or absence of coal, as well as by the distribution of the supplies of iron ore; even before coal was used for smelting, it was being used in the slitting, rolling, and manufacturing of the iron.

In the early eighteenth century iron smelting was almost as widely diffused as the woollen manufacture; but its organisation was much more capitalistic. The mining and smelting

[1] M. W. Flinn, 'The growth of the English iron industry, 1660–1760', *Economic History Review*, August 1958, pp. 144–53; B. L. C. Johnson 'L'influence des bassins houillers sur l'emplacement des usines à fer en Angleterre avant *circa* 1717', *Le Fer à Travers les Ages* (*Annales de l'Est*, Nancy, 1956), pp. 217–23.

industries were necessarily brought under capitalist control at a very early stage in their development. Iron mining was very often combined with iron smelting, and controlled by the great landed proprietors. The equipment of such an enterprise demanded a considerable volume of capital, which was most readily furnished by the landlords from whose estates the iron was to be mined. The industry was, indeed, dependent on the landowner, not only for its ore, but also for limestone and charcoal; moreover, it was the demand of the landed classes for agricultural implements and military weapons which gave the early iron industry its main markets. Capitalist organisation was necessary, also, because of the expensive equipment already in use, such as hydraulic hammers, blast furnaces with water wheels to work the bellows, machines for rolling and cutting iron. The iron workers were not merely dependent on an employer for their raw material and market; they were already organised in large workshops, and were paid wages.

By contrast with the iron-smelting industry, the iron manufacturing industries were more closely localised, but less capitalistic in organisation. Birmingham was already the centre of a growing industrial district manufacturing hardware, and specialising in such articles as nails, locks, metal buttons and shoe buckles. Sheffield had been famous for cutlery since the days of Chaucer. The metal manufacturing industries were still mainly organised on the domestic system, which at Sheffield had not yet entirely superseded the gild type of organisation, represented by the Hallamshire Cutlers' Company. The specialisation of production was already far advanced at both Birmingham and Sheffield, but not yet in the direction of a factory system. Capitalist enterprise was encroaching upon the control of industry through the travelling merchants who put out work to the small craftsmen. In some cases the merchants supplied the raw material besides commissioning the work; but usually the craftsman still owned his own tools.

32

The main change making for progress in the primary iron industry during the earlier eighteenth century was the substitution of coke for charcoal in the smelting process. From the beginning of the century inventors and ironmasters who claimed to be able to smelt iron with coal or coke became increasingly numerous; but the use of the process with commercial success seems to have been first achieved by the Darbys at Coalbrookdale. Abraham Darby was smelting iron with coke at least as early as 1709;[1] it is not easy, however, to see how Darby's method differed from the earlier unsuccessful attempts to smelt iron with coke. His furnace may have been unusually large; but probably more important was his introduction of a stronger blast. Another factor was the nature of the local coal; Newcastle coal, and the other fossil coals containing much sulphur, would not have been so suitable. Even at Coalbrookdale the new process was not at first consistently successful.

The introduction of coke smelting had emphasised the need for a stronger blast; and by 1760 satisfactory solutions to this problem had been reached. The Darbys had secured increased power by using one of Newcomen's "fire" engines to pump a better head of water for the wheel that worked the bellows of the blast furnace; by 1754 they had seven furnaces, with five fire engines, and the arrangement was working successfully. Some years later the blast apparatus itself was improved by Smeaton's invention of the compressed air pump and the introduction of his blowing cylinders at the Carron Iron Works.

Coke smelting was directly applicable only to the production of cast iron. This was as yet a relatively minor branch of the industry, and therefore the introduction of the new process in the industry as a whole was not very rapid. The greater cheapness of coke smelting extended the range of

[1] T. S. Ashton, *Iron and Steel in the Industrial Revolution*, 1924, pp. 28–30, and Appendix E, pp. 249–52.

cast-iron articles manufactured; but coke-smelted pig iron produced bar iron inferior to that made from charcoal pig, which therefore continued to be used for the production of high-grade articles. Since charcoal-smelted iron still commanded higher prices, there was no inducement to advertise the gradual introduction of the cheaper method. Until the middle of the eighteenth century the new process seems to have been almost entirely confined to the Shropshire iron district; after that time it spread rapidly throughout England, Wales, and Scotland. It was, however, not until after the introduction of the double-acting blowing cylinder, worked by steam power, that coke smelting completely superseded the charcoal process. As the eighteenth century advanced, coke-smelted cast iron encroached not only on the sphere of wrought iron but also on the use of such materials as copper, lead, brass, and wood. Cast iron was used for an extraordinary variety of articles, ranging from gun carriages, cannon and coffin nails to smoothing irons, buttons, hoes and slave bangles.

The use of mineral fuel in the fining process was even more important than its use in the blast furnace; for the fining process took much more fuel. Sixteen hundredweights of charcoal were sufficient to produce a ton of pig iron; for a ton of bar iron twenty-four hundredweights of charcoal were required. Coke-smelted iron came out of the furnace in a liquid state, and when it had cooled was always cast iron. If malleable iron or steel was required, the "sow" and "pigs" of cast iron had to be broken up, reheated, and hammered at the forge to get rid of the excessive carbon content. The reduction of the carbon content in the pig iron would be facilitated if the pig iron were reheated without coming into direct contact with the fuel. This could be effected by the introduction of a special refining furnace between the operations of the blast furnace and the forge. During the earlier eighteenth century many experiments had been made with reverberatory furnaces, in which the metal was kept separate from the fire, and heated by the action of the flame in *reverberating* or striking down from the roof of the chamber. The early experiments do not seem to have been profitable, but in 1766 the process was successfully introduced at Coalbrookdale by the two brothers Thomas and George Cranage, who were employed by the Darbys. Their method was an immediate commercial success, especially in the production of iron for the nail-making industry round Birmingham. 1808720

Another means of reducing the proportion of carbon in the pig iron was by stirring or "puddling" the molten metal while it was still in the reverberatory furnace; in this way the carbonic impurities were more directly exposed to the heat and burnt out. Something like puddling seems to have formed part of the Cranages' process; in 1784, however, patents for puddling processes were taken out almost simultaneously by Henry Cort and Peter Onions. With his puddling process Cort combined improved rolling machinery, which he had patented in 1783. This combination of puddling with improved rolling processes facilitated the production of superior bar iron, while it avoided the necessity for reheating the metal, and thus saved both time and fuel.

Alongside these developments in the primary processes many improvements were being made in the machinery already used for drawing, cutting, and working the metal. There were drills for boring cannon (which had previously been cast hollow), metal-turning lathes, machines for forging nails and turning screws. These inventions not only economised time and labour, but they also made for that precision which was now being increasingly demanded in making such new machines as the steam engine. Iron bars could now be made of any required composition; they might be hard steel on the outside and tough wrought iron in the centre. Sheet iron could now be produced of any required strength, and of great size; the making of ships' plates and engine boilers was correspondingly facilitated. Now that the metal was under such exact control, new uses were constantly being found for iron—iron railroads (1767), iron bridges (1779), iron boats (1787), and iron machinery for the textile trades. The rapid expansion of the iron industry in the 1780s was closely associated with the new methods of production and with the wider application of steam power to the various processes of the manufacture. Meanwhile the charcoal furnaces were declining rapidly in numbers as the coke furnaces increased. Considerable masses of capital were now being sunk in the industry; large integrated concerns were being built up which carried the iron through all the successive processes of mining, smelting, fining, rolling, and slitting. Some businesses employed as many as five hundred iron workers, as well as colliers and auxiliary workers.

The industrial developments of the eighteenth century called for a greatly increased output of coal, and therefore for a rapid expansion of the coal-mining industry. Even before the eighteenth century, coal was already taking the place of charcoal in a wide variety of industries, such as brewing, distilling, brick-making, pottery, sugar-refining, soap-boiling, cutlery, nail-making and the manufacture of glass. To this varied industrial consumption of coal there were added in the eighteenth century the urgent demands of the primary iron industries and of the steam engine. Capital flowed into coal-mining from several of the industries affected; but far the largest stream of capital came from the great ironmasters of the period, such as the Darbys, the Wilkinsons and the Guests. There has always been an intimate connection between coal-mining and the primary iron industries; but whereas iron-smelting was from early times carried on under a capitalist system, coal-mining remained until quite recent times at a comparatively primitive stage of technical development.

The size of the colliery undertakings of the earlier

eighteenth century varied very greatly; but even in the case of the larger collieries, employing a hundred men or more, the individual pits were very small, according to modern standards. Not many pits employed more than fifteen workers underground, except in the northern collieries, where there were already some instances of pits organised on a larger scale. Any rapid increase in the size of pits was obstructed by technical difficulties concerned with such matters as ventilation, drainage and underground transport; a minor reason for slowness in development may have been the restrictions imposed by the landed proprietors on the rate of exploitation. In spite of these obstacles a substantial increase in the scale of working did take place during the last quarter of the century; but the transition was not by any means rapid or spectacular.

The great enemies of the collier have always been water, poisonous air and fire. The modern increase in the size and depth of pits has very largely depended on the solution of these problems, together with the improvement in methods of transport underground. In early times the mines were only worked in the higher ground, and could be drained by soughs running downhill to the surface. In some collieries (such as those of the Duke of Bridgewater at Worsley) the soughs could be made to serve also as underground canals. Where the nature of the ground did not permit such direct drainage, recourse was had to such devices as the common hand pump and the endless chain of buckets. Where the pit was deep, however, the pumping could not be completed in a single operation, and this difficulty gave scope for much ingenuity in the arrangement of auxiliary pumping pits. In these deeper pits the pumps were worked by various contrivances, such as windlasses, treadmills, horse gins, windmills, and especially water wheels.

The inconstancy of wind and water soon stimulated inquiry into the possibility of using other motive forces, and led to the introduction, from 1712 onwards, of Newcomen's fire

37

engine, which attained considerable importance in the mining industries of the earlier eighteenth century, and led in its turn to the introduction of Watt's steam engine, in the generation after 1769. Actually, the Newcomen engine continued to compete with Watt's steam engine and predominated on the coalfields until well into the nineteenth century; for the great merit claimed for Watt's engine was its economy of fuel, and this was not an important recommendation to the colliery owner.

Upon the ventilation of the pit depended the miners' protection against suffocation and fire. In the earlier and smaller pits the chief source of trouble was "chokedamp" or carbonic acid gas: but in the larger and deeper pits of later generations the main danger arose from "firedamp" or marsh gas. Of these two enemies, firedamp was the more formidable, for it exploded the miner's candle without warning, whereas chokedamp usually put the candle out before it began to suffocate the miner. Explosions were appallingly frequent, and caused great loss of life; but they were regarded as an inevitable risk of the occupation, and attention was directed towards relieving the sufferers rather than towards preventing recurrences of the evil. The firedamp could be removed either by ventilation or by the deliberate production of an explosion. Ventilation was obviously the more satisfactory solution of the problem; but in many colliery districts the cost of constructing ventilation shafts was for long considered prohibitive. Where ventilation shafts were built the circulation of air was usually assisted by maintaining fires in the mine, often in special by-pits. To prevent the accumulation of gas in the waste places and in dead ends a system of vertical "stoppings", or partitions with trap doors, was gradually evolved. Another necessity in dealing with firedamp was to find some means of illumination which would not fire the gas. Flint and steel, the steel mill, and putrescent fish were all tried as illuminants without satisfactory results; but the dan-

38

ger of explosion was lessened after the introduction of the miners' safety lamp, two rival varieties of which were invented in 1815 by Sir Humphry Davy and George Stephenson. The safety lamp did not lead, however, to any considerable decrease in the number of colliery accidents. Its primary effect was to encourage the working of deeper and more fiery seams; its secondary effect was to cause an increase in the output of coal.

In most collieries there was some mechanical apparatus for winding the coal up the shaft. Sometimes a simple windlass was used, sometimes a horse gin. The winding tackle which raised the coal served also to lower and raise the underground workers. Sometimes they used the coal baskets, sometimes they rode astride a wooden "horse"; but usually they rode with their legs stuck through loops made in the winding rope. The steam engine was only very slowly adopted for the winding operation; and some of the early winding engines were afterwards converted into pumping engines, feeding the water wheels by which the coal was raised. Smeaton made this combination of steam and water power very efficient, and it persisted in some places until the early nineteenth century. By the 1780s, however, the steam engine had been adapted to produce rotary motion, and it was therefore possible from that time to wind the coals directly by steam power.

The problem of the underground transport of the coal became more serious as the pits became deeper and more extensive. Hitherto, the coal had been carried to the pit bottom either on the backs of men and women or on sledges dragged by men. Before the middle of the eighteenth century, ponies had been introduced to draw the sledges in the larger collieries of the northern counties; and this incidentally led to an extension of child labour in the pits, as the ponies could be driven by small boys. In some collieries wheelbarrows were used, and later four-wheeled waggons were introduced; these were driven along a double line of planks—the germ of the

39

modern railway. Richard Reynolds began to substitute metal rails for wooden ones at Coalbrookdale between 1768 and 1771. Wrought-iron rails began to be substituted for cast-iron in the 1780s; though the rapidly extending railroads in the northern collieries continued for many years to use mainly rails made of cast iron. The immediate result of the development of colliery railroads was to reduce the proportion of putters (or drawers) to hewers: the final result, however, was to place heavier burdens on the colliery children, who were set to draw the wheeled corves along the railroads.[1]

The direct pedigree of the modern steam engine may, perhaps, be said to begin with Savery's fire engine of 1698, which was described by the inventor as "a new invention for raising water and occasioning motion to all sorts of mill work".[2] Savery's machine was designed to use both atmospheric pressure and direct steam power; it was found to be quite workable in pumping water from ordinary wells, and was actually employed in several Cornish copper mines. It proved, however, to have a very limited lifting power, and was therefore not of much use for the deeper copper mines or the Staffordshire coal mines, although a number of Savery's machines were at work at Lancashire cotton factories in the 1790s, pumping back water into mill ponds after it had passed over the water-wheel. Thomas Newcomen, one of Savery's neighbours, produced an improved type of fire engine about the year 1705. Newcomen's engine employed only atmospheric pressure for its direct force, and used steam power merely to produce a vacuum; nevertheless, it proved much more efficient in practical use than Savery's machine, and soon received a wider application. The new atmospheric engine was at first very crude; the piston did not fit exactly,

---

[1] The best account of changes in the coal industry is to be found in T. S. Ashton and J. Sykes, *The Coal Industry of the Eighteenth Century*, 1929.
[2] See Mantoux, *op. cit.*, p. 320.

and the tap which admitted steam from the boiler to the cylinder had to be turned by hand seven or eight times a minute. In the original design the steam in the cylinder had to be condensed by the application of cold water to the outside of the cylinder; this was later avoided by the introduction of a siphon injecting water *inside* the cylinder. The tap was made automatic by attachment to the beam which connected the engine with the water pump; in 1717 a safety valve was fitted. A company for marketing the engines was formed as early as 1711, and did a fair amount of business, both in England and on the Continent. Newcomen's engines soon became almost indispensable in deep mines, and were very widely used also for the feeding of canals, as well as in the provision of drinking water for towns. Their early application to the blowing of the Darbys' blast furnaces at Coalbrookdale has already been noticed.

The principles and imperfections of the earlier fire engines were quite well known to James Watt: the idea that Watt was an uneducated, inspired genius will not square with the facts. His grandfather was a teacher of mathematics; and his father was a Greenock shipwright, who undertook the repair of ships' instruments among other nautical business. The inherited mathematical bent of the future inventor was early developed, both at home and at the local Grammar School; his mechanical ability received full play in his father's workshop. James Watt developed one of his father's trades as a maker of scientific instruments, and became a scientific-instrument maker to the University of Glasgow at the age of twenty-one. He studied chemistry in the University under Dr. Black, and conducted research on the properties of latent heat. In 1761–2 Watt made a series of systematic experiments on steam pressure, using the engine invented by Papin in the later seventeenth century. In 1763–4 he was employed in repairing a model of Newcomen's engine, which belonged to the University and was used in the practical physics course. His study of Newcomen's engine impressed him with the low efficiency of atmospheric pressure compared with direct steam pressure. It also became clear to him that Newcomen's engine wasted a great deal of fuel in the alternate cooling and reheating of the cylinder in the process of condensation. Watt's remedy for this latter defect was to design a special condensing chamber, separate from the cylinder; and this first improvement led to an equally fundamental change in the character of the engine. In order to avoid the necessity of using water to keep the piston air-tight, and also to prevent the air from cooling the cylinder during the downstroke of the piston, Watt operated the piston entirely by direct steam pressure, and thus diverged sharply from the principle of Newcomen's atmospheric engine.

The main principles of Watt's steam engine were clearly laid down by 1764. By 1769 the engine had been made to work, after many failures, and was patented as a "method of lessening the consumption of steam, and consequently of fuel, in fire engines".[1]

To "invent" the steam engine had been comparatively easy; to produce the new machine on a commercial scale with financial profit was quite beyond Watt's resources. To bring the steam engine into general use a new class of operative engineers and fitters had to be trained and organised; this was for Watt a much less congenial task than that of scientific research and invention. One of Watt's chief practical difficulties was to get cylinders sufficiently accurate in bore to prevent the leakage of steam. To work in metal with such precision, and rapidly enough to turn out engines in large numbers, demanded not only a body of highly specialised workers, but also many technical improvements in metal working. Accuracy in boring was achieved by the use of John Wilkinson's cylinder-boring lathe. For twenty years, 1775–95,

[1] Patent of 1769 (No. 913) quoted in full in the Act of 1775 (15 Geo. III, c. 61) which extended the period of the patent's validity.

nearly all the cylinders for Watt's engine were supplied by Wilkinson from his works at Bersham and Bradley; some other parts of the engines were supplied from his works at Broseley. Watt's final victory owed a great deal on the technical side to such men as Wilkinson and the Darbys. On the business side Watt owed no less a debt to his successive partners, John Roebuck of Carron and Matthew Boulton of Birmingham. Roebuck, Watt's first partner, became bankrupt in 1773, and his rights in the invention were then taken over by Boulton. Boulton from the first realised the world-wide possibilities of the steam engine much more clearly than Roebuck, and was able to apply to its construction a specialised technique which resulted in much more accurate workmanship. He planned to "execute the invention twenty per cent. cheaper than it would be otherwise executed and with as great a difference of accuracy as there is between the blacksmith and the mathematical instrument maker".[1]

Watt's patent rights, which were due to expire in 1783, were in 1775 specially extended for a period of twenty-five years, and his partnership with Boulton was finally settled. Then came several long years of costly experiments and unprofitable contracts, during which time the development of the steam engine was only one among several enterprises which Boulton kept simultaneously afloat.[2] The profits of the engineering enterprise did not become tangible before 1786; though by that time steam engines of the new model were being used in many English industries, and were even being introduced into France and Germany.

Between 1775 and 1800 Boulton and Watt were responsible for a large proportion of the total output of steam engines in this country; and from the records of the firm it is possible to

---

[1] Letter from Boulton to Watt, of February 7th, 1769; quoted by H. W. Dickinson and R. Jenkins, *James Watt and the Steam Engine*, 1927, p. 31.
[2] On this point see J. E. Cule in *Economic History*, Vol. IV, No. 15, February 1940, pp. 319-25.

discover which trades were adopting steam power, to what extent, and from what date. Information concerning the use of the older atmospheric engines is not so adequate. Newcomen himself probably only erected about six or seven; but engines of the same type increased rapidly in numbers, especially for use in coal mines. Altogether, there might be in the middle 1770s about a hundred and thirty engines of the old type working in England. At that time the new steam engine had not emerged from the experimental stage; so late as 1777 only a bare half-dozen of Watt's engines were in operation. The penetration of industry by steam power took on a new significance in 1781, when Watt patented his rotary motion. The engines erected before 1782 were all of the older reciprocating type; at that date there seem to have been between forty and fifty in operation. These earlier engines were mostly used for draining mines, though some were erected in iron works, and some on water works. Of sixty-six engines built by Boulton and Watt between 1775 and 1785, the majority were for copper mines in Cornwall and iron works in Shropshire or Staffordshire. By the latter date, however, the importance of the new type of engine had been generally recognised. The rotary motion made it possible to apply steam power directly to all kinds of industrial undertakings; and applications for engines were already being received from many quarters. Between 1785 and 1795 Boulton and Watt erected 144 engines. Many of these still went to collieries and iron works in Shropshire and Staffordshire; but far greater numbers were now being ordered for cotton mills in Lancashire, Nottinghamshire, Cheshire, and Yorkshire. During the concluding five years of the century this preponderance of orders from the textile districts continued; on the other hand, the orders from the midland iron districts had now apparently fallen off.

Taking the last quarter of the eighteenth century as a whole, out of 289 engines erected by the firm there were eighty-four in cotton mills, thirty in collieries, twenty-eight in iron works, twenty-two in copper mines, eighteen on canal work, and seventeen in breweries. Of these same engines eighty-nine were in the northern textile counties of Lancashire, Cheshire, and Yorkshire, fifty-six were in the midland iron counties of Staffordshire and Shropshire, forty-one were in Middlesex and twenty-one in Cornwall. Concerning this geographical distribution of the engines it may be remarked that the bad state of the roads caused most of the engines to be erected either on the coalfields or in districts to which coal could easily be transported by water.[1]

[1] My information concerning the number and distribution of steam engines erected before 1800 comes from J. Lord's *Capital and Steam Power, 1750–1800*, 1923, Chapter VIII. I have reason to believe, however, that Mr. Lord's lists are not exhaustive, and some of his conclusions have been criticised by A. E. Musson and E. Robinson, 'The early growth of steam power', *Economic History Review*, April 1959, pp. 418–39.

CHAPTER FOUR

The Industrial Capitalists

THE CAPITALIST ORGANISATION of industry, accompanied by a social cleavage between the employing and the labouring classes, had been steadily growing in importance for centuries. During the eighteenth century, however, industrial capitalists certainly became more numerous, more class-conscious, and more closely organised for the defence of their common interests: in this sense it is not incorrect to say that the economic changes of that century gave rise to a new class in English society, a class which was soon to compete with the landed aristocracy for political as well as economic importance. Such "captains of industry" as Richard Arkwright were not isolated figures in their generation; they were simply prominent examples of a type which was becoming increasingly common in all branches of manufacture. In the cotton industry were such families as the Peels, the Grants, the Gregs and the Fieldens; among the individual leaders were men like Samuel Oldknow of Mellor, and Robert Owen of New Lanark. Of all such men it may be remarked that they were more important as industrial organisers than as inventors. Their success was due mainly to general business capacity, to their skill in the manipulation of capital and in the management of labour. Many of them were Dissenters; of the Nonconformist sects, the Quakers, the Presbyterians, and later the Unitarians, seem to have been the most numerous and influential.[1]

[1] Charles Wilson, 'The entrepreneur in the Industrial Revolution in Britain', *History*, June 1957, pp. 111–17.

Richard Arkwright's fame as an inventor rests on very doubtful ground; but his genius for the mobilisation and control of capital cannot be doubted. It was his abnormal financial capacity which made him the first great "cotton lord", and one of the most successful of the early factory masters.[1] It was for the purpose of seeking financial backing that Arkwright migrated from Lancashire to Nottingham. There for a short time he received support from local bankers named Wright; but his financial position was not securely established until 1771, when he entered into a contract with two merchant employers in the hosiery trade, Samuel Need of Nottingham and Jedediah Strutt of Derby. Arkwright's original manufactory might more properly be called a workshop; it contained only a few frames, which were worked by a horse gin. In 1771, however, after he had joined forces with Need and Strutt, Arkwright set up a much bigger factory at Cromford, on the model of the silk mill established by the Lombes in 1718 at Derby. By 1779 the Cromford mill was giving employment to three hundred workers. Meanwhile, Arkwright and his partners had not only introduced the machine-spun cotton yarn into the hosiery industry, but had become pioneers in the weaving of pure cotton calicoes. In 1775 Arkwright took out his second patent, covering several distinct inventions, of which the most important were the carding machine and the roving frame. With some minor supplementary devices, these new machines completed the mechanisation of the preparatory processes in the cotton trade, and left only weaving as a hand industry. After his initial success, Arkwright formed various partnerships, and financed the opening of cotton mills (using his patented machinery) in many parts of England, Scotland, and Wales. By 1785, when his patents were revoked, he was firmly

---

[1] The best recent account of Arkwright's career is to be found in R. S. Fitton and A. P. Wadsworth, *The Strutts and the Arkwrights, 1758-1830* (1958), pp. 60-107.

47

established as the leading capitalist in the cotton industry, and no mere legal decision could check his triumphal progress. He was knighted in 1786, and was appointed Sheriff of Derbyshire in the following year; when he died in 1792 he was worth half a million, and is said to have cherished the ambition of accumulating enough money to pay off the National Debt.

In the iron-founding industry, John Wilkinson may be taken as typical of the race of pioneering ironmasters, to which belonged such families as the Darbys of Coalbrookdale, the Guests of Dowlais and the Crawshays of Cyfarthfa. John Wilkinson was born in 1728 at Clifton, in Cumberland, where his father was a working iron founder. As young boys, John and his brother William helped their father in more than one independent iron-founding enterprise. By 1770 the two brothers were in control of important ironworks at Bersham (near Wrexham), Broseley (near Coalbrookdale), and Bradley (near Bilston). In 1774 John Wilkinson patented a new method of boring cannon; this led to extensive contracts with the Office of Ordnance; a second machine for the boring of cylinders became an important factor in the development of Watt's steam engine. Conversely, the development of the steam engine contributed (as we have already seen) to the technical improvement of Wilkinson's iron founding. The Darbys, in an earlier generation, had gained a stronger blast by assisting their water wheel with one of Newcomen's fire engines; Wilkinson in 1776 installed one of Watt's steam engines to blow his blast furnaces at Broseley. This was one of the first steam engines sent out from the Soho works, and the first to be applied to purposes other than pumping. Wilkinson extended the Bradley works, started a brickyard there, and connected them with the Birmingham Canal by a private branch. At Broseley he built several blast furnaces, which he supplied with coal from his own mines. He was financially interested in copper works in South

Wales, lead mines and lime kilns in North Wales, and copper mines in Cornwall. He had a London warehouse, and a large wharf at Rotherhithe; his reputation and his business activities extended also to France and Germany. Between 1787 and 1808 his private coinage of silver and copper circulated throughout the Midlands and West of England, bearing his likeness and the modest inscription: "JOHN WILKINSON, IRON MASTER". He may truly be said to have been "iron mad" in his passion for extending the uses of the metal. With the third Abraham Darby, Wilkinson helped to finance the first iron bridge in 1777–9, and in 1787 he launched the first iron boat. He built a "cast-iron chapel" for the Methodists at Bradley, and provided by will that he should be buried in an iron coffin.

Matthew Boulton was born in the same year as John Wilkinson, and became even more pre-eminent as an iron manufacturer than Wilkinson became as an iron founder. Boulton's father was a manufacturer of Birmingham "toys", that is to say miscellaneous metal articles like buttons, watch chains and shoe buckles. To this trade Matthew Boulton was brought up, and he inherited a considerable fortune with the business when his father died in 1759. In addition, Matthew had married an heiress, and might have been expected to settle down to the life of a leisured gentleman. Instead of doing this, however, he employed all his resources (including as much credit as he could command) in extending the scope of the family business. In the year of his father's death, Boulton began to build his great Soho works on a desolate heath to the north of Birmingham. The work of construction and extension went on from 1759 to 1765; by the latter date there were at Soho five blocks of buildings, and working accommodation for six hundred workmen. The machinery was driven partly by horse gins, and partly by a water wheel which was fed from a private reservoir. "Toy" making on such a large scale was unusual in Birmingham, and Boulton (with his partner

Fothergill) had an immediate success; even in 1763 their turn-over already amounted to £30,000. But Boulton not only made at Soho the usual Birmingham wares; he added to the trade many novelties, and planned "to work for all Europe in all things that they may have occasion for: gold, silver, copper, plated, gilt, pinchbeck, steel, platina, tortoiseshell, or anything else that may become an article of general demand".[1] This was several years before Boulton took James Watt into partnership. By 1778, however, the toy-making firm of Boulton and Fothergill was "a losing concern and its credit was bad".[2] Boulton would have followed Watt's first partner into bankruptcy, if he had not been able to draw upon the credit and profits of the steam-engine business to make good the losses in his other enterprises.

These early industrial capitalists sprang from very diverse origins. It will be noticed that the famous inventors of the period were not particularly prominent as business men. Hargreaves, Crompton and Cartwright benefited little from their discoveries; Cort went bankrupt, and Watt, although he eventually proved to be an excellent business man, might never have developed his steam engine if it had not been for the initial opportunity afforded by his partnership with Matthew Boulton. Arkwright and Wilkinson had inventions to their credit; but in neither man was the inventive faculty predominant. In the textile industries many of the early factory masters came from country districts and from families which had previously combined manufacturing industry with peasant agriculture. This is hardly surprising, indeed, when it is considered how widespread the combination had hitherto been. The Peels had been peasant proprietors and "hardy yeomen" since the fifteenth century, and com-

---

[1] S. Smiles, *Lives of Boulton and Watt*, 1865, p. 172, note 1.
[2] J. E. Cule, *loc. cit.*, p. 320. See also E. Robinson, 'Boulton and Fothergill, 1762–1782, and the Birmingham export of hardware', *Univ. of Birmingham Hist. Journal*, VII, no. 1, 1959, pp. 60–79.

bined hand-loom weaving with small farming long before the first Robert Peel known to history left the country for town industry in the middle of the eighteenth century. In 1780 Joshua Fielden was still living as a yeoman in Todmorden, though he had also, like many of his neighbours, two or three looms in his house, weaving woollens for the Halifax market. He made his entrance into the cotton industry by setting up several jennies in three converted cottages; his nine children were turned into cotton spinners, and the family fortunes were founded. David Dale tended cattle as a boy in Ayrshire; and many of the other Scots who swarmed into the cotton trade in the 1780s were of equally bucolic origin. The factory masters who did not come from agriculture were a very mixed lot. Richard Arkwright began as a barber, John Horrocks as a stone cutter; Robert Owen was the son of a village saddler, and began his working life as a linen draper's assistant.

This diversity of origin among the pioneers of the new industrial system must not be over-stressed. Many of the early factory masters came from families which had been connected with the textile industries for several generations; and this industrial continuity was even stronger in the case of the metal industries. With few exceptions the great ironmasters were from childhood connected with the metal industries in one way or another. The father of the first Abraham Darby was a locksmith; Aaron Walker was a nailer; Benjamin Huntsman was a clockmaker; Samuel Garbett began as a brass worker; Ambrose Crowley and Richard Crawshay received their early training in ironmongers' shops. John Roebuck, though a doctor of medicine, was the son of a Sheffield manufacturer. Of course, if research were pushed far enough back, most of these families could be shown to have originated among the peasantry; but the divorce from agriculture was fairly remote in some of the cases.[1]

[1] With Mantoux, *op. cit.*, pp. 379–81, *cf.* Ashton, *Iron and Steel*, pp. 209–10.

Among the qualities necessary for success in large-scale industrial operations, fighting spirit was evidently more important than inventive genius; but courage and initiative did not always survive, in that unsettled age, unless they were backed by more prosaic business qualities. The industrial pioneers needed above all the capacity for mobilising and co-ordinating large masses of both capital and labour. Neither task was easy; but the recruiting and management of labour was perhaps the harder. Down to the end of the eighteenth century, the established textile workers under the domestic system had no strong inducement to go into the new factories; and there was a prevalent feeling that factory work was not respectable. The early factory workers were, therefore, necessarily recruited from the less stable and less responsible elements in the population.[1] The contemporary records all confirm this impression; displaced agricultural workers, discharged soldiers, broken tailors and cobblers, paupers and vagrants, all tried their hands in the new factories, and left when the discipline grew irksome. Contrary to earlier belief, the Settlement and Removal Act of 1662 did not present any serious obstacle, after 1697, to artisans and labourers who were really determined to move from one parish to another.[2] The task of organising such casual workers into a settled industrial population was probably harder even than the task of persuading the private bankers of the day that large profits could not be made without large overdrafts. The industrial pioneers had also to face new marketing problems, for industry was now international in its scope; the new machines and engines could not reach their full efficiency of operation unless they were producing for a world-wide market. Matthew Boulton, in negotiating for a partnership with Watt in 1769, stated very emphatically the necessity for producing steam

[1] See below, pp. 64-5.
[2] D. Marshall, 'The Old Poor Law, 1662-1795', *Economic History Review*, Nov. 1937, pp. 38-47.

engines in large quantities if the business was to be profitable. "It would not be worth my while to make for three counties only," he said, "but I find it very well worth my while to make for all the world."[1] Eventually, the firm of Boulton and Watt sold engines not only throughout England, but also in Scotland, Wales, France, Holland, Germany, Spain and Russia; for a long time, however, the marketing problems raised merely by their English business were formidable enough.

The early industrial capitalists needed, then, to possess exceptional organising capacity, among other business qualities; but apart from their ability as men of business they were not remarkable, as a class, for general intelligence. Watt, Boulton and Wedgwood were men of wide culture and high moral qualities; but in that respect they were not typical of their class. Most of the manufacturers were ill-educated, coarse, and rough, with an extremely limited range of ideas; intellectually they were in most cases not markedly distinguishable from their foremen, save in their knowledge of business method and their ruthless determination to make money quickly. Arkwright, the "bag-cheeked, pot-bellied barber",[2] with his "fat vulgar face, his goggling, heavy-lidded eyes" was more typical of the new class of manufacturers than James Watt, with his fine-drawn features and perpetual air of self-distrust, or Samuel Crompton, whose portrait "combines the features of Bonaparte in his younger days with the expression of a Methodist preacher".[3]

If the early industrial capitalists lacked culture and social conscience, they were at any rate not lacking in consciousness of their common interests. Agreements and organisations for collective action were continually being formed among the manufacturers during the later eighteenth century, while attempts to form similar organisations among

[1] Quoted by Dickinson and Jenkins, *loc. cit.*
[2] T. Carlyle, *Chartism*, 1840, Chapter VIII, p. 85.
[3] Mantoux, *op. cit.*, pp. 225, 242.

their workpeople were being prohibited by one special Act
after another. One instance of such agreements occurred
in 1762, when the Darbys and the Wilkinsons agreed on uniform prices for cylinders, pipes, etc., in all markets except
London; but the ironmasters were not solely dependent on
such private compacts. By 1777 a midland association of ironmasters was in existence, with quarterly meetings for the
regulation of trade policy in such matters as the determination of prices and conditions of sale. Such industrial and commercial activities went on steadily, quarter by quarter, from
that time; and in later years many other districts copied this
organisation of the midland iron trade. Thus, in 1799, a
"Friendly Association" of the ironmasters of Yorkshire and
Derbyshire was established, with quarterly meetings and a
regular constitution, including an annual subscription of a
guinea. After 1810 special representatives were sent from this
association to attend the Gloucester meetings of ironmasters,
and frequent communications were maintained with the
organised ironmasters of Wales, Shropshire, and Staffordshire. The Welsh quarterly meeting, held at Newport, had
been instituted in 1802, with an annual subscription of a
guinea and an entrance fee of a bowl of punch. All these meetings were concerned with the fixing of prices and conditions
of sale; and decisions made by one meeting were often agreed
to by the meetings in other districts, so that there was some
approach to national uniformity of trade policy. Nor were
the activities of such organisations entirely industrial; the
manufacturing interest also exercised a strong influence on
political policy, long before the new manufacturing towns received direct representation in Parliament.[1]

Their indirect influence on public policy, and their pre-
occupation with money-making, made the industrial

[1] See, for example, J. M. Norris, 'Samuel Garbett and the early development of industrial lobbying in Great Britain', *Economic History Review*, April 1958, pp. 450–60.

capitalists indifferent to the agitation for parliamentary reform during the later eighteenth century; they declined to send petitions on the subject, and even resented any attempt to involve them in party controversy. Yet powerful organisations of the employing classes already existed, not only in the iron industry, but in many other branches of trade and manufactures. The Norwich "Committee of Trade" was already in active operation by 1736. The Manchester "Committee for the Protection and Encouragement of Trade", which was established in 1774, included manufacturers as well as merchants; as reorganised in 1781 the Committee represented not only the cotton manufacture but also the linen, silk, and small-ware industries. Moreover, there were other organisations for various special branches of the textile industries, such as the fustian manufacture, dyeing, bleaching, and calico printing. A parallel organisation of the worsted clothiers and manufacturers of the West Riding, Lancashire, and Cheshire was established in 1777. It was in the first instance concerned with the legislation against workmen's combinations and against the embezzlement of yarn; but it soon assumed other functions, such as opposition to the export of wool and of machinery. Many less formal and less public organisations were already operative throughout the main industrial districts.

Employers' organisations were being established in most of the metal trades, among the steel manufacturers, the nail makers, the cutlers, the silver-plate manufacturers, the steel tilters, the file makers and tool makers. In the brass and copper industries capitalist organisation became so strong as to constitute a monopoly. In the early years of the eighteenth century there were only four or five copper-smelting works in England; and it was alleged that the companies had already come to an understanding about the price of cake copper. Various other brass and copper companies appeared in the course of the eighteenth century, and some became very large concerns; but the total number of large-scale producers remained small, and concerted action continued to be easy. In the 1780s, however, the associated smelters, who relied mainly on their control of the Cornish copper mines, met with serious opposition from the development of extensive copper-mining operations in Anglesey, under the leadership of Thomas Williams. By 1785 competition with Anglesey had reduced the Cornish miners to extreme distress, and the associated smelters had to agree to a partition of the market. By agreement between the two main districts the Cornish Metal Company was formed, with the object of buying up the copper from the mining companies, getting it smelted under agreement with established smelting companies, and marketing the whole product at fixed prices. Before the end of 1787, however, the Cornish Metal Company had been forced by its financial losses to make Williams its sole selling agent. In 1790 Williams, with ten of the main smelting companies behind him, took over the whole business of the Cornish Metal Company, and became the dominant figure in the copper trade of the country. It is true that the monopolistic control of the copper trade seems to have broken down after 1793; but that may have been because it was no longer necessary. The outbreak of the French wars cut off the imports of copper from the Continent, while large exports of copper at low prices were permitted through the East India Company. The increased demand for copper for ship sheathing and other war purposes compensated the miners and smelters (though not the Birmingham manufacturers) for the loss of the export trade in "Brummagem toys". The price of copper rose rapidly, and limitation of output became unnecessary.[1]

It was the existing organisations in the separate industries which made possible the formation of the General Chamber of Manufacturers of Great Britain in 1785; though the direct

[1] See H. Hamilton, *The English Brass and Copper Industries*, 1926, Chapters VI–VIII.

incentive to this federation of interests must be sought in the economic policy of the Government at the end of the American War. Pitt's new excise scheme of 1784, which included a fustian tax, led to special committees of the textile manufacturers being formed in such towns as Manchester and Glasgow, and the sending of delegations to London. In this movement the textile manufacturers were strongly supported by the midland ironmasters' quarterly meeting and by the Birmingham Commercial Committee, which had been formed in 1783. Within a short time Pitt's proposals for a treaty of commercial reciprocity between England and Ireland called for still more united action from the manufacturing employers, who feared the effect of allowing Irish manufactured goods to be imported freely into England. The General Chamber of Manufacturers was organised in March 1785, on the initiative of Josiah Wedgwood, to resist the Government's proposals. During the next few months a good deal of indirect pressure was exerted by the General Chamber; prominent manufacturers met members of the Government in London to discuss the difficulty, and eventually the agitation was successful in securing such a modification of the Government's proposals as was sufficient to cause the failure of the negotiations with the Irish Parliament.

The Government's negotiations for an Anglo-French commercial treaty in 1786 caused a sharp division of opinion among the various industries represented in the General Chamber of Manufacturers. Eden's treaty was an important advance towards freer trade; but while it benefited the cotton, iron and pottery interests (which were predominant in the General Chamber) it seemed less likely to benefit such old-established industries as silk, ribbons, leather, paper, clocks and glass.[1] The General Chamber voted in favour of the treaty; but the dissentient interests were strong enough to

[1] W. O. Henderson, 'The Anglo-French Commercial Treaty of 1786', *Economic History Review*, August 1957, pp. 104–12.

cause serious disunion afterwards within the Chamber, which therefore became somewhat discredited with the public and the Government. Pitt had from the first declined to regard the Chamber as representing the interests of the general body of manufacturers; though after 1785 he was always careful to take the individual opinions of the leading industrialists on points of economic policy.

In later years, organised action by bodies of traders and manufacturers followed closely the precedents laid down by the General Chamber. In 1796–7 fresh proposals to put excise duties on coal and pig iron, with customs duties to correspond, roused the ironmasters to renewed activity. The Birmingham Meeting organised a strong agitation against the excise on iron, and arranged for common action with the Welsh and Scottish districts. Eventually Pitt abandoned the proposed excise on iron, but carried through the proposal for increased customs duties; the ironmasters thus secured increased protection, instead of increased burdens. A similar situation arose ten years later, when the proposal for an excise on pig iron was revived by Lord Henry Petty, at a time when the economic warfare with Napoleon was creating an urgent need for increased revenue. The ironmasters without hesitation set up in London a standing committee of fourteen representatives, drawn from the various iron districts. Propagandist pamphlets were published, and interviews were arranged with members of the Government. At these interviews the proposed tax was alleged to be threatening the whole fabric of British industry, which was the mainstay of national defence; in the end, the obnoxious proposal was withdrawn and a tax on brewing substituted.

In many of the early organisations of capitalists there was no clear differentiation between merchants and manufacturers. Even where distinct manufacturers' and merchants' committees existed side by side, they commonly overlapped considerably in membership. The Birmingham Commercial

Committee had as its president a prominent manufacturer, Samuel Garbett. The Manchester Commercial Society, which was founded in 1794, consisted of both merchants and manufacturers. The establishment of a Mercantile and Manufacturing Union of all Sheffield trades in 1814 shows the same close co-operation between the industrial and commercial capitalists; no doubt a similar combination of interests might be traced in the early history of the Commercial Societies and Chambers of Commerce in other manufacturing towns.[1] Nevertheless, while the manufacturers found it expedient to work alongside the merchants in dealing with matters of common interest, this did not prevent them from possessing also their own separate organisations. The new class of industrial capitalists was in no danger henceforth of losing its solidarity. The constant warfare against the rudimentary labour organisations, which were springing up in almost all the main industries of the country, was in itself enough to strengthen the class consciousness of the industrial employers.

[1] See Redford (and others), *Manchester Merchants and Foreign Trade, 1794–1858* (1934), Chapters I–V.

CHAPTER FIVE

The Industrial Wage Earners

THERE HAVE BEEN industrial wage earners and labour organisations of one sort or another since the Middle Ages; in a few trades, indeed, there may have been some degree of continuity between the mediaeval form of journeymen's associations and the modern form of trade unionism. In the majority of trades, however, no such continuity of development is traceable: the early wage earners' associations were mostly sporadic and short-lived. It is not until the early eighteenth century that there can be traced in English industry the general spread of labour unions; and even then the organisations formed did not in most cases show any close similarity to modern trade unions in either scope or structure. There is, therefore, substantial justification for the belief that modern trade unionism is a by-product of the industrial changes which were taking place during the eighteenth century. Nevertheless, the movement towards trade-unionist organisations showed itself before the period of famous inventions, and was not confined to those branches of industry which were directly affected by rapid technical progress.

The labour organisations of the earlier eighteenth century were local trade clubs rather than national trade unions. Such local trade clubs were found in almost all the main trades of the country, and many survived into the nineteenth century, in spite of much legislation aiming at their suppression. Examples of this persistence in labour organisation were especially numerous in the textile industries. In such old trades as tailoring the distinction between the capitalist employers and the permanent journeymen was already well established. It is not surprising, therefore, to find the master tailors of London petitioning Parliament in 1720 against journeymen's combinations organised for the purpose of raising wages and shortening hours of labour. Parliament replied by prohibiting such combinations in the tailoring trade, and by fixing maximum rates of wages. Evidently the journeymen's association persisted in spite of this legislative prohibition, for a Privy Council Order to the same effect was issued in 1744. In 1767 further legislation was passed against such combinations; yet a witness giving evidence in 1810 said that the organisation had existed for over a century.

In the various districts of the woollen manufacturing industry reports of workmen's combinations are frequent from the very beginning of the eighteenth century; and in this industry, also, repressive legislation and royal prohibitory proclamations seem to have been equally ineffectual to prevent the persistence of the labour organisations. The case of the worsted smallware weavers of Lancashire is especially interesting, partly because it provides a background to the rapid technical changes which were taking place in the Lancashire textile industries, partly because it shows the remarkable resilience of a labour union apparently shattered. The regulations of the worsted smallware weavers were framed in 1747, and dealt with such matters as the conditions of apprenticeship and entrance to the trade. In 1756 the weavers began to hold regular monthly meetings to which delegates were sent from each shop. By this time the master manufacturers had become alarmed at the development of the combination, and began to contemplate legal proceedings. Warning notices were issued in 1759, and in the following year a number of the weavers were prosecuted at the Lancaster Assizes for unlawful combination to raise wages. This prosecution was withdrawn only after the defendants had promised in open court and in writing to renounce the combination, and to refrain from such action in the future. Meanwhile similar measures had been taken against a combination among the Manchester check weavers, eighteen of whom had been fined at the Lancaster Assizes in 1759. To all appearances these legal prosecutions must have driven the combinations out of existence; yet in actual fact the organisations seem to have gained in strength during the next generation. The choice before the employers and judicial authorities was not between combinations and individual contracts, but between open trade clubs and less responsible secret societies.

The preceding examples of labour organisation concern trades which had not been directly affected by the introduction of power-driven machinery and a factory system. But the aggregation of workpeople into factories, and the more obvious cleavage of interests which the factory system involved, naturally accelerated the formation of workmen's combinations. The rapid spread of cotton-spinning factories in the North of England after 1780 led at once to the establishment of cotton spinners' unions in such rising industrial towns as Stockport and Oldham. So early as 1785 the "Friendly Society of Cotton Spinners of Stockport" was issuing its notices in the public newspapers.[1] Such societies were the forerunners of a great number of spinners' unions in the northern counties of England and the south-western shires of Scotland.

These early cotton spinners' unions, like the other textile workers' organisations already mentioned, were on a narrowly local basis; as yet there was no general movement towards the formation of national organisations comparable with the typical trade unions of modern times. Curiously enough, the first known instance of an attempt at labour organisation on a national basis was in the hatting trade, in which there is strong evidence for continuity of association

[1] G. Unwin, *Samuel Oldknow and the Arkwrights*, 1924, pp. 32-34.

among journeymen since the Middle Ages. In 1771 the journeymen hatters seem to have "established a national federation of the local trade clubs existing in more than a dozen provincial towns with those of Southwark and the West End of London".[1] The original objects of the federation were mainly concerned with the maintenance of the statutory apprenticeship regulations, which were being broken down by the rapid development of capitalist organisation; but in 1775 the journeymen hatters also forced their employers to pay higher rates of wages, and secured the exclusion of non-unionists from employment. Hatters' congresses were held in 1772, 1775 and 1777, and there was evidently a substantial trade organisation behind them; members paid a uniform contribution of twopence a week, and when "tramping" in search of work were given regular relief from the funds of local branches.[2] In 1777 the master hatters obtained from Parliament the repeal of the old limitation of apprentices for their trade and a further prohibition of workmen's combinations; but the journeymen's organisation evidently persisted in some form or other, though the national journeymen hatters' trade union of later times does not claim to have been founded before 1798.

The general movement towards labour organisation, in both the mechanised and the non-mechanised branches of manufacture, may be taken as evidence that the working classes were definitely hostile to the new developments in industry, and felt that their customary standard of life was being threatened. Nor is it difficult to find more direct evidence of hostility to power-driven machinery and prejudice against the factory system. Throughout the later eighteenth century machine-breaking riots occurred spasmodically in

---

[1] Webb, *History of Trade Unionism*, 1920 ed., p. 29.
[2] For the existence of this custom among skilled craftsmen, see E. J. Hobsbawm, 'The Tramping Artisan', *Economic History Review*, 2nd series, III, no. 3, 1951, pp. 299–320.

various parts of the country, in spite of much repressive legislation. Every period of distress brought fresh proof to the popular mind that the machines were "taking the bread out of the mouths of the poor"; though some of the distress was certainly due to abnormally bad harvests, and much more to the economic dislocation caused by warfare and currency derangements.

Behind the spasmodic outbreaks of machine-breaking fury there was, however, a more general prejudice against factory work, which seems to call for special explanation. There were, of course, many features of employment in the early factories which might well make any intelligent being dislike it; though how far factory conditions were worse than the conditions in domestic industry is a separate question. But factory work was not merely disliked because it was disagreeable; there was also a prejudice against it as being disreputable. William Hutton, who was an apprentice in Lombe's mill at Derby from 1730 to 1737, objected not so much to the nature of the work as to the low social and intellectual level of his fellow workers, "the most vulgar and rude of the human race".[1] When the brothers John and George Buchanan established the Deanston Mills in 1785, they found that "the more respectable part of the surrounding inhabitants were at first averse to seek employment in the works, as they considered it disreputable to be employed in what they called 'a public work'." [2] A similar prejudice was encountered by David Dale at New Lanark, by Samuel Oldknow at Mellor, and by most of the early factory masters about whom information is available.

The early factory population was certainly to a large extent composed of casual and not very respectable workers. For most of their adult workers the early factory masters seem

---

[1] *The Life of William Hutton*, ed. Ll. Jewitt, 1872.
[2] *Factory Inspectors' Reports*, December 1838, Appendix V, p. 98; see Redford, *Labour Migration in England*. pp. 19–22.

to have relied on pauper or tramp labour; a considerable proportion of the child labour employed was recruited by an extension of the old-established system of parish apprenticeship, which even before the factory period was already subject to grave abuses. The aversion of the settled respectable population from factory work in such company was quite natural; but since the factory masters seem to have been confronted with this general prejudice from the first, it is not easy to determine whether the disreputable character of the early factory population was a cause or an effect of the prejudice. It seems quite likely that the general disinclination to enter "a public work" may have arisen from an idea that factories were a kind of poor-law workhouses. Nicholls was probably reflecting the popular opinion fairly accurately when he wrote that "the workhouse was in truth at that time a kind of manufactory . . . employing the worst description of the people".[1] Moreover, in the seventeenth and eighteenth centuries workshops and works were sometimes called "workhouses", apart from any connection with the Poor Law.[2] It was therefore quite natural that the new factories should be popularly confused with the older system of houses of industry. This being so, it was equally natural that the early factory masters should turn to the workhouses for a large part of their labour supply, whether they needed children or adult workers. Indeed, the workhouse was used by some factory masters as a convenient labour-recruiting agency, not only in the eighteenth century but until comparatively recent times.

If the prejudice of the settled population against the factory system can be thus explained, the more active hostility of the industrial workers to the new machines should be even easier to understand. The main advantage of the new machinery, at any rate in the eighteenth century, was its economy of labour,

---

[1] Nicholls, *History of the English Poor Law*, Vol. II (1854), pp. 18, 58.
[2] See *Oxford English Dictionary*, s v. "workhouse".

especially poorly paid, semi-skilled labour.[1] The workers so
affected had to face the prospect of unemployment and loss of
livelihood, and were inevitably hostile to the inventors and
their creations. Actually, it is difficult to believe that the new
machinery and the new methods did cause much industrial
unemployment during the eighteenth century. The machine-
smashing riots of the period reflected the spasmodic recurrence of severe economic distress; but this recurrent distress
should probably be attributed to high prices caused by harvest
failures or the currency derangement of wartime, rather than
to any serious scarcity of industrial employment. Nevertheless, recurrent distress in a period of rapid industrial transition inevitably raises the question whether the industrial
changes tended to improve or to injure the welfare of the
working classes.[2] Admittedly, the working and living conditions of the industrial population during the later eighteenth
century were deplorable, judged by modern standards. A
working day of fourteen hours was quite usual in the early
factories; in busy seasons the mills worked night and day on a
shift system, and the factory "hands" sometimes had to work
double shifts. The working rooms were often low, dark, and
filled with a fine fluff which caused bronchial and lung
troubles. "Factory fever", a disease somewhat similar to the
"prison fever" of the period, broke out in the Manchester
district in 1784. The origin of the epidemic remained uncertain; it may possibly have been Irish "famine fever", imported along with the increased stream of Irish immigrants
after the great famine of 1782. While the origin of the fever
was uncertain, however, the medical investigators were quite
convinced that the disorder had been "supported, diffused,

[1] Ashton, *Economic History of England: the Eighteenth Century*, 1955, pp.
108–9.
[2] On this question see T. S. Ashton, 'Changes in the standards of comfort in eighteenth-century England' (*Proc. British Academy*, Vol. XLI, 1955,
pp. 171–87), and T. S. Ashton, 'The standard of life of the workers in
England, 1790–1830', in *Capitalism and the Historians*, ed. F. A. Hayek
1954, pp. 127–59.

and aggravated, by the ready communication of contagion to numbers crowded together; by the accession to its virulence from putrid effluvia, and by the injury done to young persons through confinement and too long-continued labour: to which several evils the cotton mills have given occasion".[1] Frequent recurrences of these "low fevers" in the manufacturing districts were brought prominently to the public notice during the succeeding generation by Dr. Thomas Percival and his friends on the Manchester Board of Health. Housing conditions may have helped factory confinement in spreading such diseases; the rapid growth of large industrial towns necessarily gave rise to much overcrowding in the working-class quarters. In Manchester and the neighbouring towns many of the newcomers found a lodging in cellars, which were dark, damp, and unhealthy. The water supply, drainage, sanitary arrangements and street-cleansing services were all alike primitive and inadequate.[2]

There was, however, another side to the question. Housing and sanitary conditions seem to have been at least as bad in London as they were in the new factory towns; and yet the sanitary condition of London was much better in the later eighteenth century than it had been in earlier times.[3] It is possible, therefore, that the sanitary shortcomings of the manufacturing districts were not wholly to be attributed to the new machinery and the factory system. Actually, the housing conditions even in the most rural districts were not much better than the urban conditions in many respects. There was a good deal of overcrowding in the country districts, partly arising from the demolition of cottages by the landed proprietors, in the hope of keeping down the poor rates. The "entire villages just out of the hands of the masons,

[1] Dr. T. Percival, quoted by Hutchins and Harrison, *History of Factory Legislation*, 1911 ed., p. 8.
[2] The problems of urban sanitation are discussed more fully in Chapter XI, below.
[3] M. Dorothy George, *London Life in the XVIIIth Century*, 1925, *passim*.

consisting of beautiful little cottages",[1] which an American-born observer noted in Yorkshire in 1833, may have compared quite favourably with the "miserable mud cottage, in a low, damp situation, adjoining a large tract of open field land, with a filthy pond close to the door",[2] which some of the Bedfordshire migrants left behind when they moved to Yorkshire in 1836. Whether the factory fever of the period was related to the Irish famine fever or not, it had its counterpart in the ague which was prevalent over wide stretches of low-lying marshy country in the southern agricultural counties. Even the damp cellars of Manchester were no worse than the Irish cabins from which many of the cellar dwellers came.

Bad living conditions were not, then, confined to the industrial towns; nor were bad working conditions peculiar to the factories. Many domestic workers found it necessary to keep to their tasks for as long hours as the factory workers; moreover, domestic workshops were usually smaller and often damper than the factory rooms. According to some contemporary accounts, the rooms in which domestic workers "batted" cotton and ate their meals were as thick with fluff as any spinning room in a factory. Probably the really hateful feature of factory life from the contemporary point of view was its compulsory uniformity and strict discipline. Such a life was no doubt distasteful to domestic workers who had been able to take a day off now and then to follow the hounds afoot, or a week off to get thoroughly drunk; but discipline and uniformity are such general and necessary features of working life nowadays that it is hard to think of them as major grievances. Even in those days many agricultural workers found the heat of the spinning rooms as tolerable as the cold damp of the fields. There must have been many who agreed with the Suffolk migrant who wrote home in 1836: "I do not know that I would like to work abroad now; I would rather

[1] *Report on Manufactures, Commerce, and Shipping*, 1833, p. 48.
[2] *Second Annual Report of the Poor Law Commissioners*, 1836, Appendix B, No. 21, p. 439.

work in the mill than in the field." [1] Bronchitis may have seemed no worse a danger than rheumatism.

So far as wages were concerned, the advantage rested (and still rests) with the factory "hand" as against either the domestic industrial worker or the agricultural labourer. It is true that the statistical evidence available is very defective, and that no exact comparisons are possible. The question is, moreover, complicated by the contemporary irregularity of employment in both manufacturing industry and agriculture, as well as by the income from secondary occupations. The rent-free occupation of a cottage with a vegetable garden often made a considerable difference to a man's real wages. Another difficulty in interpretation arises from the fact that wages in the eighteenth century often represented the earnings of the family rather than of the individual. Another factor obscuring the real rates of wages was the prevalence of the truck system.[2]

After taking into consideration all the various sources of possible error, however, it seems possible to make one or two rough generalisations, so long as it is recognised that they do not state any final truth. Throughout the later eighteenth century, industrial wages were higher than agricultural, and the wages of factory workers were higher than those of corresponding grades of domestic industrial workers. The wages of all classes of workers were rising during the period, but the increase was less marked in agricultural than in industrial wages, and much less marked in some of the older industrial areas than in the "new" manufacturing districts of the North of England.[3] Certain classes of the domestic industrial workers suffered wage reductions, and many agricultural labourers lost industrial by-occupations. On the other hand, some

[1] *Second Annual Report of the Poor Law Commissioners*, 1836, Appendix B, No. 20, p. 421.
[2] For this problem, see the authorities cited by G. W. Hilton, 'The British truck system in the nineteenth century', *Journal of Political Economy*, Vol. LXV, June 1957, pp. 237–56.
[3] E. W. Gilboy, *Wages in Eighteenth Century England*, 1934, pp. 112–13, 214–15, and *passim*.

classes of domestic industrial workers benefited greatly, though not permanently, from the technical changes, while many of the rural by-industries showed a surprisingly persistent vitality right down to the middle of the nineteenth century. In the cotton industry, which was the most progressive of the textile trades, there was during the last quarter of the eighteenth century a general displacement of domestic labour in the spinning and other preparatory processes; but this was not yet a serious social evil, owing to the contemporary prosperity of hand-loom weaving. It is true that there was a swift and persistent deterioration in the weavers' economic and social condition after the beginning of the French wars in 1793; but after that date there were also new factors which require to be taken into consideration in accounting for this economic retrogression and social collapse.

The general rise in wage rates during the later eighteenth century was, to a large extent, nullified by the coincident rise in prices. The recurrent outbreaks of social unrest during the period were caused more directly by the high prices (especially of foodstuffs) than by either wage reductions or industrial unemployment. In order to determine the fundamental causes of the social distress it is necessary, therefore, to discover what caused the high prices. The new machinery and the factory system can hardly be included among the direct causes of increased prices; for the industrial changes surely tended to cheapen manufactured goods by increasing the quantity produced. Similarly, it can be shown that the agricultural changes increased the production of foodstuffs; why, then, did the prices of foodstuffs rise with especial rapidity?

One important reason for the rising level of prices was the rapid growth of population.[1] The food supply was increasing, but was not keeping pace with the increase of population and the rising conventional standard of comfort. England had

---

[1] Other causes of high prices, such as wartime scarcity and currency derangements, are discussed in Chapter VII, below.

hitherto been a grain-exporting country in normal years, though there had always been the danger of food scarcity, and the necessity for importing grain in years of abnormally bad harvests. After the middle of the eighteenth century the balance gradually swung from a small normal surplus of grain to a small normal deficiency. Even at the end of the century England was not seriously dependent on foreign grain; but the demand for bread (and so for grain) was very inelastic, and a comparatively small deficiency in the supply might send prices almost to famine height. Many of the social disturbances which resulted in machine-breaking were really food riots caused by the high prices of grain; bad harvests may have been the immediate occasion of the high prices, but one of the main underlying causes was the steadily increasing pressure of population upon the food supply.

It has often been said that this increase in population was called forth by the "industrial revolution". Apparently the assumption is that, since the early factories gave employment to far more children than adult workers, it became financially profitable to marry and have children; and thus a stimulus was given to the marriage rate and the birth rate. Actually, however, the official statistics of the period seem to suggest that the unprecedented increase of population was due rather to a sharply decreasing death rate than to any extraordinary increase in the birth rate.[1] It is true that there was a persistent rise in the birth rate during the eighteenth century,

---

[1] G. Talbot Griffith, *Population Problems of the Age of Malthus*, 1926, Chapter II. See, however, T. H. Marshall's article on 'The Population Problem during the Industrial Revolution', in *Economic Journal*, Economic History Supplement No. 4, January 1929, pp. 429–56; also H. J. Habakkuk, 'English Population in the Eighteenth Century', *Economic History Review*, December 1953, pp. 117–33, and J. T. Krause, 'Changes in English fertility and mortality, 1781–1850', *ibid.*, August 1958, pp. 52–70. Mr. Krause concludes that his researches and calculations "suggest strongly that a rising birth rate was the major cause of the growth of the English population in the period," but adds: "Only after detailed local studies have been completed will a relatively exact explanation of English demographic growth during the Industrial Revolution become available".

and this must certainly be included among the causes of increased population; but it was by no means so spectacular as the contemporary fall in the death rate. Moreover, it appears from the statistics available that the birth rates in such manufacturing and mining counties as Lancashire, the West Riding of Yorkshire, Durham and Monmouth were not much higher than that of the country as a whole; though it must be remembered that the statistics recorded for the industrialised counties were likely to be inaccurate and ambiguous. Among the factors tending to increase the birth rate many responsible writers included the prevalent system of giving poor-law allowances in aid of wages. The system was said to sap the independent spirit of the labourer and diminish his prudence, to promote early marriages, and to be conducive to large families. On this point it may be remarked that the allowance system was more important in the agricultural counties than in the industrial districts; but it was in the industrial districts that population was increasing with especial rapidity. Even if all urban population is omitted from the calculation, the counties most affected by the allowance system seem to have been increasing in population less rapidly than the others. On the whole, it may be considered improbable that the operation of the poor laws stimulated the birth rate to any appreciable degree. It is, however, quite possible that the poor laws encouraged the growth of population by reducing the death rate, especially through the provision of medical relief; this would be particularly important in the reduction of infantile mortality. Probably the strongest force making for a reduction in the death rate during the eighteenth century was the advance of medical science, and its more general influence upon social welfare through the spread of such institutions as hospitals and dispensaries.[1] Many dreaded diseases, such as typhus, dysentery,

[1] With G. T. Griffith, *op. cit.*, compare M. C. Buer, *Health, Wealth, and Population, 1760–1815*, 1926, *passim*.

and scurvy were practically extinguished in this country, or at any rate ceased to be of primary importance. It has recently been argued that medical advances, with the exception of inoculation and vaccination against the smallpox, were not important, but this view is not founded on an examination of the historical evidence relating to the work of individual hospitals and dispensaries.[1]

In general terms, it may be asked whether the English working classes were better off or worse off in the later eighteenth century than they had been in earlier generations. So many incalculable factors are involved in this problem, however, that no final solution seems possible; even the simpler questions, as whether wages rose more or less in proportion to prices, are difficult to answer convincingly. Any exact comparison between wages and prices is, of course, impossible for that period. On a rough approximation, however, it seems likely that wages in general rose more in proportion to prices, though some classes of workers suffered a reduction in real wages, if not also in money wages. This tentative generalisation is supported by investigations which have been made into the relation between wages and prices over the very critical period of warfare between 1793 and 1815, when the increase of prices was much more rapid than in the preceding generation. According to the information at present available, the measurable changes in social welfare seem to have been surprisingly slight when compared with the violent statements which have often been made on the subject. Professor Clapham's summary is a model of scientific caution: "The conclusion of a difficult problem, which contains a number of doubtfully known quantities, is that whereas on the average the potential standard of comfort of an English (with Welsh) labouring family in 1824 was probably

[1] T. McKeown and R. G. Brown, 'Medical evidence relating to English population changes in the eighteenth century', *Population Studies*, Vol. IX, No. 2, November 1955, pp. 119–41.

a trifle better than it had been in 1794, assuming equal regularity of work, there were important areas in which it was definitely worse, others in which it was probably worse, and many in which the change either way was imperceptible." [1] Professor Clapham's statement has all the superficial marks of a guarded approach to quantitative accuracy. Nevertheless, it must be confessed that even this cautious generalisation has been vigorously denounced as fallacious. [2]

[1] J. H. Clapham, *Economic History of Modern Britain*, Vol. I, 1926, p. 131.
[2] J. L. Hammond, 'The Industrial Revolution and Discontent', in *Economic History Review*, Vol. II, No. 2, January 1930, pp. 215–28. See also the more recent study by E. J. Hobsbawm, 'The British standard of living, 1790–1850', *Economic History Review*, August 1957, pp. 46–68; R. M. Hartwell, 'Interpretations of the Industrial Revolution in England: a methodological inquiry' [Part I] *Journal of Economic History*, Vol. XIX, 1959, pp. 229–49; and A. J. Taylor, 'Progress and poverty in Britain, 1780–1850: a reappraisal', *History*, Vol. LXV, February 1960, pp. 16–31.

CHAPTER SIX

Changes in Agriculture

DURING THE EARLIER eighteenth century agriculture had been quietly prosperous, without any great increase in the cultivated area. Then from 1730 to about 1750 a more harassing time was experienced by landlords and farmers. It was marked by a fall in the price of wheat, a tendency for agricultural rents to fall in sympathy, and the piling-up of heavy arrears of rent in the countryside.[1] There was a considerable export trade in grain, aided by State bounties, yet home prices remained moderate. Much land was re-converted from pasture farming to tillage. Cheap grain prices benefited the mass of the population. Poor rates fell, and real wages were as high as they had been since the fifteenth century. The standard of living rose, and more flesh meat was eaten; by 1760 wheat had become the chief breadstuff of half the population of the country. The main force making for rapid changes in agriculture was, perhaps, the steady pressure of a population which was growing both in numbers and in standard of living. By the middle of the century a good deal of pioneering work in the improvement of agricultural methods had already been carried out; but the new methods were not likely to be taken up quickly, except by large capitalists or substantial tenant farmers working large enclosed estates.

Gregory King had estimated in 1696 that the heaths, moors, mountains, and barren lands of England and Wales amounted to ten million acres, or more than a quarter of the

[1] G. E. Mingay, 'The agricultural depression, 1730–1750', *Economic History Review*, April 1956, pp. 323–38.

whole area; and even this was probably an underestimate. The proportion of waste land still remained large, even after the enclosures of the next hundred years. Lancashire in 1794 still had 108,500 acres of waste, and Yorkshire had 265,000 acres. Great tracts of waste also occurred, not only in mountainous regions like Westmorland and Derbyshire, but also in Nottinghamshire, Lincolnshire, and the Fen counties. Even round London matters were not much better; such places as Hounslow Heath, Finchley Common, Epping Forest, and the Surrey Weald were still desolate tracts of waste land, known to be resorts "of the most idle and profligate of men".[1] According to an estimate of the Board of Agriculture, in 1795, there were nearly eight million acres in England and Wales still uncultivated. This, again, was probably an underestimate, but if there is any validity in comparing it with Gregory King's estimate a century earlier, it appears that the agricultural changes of the eighteenth century had added rather more than two million acres to the cultivated area.

At the beginning of the eighteenth century about a half of the arable land of the country was still cultivated on the old open-field system. The economic loss was considerable; many features in the traditional organisation of the open-field villages hindered the adoption of improved methods. All the cultivators were bound by customary rules, obliged to do what everybody else did, and at the same time. Special winter crops could not be grown, because the arable fields were subject to common pasture rights after the summer harvest until the spring ploughing. Efficient drainage was often impossible, and the strips were too narrow for cross-ploughing. A great deal of time was wasted in going about among the scattered strips, and other expenses (such as carting and manuring) were correspondingly high. Labouring under such difficulties, the strip holders quarrelled frequently

[1] See Ernle, *English Farming, Past and Present*, 5th ed., 1936, pp. 152–54.

among themselves, and ill will was added to the other factors making for inefficient agriculture. The common pastures, which formed an integral part of the open-field economy, were also in a very bad condition except where the number of cattle which could be turned on to the common had been 'stinted', i.e. limited by communal regulation. Livestock was reared only with difficulty; the animals were ill-fed and subject to disease. Many commons were over-stocked with animals belonging to speculative jobbers. In this way the beasts of the small holders were often crowded out, and the pasture rights became of negligible value. The cottager's cow could hardly find a living on a common pasture overrun with sheep. In most cases, indeed, the cottager's profits from the commons consisted mainly in fuel, geese and perhaps scanty grazing for a pony. So long as the growth of population remained fairly slow, the inefficiency of the open-field system might be tolerated out of respect for ancient tradition. In the later eighteenth century, however, the pressure of a growing population and a rising standard of living was aggravated by the almost incessant strain of warfare and wartime scarcity. It is true that the scarcity of food was to some extent relieved by the increasing cultivation of potatoes during the eighteenth century. Nevertheless, there was still an urgent necessity for increased supplies of foodstuffs, both corn and meat. This necessity forced on a relatively rapid transition in agricultural organisation and technique; and, among other necessary changes, the enclosure of the common pastures and open-field arable was accelerated.

The urgent need for increased food supplies may justify this quickening of the enclosure movement; it is, however, important not to exaggerate the rapidity of the changes. The number of Enclosure Acts certainly increased very markedly after 1760;[1] but enclosure might take place by private agree-

[1] See Gilbert Slater, *The English Peasantry and the Enclosure of Common Fields*, 1907, Appendices A and B, pp. 267–68.

77

ment without any Act, and without leaving any contemporary record available to the historian. Enclosure by private Act of Parliament only gradually established itself as the normal procedure; therefore, if the progress of enclosures is measured in terms of the Enclosure Acts passed, the quickening of the movement tends to be over-emphasised. Actually the movement was comparatively slow, down to the period of warfare at the end of the century. The area of land enclosed during the eighteenth century cannot be estimated very accurately; but it was probably not less than five million acres in England and Wales. The districts enclosed during that period were mainly the corn-growing regions of the east, north-east, and east-midland counties. There was, indeed, a strong correlation between the number of Enclosure Acts and the price of wheat; when wheat was dear, the number of Enclosure Acts increased. This tendency was especially marked during the periods of wartime scarcity between 1793 and 1815; but it can be traced fairly clearly throughout the later eighteenth century.

Efforts to improve the cultivation of crops could not yield their full benefits until the stock-farming of the country was improved; conversely, the improvement of stock-breeding depended on the field cultivation of roots, clover, and artificial grasses, which the pioneers of the seventeenth and earlier eighteenth centuries had done much to extend. In stock-breeding the most famous innovator was Robert Bakewell, who in 1760 succeeded his father in the tenancy of a 440-acre farm at Dishley, Leicestershire. Bakewell's experiments in improving the breed of sheep were remarkably successful, and his methods were taken up more readily than the improvements in crop cultivation popularly associated with the names of Tull and Townshend.[1] But even in stock-breeding, reforms

[1] Tull's importance has been greatly exaggerated, and Townshend neither introduced the turnip to Norfolk nor invented the Norfolk system of husbandry. See T. H. Marshall, 'Jethro Tull and the "New Husbandry"

78

could not be quickly adopted by open-field farmers; and therefore the enclosure movement received a further indirect stimulus from the work of Bakewell, as it had done from that of the earlier reformers.

Hitherto neither sheep nor cattle had been bred primarily for meat. Sheep had been valued for their manure in agriculture, and in commerce for their skins and their wool; wool was the chief source of trading profit to English farmers. As yet no scientific attempts had been made to improve the shape (as distinct from the size) of either sheep or cattle. Length of leg was the chief "point" looked for; long legs were certainly necessary to animals which had to seek their food over miles of miry, undrained pasture, and would eventually be driven on hoof over the execrable roads of the period to markets scores or hundreds of miles away. In breeding livestock for the butchers, Bakewell's object was to produce animals which were heaviest in the best joints, and matured most quickly. He secured his most striking success in the breeding of sheep. His New Leicesters were ready for the market in two years; they were said to be the hardiest when alive and the heaviest when dead. With cattle Bakewell had less success, mainly because the Craven Longhorns on which he worked were unsuitable for his purposes. He improved the breed for butchering, but impaired their milking qualities; this was fatal in Leicestershire, where the Stilton cheese manufacture demanded good milkers. In the end an improved breed of Durham Shorthorns became recognised as supreme, both for milk and meat.

Although it is often stated that English sheep and cattle were on the average more than twice as heavy at the end of the eighteenth century as they were at the beginning, thanks

---

of the eighteenth century', *Economic History Review*, January 1929, pp. 41–60, and N. Riches, *The Agricultural Revolution in Norfolk*, 1937, also J. H. Plumb, 'Sir Robert Walpole and Norfolk husbandry', *Economic History Review*, 2nd series., Vol. V, No. 1, 1952, pp. 86–89.

to the efforts of Bakewell and his rivals, this statement is open
to serious doubt. The average weight of animals slaughtered
at Smithfield does not seem to have been much higher in 1800
than in 1700. The main increase in the supply of meat in the
eighteenth century came, not from this cause or from any
spectacular increase in total numbers, but rather from better
methods of fattening, and slaughter at an earlier age. There
was some improvement in the quality of the meat.[1] In the
case of sheep, however, there was a drawback to this improvement; the quality of the wool had been sacrificed to the
improvement of the mutton. Hitherto English wool had been
noted for its fineness, which had made it very valuable both
for the native textile industries and for export to the Continent. This quality had been partly due to the hard living
and scanty feeding of sheep on the congested common pastures and the unimproved wastes. As sheep were now being
bred for mutton, the heavier, coarse-wooled breeds were developed and the lighter, short-wooled sheep became less common; whereas hitherto not more than a quarter of the sheep
in England had been of the long-wooled breed. New
machinery and new fabrics were being introduced which
made use of the longer-fibred wools; but for the finer kinds of
cloth the English manufacturers became dependent on
foreign supplies of short-fibred wool from Spain, Saxony, and
(later) from New South Wales.

It is important not to over-estimate the rapidity of agricultural progress at this period; between the theories of the
reformers and the practice of the ordinary farmer there was a
great gap. In many parts of the country agricultural methods
had changed very little for centuries, and there were many
factors making for the continuance of this stagnant condition.
The prevalence of unreclaimed waste land, the insecurity of
tenants-at-will, the poverty and ignorance of the small

---

[1] G. E. Fussell, 'The size of English cattle in the eighteenth century',
Agricultural History, Vol. III, 1929, pp. 160–81.

farmers, the lack of markets and the difficulties of transport, all helped to prevent the backward districts from overtaking the more progressive. The standard of English agriculture needed levelling up more urgently than it needed raising.

It was as an agent in this process of levelling up the standard of English farming that Arthur Young was especially important. Young had failed both as a journalist and as an agriculturist before he became an agricultural journalist; but his earlier failures ought not to detract from his later brilliant success as a populariser of agricultural science. After 1767 he began to publish agricultural books and pamphlets at a prodigious speed, transmitting up-to-date ideas about farming, the latest results of observation and experiment, together with news about the establishment of farmers' clubs and agricultural societies. In his agricultural tours Young found a sharp contrast between the progressive farming of many great landlords and the backward condition of the open-field districts. It seemed obvious to him that the way to get the most out of the soil was to sweep away the common fields and common pastures, and to develop the system of large farms and long leases which had achieved such striking success in particular localities. He thus became the mouth-piece of the enclosing landlords. Helped by their backing, as well as by the pressure of wartime scarcity and the increasing demands of the industrial population, Young's propagandist writings became a strong influence in the direction of large-scale capitalist farming and scientific agriculture. Farming became more fashionable among the nobility than ever before, and every aspect of agriculture was taken up with energy and enterprise. Rents rose rapidly, but not so rapidly as farming profits. Many new crops were introduced, and new machinery invented; agricultural societies and cattle shows were started in various parts of the country.

The typical agricultural capitalist of the later eighteenth century was Thomas William Coke, who in later life was raised to the peerage as Earl of Leicester. In 1776 Coke succeeded to considerable estates at Holkham (in Norfolk) and elsewhere, and soon began to farm his own land with great profit. As a result partly of wartime conditions, but partly also of his personal energy and enterprise, the annual rental of that part of his estate which had brought in £12,332 in 1776 increased to £25,789 by 1816.[1] Originally much of his land was of a thin, sandy soil, growing only rye and producing very poor livestock. Coke continued the expensive policy of his immediate predecessors by enriching the land with marl and clay. He bought a good deal of manure from elsewhere, drilled his wheat and turnips, grew sainfoin and clover and trebled his livestock. He introduced into his neighbourhood the use of bone manure, and of artificial foodstuffs such as oil cake; he practised stall feeding. Coke's farm buildings and cottages were models for other landlords. Tenant farmers on the Coke estates were usually given long leases of twenty-one years, and the leases contained management clauses to prevent backward farming. During his lifetime Norfolk, which was at this time also one of the chief industrial counties of England, became steadily more important both as a wheat-growing area and as a fattening ground where Scotch cattle were got into condition for the London market.

The traditional conservatism of English agriculturists was to some extent broken down by the work of such men as Young and Coke; but a good many local prejudices persisted. Farmers were backward in growing wheat and potatoes; landlords were unwilling to give leases, and sometimes bound their tenants with restrictive clauses to continue old-fashioned methods. Landlords were not willing, and tenants could not afford, to spend money on permanent improvements. Generally speaking, the most rapid progress was on the large estates and the large farms; the small farmers

[1] R. A. C. Parker, 'Coke of Norfolk and the Agrarian Revolution', *Economic History Review*, December 1955, pp. 156–66.

were still stagnating, and this stagnation was most complete in the districts still under the old open-field system.

There has been almost interminable controversy about the social effects of the "Agrarian Revolution"; and it is still hazardous to make wide generalisations on the subject. To some extent the conflict of opinion has been due to the fact that changes which were economically desirable sometimes had unfortunate social reactions. To some extent, also, the controversy has persisted because the term "Agrarian Revolution" covers changes which had divergent economic and social results; even the narrower term "enclosure movement" suffers from a similar ambiguity. Enclosure might mean, for instance, the reclamation of waste land, or the extinction of open-field arable farms, or the appropriation of common pastures. The reclamation of waste would usually be justifiable on both economic and social grounds. The extinction of open-field arable was desirable for economic reasons, but might be socially disastrous. The appropriation of common pastures was a more dubious step, from both points of view, though it might be held to be necessarily bound up with the enclosure of the open-field arable. It has to be remembered, too, that the immediate effects of enclosure were not always in line with the permanent results. Moreover, enclosure in one part of the country and at one particular time was not necessarily similar in effect to enclosure in another district or at another time. The effects of enclosure might vary also according to the nature of the soil, the use made of the land before and after enclosure, and the degree in which the people of each district depended on agricultural employment.

Contrary to the views expressed by an earlier generation of historians, it may now be maintained that the enclosures of the eighteenth and early nineteenth centuries were carried out with a due regard for the interests of persons holding established property rights. The procedure by private Act was, on the face of it, liable to many abuses, but the evidence for the undue use of social or financial influence is slight in proportion to the total number of Acts passed. The enclosure commissioners appointed by these Acts seem in the main to have acted honestly and impartially. It is true, however, that the procedure might prove very expensive, and that the smaller land holders were often too poor to contest the cases. The owners of cottages with common rights received allotments of land on enclosure, but the plots were sometimes too small to be of any significant value, especially since the expense of fencing and hedging was disproportionately greater for the smaller plots, although the cost of fencing and hedging differed greatly from enclosure to enclosure. Moreover, a small compact allotment did not yield the same *variety* of benefits as common rights over a wider area; the cottager might now grow vegetables, but he could no longer pasture sheep, or cut his winter's fuel. In any case, the land allotted belonged to the cottage owner, not to the occupier. Poor people who lived near commons, but not in cottages possessing common rights, suffered especially heavily through the loss of many non-legal benefits. One remedy for this, when non-legal claims were considered at all, was to set aside some land or money for the use of the labouring poor; such grants were not general, however, and were never adequate as compensation for the loss.[1]

Apparently the enclosures had disastrous effects also on the position of the independent small farmers and yeomen, although these two classes had ceased to be an important element in the rural economy over wide areas of the country even before 1780. Nevertheless, from all quarters of the country came complaints about the steady diminution in the numbers of small holders, and the corresponding consolida-

[1] For recent work on enclosure, see W. H. Chaloner, 'Bibliography of recent work on enclosure, the open fields and related topics', *Agricultural History Review*, Vol. II, August 1954, pp. 48–52.

tion of holdings into large estates. It is evident that enclosure favoured consolidation, owing to the relative cheapness of fencing and hedging larger holdings. Moreover, the adoption of improved agricultural methods, for which enclosure was usually a preparation, demanded more capital than most small holders could command; and small holders who persisted in the older methods found it difficult to compete with the larger farmers, except in abnormal times. Small holders who combined agriculture with by-industries would be hit by the growth of large-scale industry and the factory system; though cottage industries retained a surprising vitality until the second quarter of the nineteenth century. The new commercial and industrial wealth had also an indirect effect on the problem; successful business men were buying country estates for non-economic purposes, and were prepared to pay more than the economic price for them.

Enclosure was not the only factor, then, which may have been causing a diminution in the numbers of small holders. Indeed, there are one or two considerations which suggest that the "disappearance" of the yeomanry was not *necessarily* connected with enclosure at all. The consolidation of holdings was proceeding where no enclosures of open-field villages were taking place; and it is agreed that the enclosure of other kinds of land was not a considerable factor in the displacement of the peasantry. Moreover, if there was a *necessary* connection between enclosure and consolidation, the period of most rapid enclosure might be expected to have seen the most marked quickening in the process of consolidation. Yet during the long French wars at the end of the eighteenth century, when enclosures increased enormously, the numbers of small owners and small farmers were also increasing, both in England and in France. It is true that in Lancashire and Kent the shrinkage in the number of small holders continued even during the wars; but in these two counties, significantly enough, no open-field enclosures were taking place.

Such conflicting considerations suggest the necessity for caution in discussing the common charge against enclosure throughout modern times, that it decreased agricultural employment and led to rural depopulation. If by depopulation is meant the actual decrease of population, there is not much evidence of serious rural depopulation in England during either the eighteenth or the earlier nineteenth centuries. It may be agreed that where arable land was enclosed and converted to pasture there would usually be a decrease in agricultural employment; though this did not always happen, where the enclosed land was used for scientific stock-breeding. On the other hand, where pasture or waste land was enclosed for arable farming, it was fairly certain that agricultural employment would be increased, e.g. in fencing, hedging and roadmaking, and the growth of rural population encouraged. The enclosure of extensive tracts of waste land, such as the marshes, moorlands, and heaths which formerly covered a great part of England, led almost inevitably to local increases of population, at any rate for a time. In all cases of local depopulation the effects of non-agricultural causes are to be considered; in some districts it is almost certain that the positive attraction of new industrial development was a more potent stimulus to movement than was the negative repulsion of agricultural changes.

To some extent the social effects of the agrarian transition depended on whether enclosure was followed by the conversion of the land from tillage to pasture. On this point, and on the related question whether enclosure diminished corn-growing, there has been fierce controversy. The use of the land was certainly very often changed after enclosure, sometimes from tillage to pasture, sometimes from pasture to tillage. The acreage under wheat diminished in some midland counties, such as Leicester and Northampton, and this was probably general, so far as concerns districts formerly cultivated under the open-field system; but the contrary was

true in districts where large tracts of waste had been enclosed. Taking the enclosed land as a whole, there was apparently an increase in the area under wheat during the later
eighteenth century; and even in the areas where the wheat
acreage diminished, there were often compensations. In such
counties as Leicester, where great progress was being made in
stock-breeding, the diminished acreage under wheat was
partly offset by the increased acreage under other arable crops,
such as oats and barley. In any case, a diminution in the acreage under wheat did not necessarily mean a decrease in the
aggregate yield of wheat; for one usual result of enclosure was
the adoption of improved methods, and from this followed an
increase in the yield per acre. In the districts which were enclosed by private Act between 1755 and 1800, there was a net
gain in the area under wheat of 10,625 acres, out of 1,767,651
acres enclosed; the area under wheat had been 155,572 acres
before enclosure, and was 165,837 acres when investigation
was made in 1800. On the whole, it seems fairly reasonable to
assume that the agricultural changes of the later eighteenth
century did not cause any diminution in the arable land of the
country, or any decrease in the aggregate yield of grain; and
it is probable that the enclosures of the period were not an
active force in lessening agricultural employment or depleting
the rural population.[1]

[1] See Redford, *Labour Migration in England, 1800–1850*, 1926, pp. 60–61.

CHAPTER SEVEN

The Economic Effects of the French Wars

THE DIFFICULTY OF explaining exactly how the economic changes of the later eighteenth century can have caused the intense social distress of the period suggests that some of the main sources of the evil must be sought elsewhere. The experience of the last two generations makes it clear that war is one of the most potent causes of economic dislocation; it is, therefore, not unreasonable to assume that much of the social distress, for which the economic changes have been blamed, was really due to the numerous wars of the eighteenth century, and especially to the long struggle against France between 1793 and 1815. Two of the most important and immediate causes of distress were the persistent rise of prices and the irregularity of industrial employment: but these were largely attributable to the effects of the wars. Contemporary writers emphasised the danger involved in the transference of the country from the stable basis of agriculture to the fluctuating basis of trade. It may be doubted whether this was a fair description of the transition which was in progress; but even so, the commercial fluctuations which caused irregularity of industrial employment were themselves in close correspondence with the varying fortunes of war and the uncertain tenure of peace.

Throughout the eighteenth century, commercial warfare and mutual embargo had been almost the normal state of Anglo-French relations. Trade tended to be hampered by a succession of commercial blockades, even in times of peace;

88

and in time of military or naval warfare, the economic warfare would naturally be intensified. This did not prevent trade from being carried on between the different countries; the prohibitions and regulations were very generally evaded by means of smuggling. According to contemporary opinion, smuggling was almost as extensive as legitimate trading, and was assumed to be the natural reaction to the existing commercial policy.

The new industrial techniques of the eighteenth century, and the more liberal trend of economic thought, tended towards the breaking down of this long-standing system of commercial regulation; the movement towards greater freedom of trade was, however, checked by the outbreak of the French Revolution and reversed during the ensuing generation of warfare. After the outbreak of war in 1793, French policy soon worked up to a general prohibition against the importation of any manufactured goods from countries subject to Great Britain; in 1796 the prohibition was even extended to cover all goods derived from British trade. In effect, French policy was already aiming at a self-blockade which foreshadowed the later Continental System. Throughout the earlier period of the wars there were French schemes to cut off the Continent from intercourse with Great Britain, and so to glut the English markets with colonial and eastern produce; the English were to be *vaincus par l'abondance*. Alongside this French commercial blockade there developed a British naval blockade. Not only did British ships block many enemy ports, but the British Government also declared a paper blockade over long stretches of enemy coastline, as a pretext for capturing neutral vessels bound for enemy ports.

The economic warfare between France and England became more intense after 1806. In the immediately preceding years the policy of England had been to destroy French maritime commerce by the vigorous use of naval supremacy. This policy had been successful in driving French shipping off the seas; but the produce of the French colonies was still able to reach Europe in American ships. France was still receiving goods from overseas through the neutral markets of Germany, Denmark, Sweden, and Spain. From the English point of view this situation became more serious after 1805 through Napoleon's seizure of Holland, which involved the French control of Dutch trade. Napoleon considered that he had already effectively closed French, Italian and Swiss markets against British goods; it now remained to close the rest of the continental outlets in the same way. The battle of Jena (1806) gave Napoleon control of the Weser, Elbe, Oder, and all the Baltic coastline as far as the Vistula; the time seemed ripe for the application of stronger economic pressure upon England. As a reprisal against Napoleon's seizure of Holland, the British Government had declared a naval blockade along the whole of the Channel coast, from Brest to the mouth of the Elbe. To this extreme statement of naval policy Napoleon replied with the Berlin Decree of November, 1806, which declared that all the British Isles were in a state of blockade. All commerce or correspondence with Britain was prohibited, all British subjects in French territories were declared to be prisoners of war and their property fair prize.

Several lines of policy were open to the British Government in framing counter-measures to Napoleon's threat of economic pressure. A modern government would doubtless have attempted to cut off the imports of the continental countries; but to the governments of the time this looked too much like supporting Napoleon's own policy. A more directly retaliatory policy was to cut off the export trade of France and her allies; but such export trade had been practically killed already, and was never so important to the continental states as British trade was to Great Britain. A more profitable policy was to break down the blockade by forcing (or smuggling) British goods into the continental markets; and this was the policy actually pursued by British merchants. The policy of the British Government is not easy to disentangle from among the twenty-four Orders in Council issued in 1807, or from the six supplementary statutes of 1808. The Orders in Council were tantalisingly obscure and conflicting, but the general line of thought underlying them is fairly clear. The main object of policy was that no goods should be carried to France unless they first touched at a British port and paid duties, which would raise their price and so handicap them in competition with British goods. This principle was very clearly expounded in 1812 by Lord Bathurst, the President of the Board of Trade: "France by her decrees had resolved to abolish all trade with England: England said, in return, that France should then have no trade but with England." [1]

On the French side the economic warfare had been made more intense by Napoleon's Milan Decrees of November and December, 1807. Any vessel which submitted to the British Orders in Council, either by permitting inspection, or by calling at an English port, or by paying British customs duties, was declared to be denationalised, and became lawful prize whether in port or at sea. This meant in effect that many neutral ships would be liable to capture and confiscation by the French, since they could not rely on escaping inspection; the measure had, therefore, a protectionist tendency against all shipping which was not purely French. Incidentally, the policy acted as a further aggravation to the friction which had already arisen between America and the belligerent countries.

The state of economic warfare was not confined to maritime hostilities. Napoleon's Continental System included also schemes for the stimulation of agriculture and manufacturing industry on the Continent; such schemes were, indeed, a necessary counterpart to the attempt at boycotting the wares of English trade. English industry and commerce did

---

[1] Hansard, Vol. XXI (1812), p. 1053; quoted E. F. Heckscher, *The Continental System*, 1922, p. 120.

not collapse, however, so completely as might have been expected. Napoleon's system was ultimately a failure in both its main aspects; his attempts at fostering the growth of French industry were largely ineffective, and his boycott of English trade was partly nullified by the smuggling of English goods, although it achieved a considerable measure of success in 1810–12.[1] It cannot be maintained that in its direct effects Napoleon's Continental System dealt a very deadly blow at English industry and commerce, especially as the whole scheme collapsed after the disastrous Russian expedition of 1812. In the end, however, the indirect effects of the Continental System raised up a serious menace to the economic stability of England, by causing increased friction between this country and the United States.

During the early stages of the European wars, America had reaped a profitable harvest from her position as a neutral maritime country, and had developed a considerable transit trade in the colonial produce of the French, Spanish, and British West Indies. This carrying trade was badly hit by the Orders and Decrees of 1806–7, and the Americans were sorely aggrieved at a policy which they regarded as an unwarrantable interference with the rights of neutral traders. The American policy of neutrality was eventually broken down by British severity towards neutral shipping, which led in 1806 to an American Non-Importation Act: this prohibited the importation, from any country, of most of the main groups of British manufactured goods, except cottons. It is true that the Non-Importation Act had soon to be suspended, and was important mainly as a precedent for future action; during 1807 American trade and shipping not only continued to grow, but actually reached their high-water mark. By the end of that year, however, American trade was being seriously restricted by the European blockade measures,

---

[1] F. Crouzet, *L'Economie Britannique et le Blocus Continental, 1806–1813*, 2 vols., 1958, II, pp. 525–804.

and the United States had followed the European precedent by declaring a deliberate and direct self-blockade. In December, 1807, a general embargo was laid on all vessels lying in American ports and bound for European ports; vessels in the American coasting trade were required to give security that their cargo would be discharged in an American port. In addition, the Non-Importation Act of 1806 was again put into operation against British manufactures, which were the only goods likely to be imported from Europe. Actually, these restrictions on trade could not be completely enforced; but their effect was strong enough to cause serious economic dislocation, both in England and in America. About one-third of England's commerce was cut off, including a large proportion of the raw cotton on which the industrial welfare of Lancashire depended.

The restrictive effects of the embargo were resented almost as fiercely in America as in England and a milder policy had soon to be substituted; but friction between the two countries continued and led eventually to open warfare in 1812. The Anglo-American War of 1812–14 did not seriously affect the issue of the European conflict, which was now definitely becoming disastrous to Napoleon's armies. Nevertheless, the futile struggle damaged both American and English commerce, and gave a sufficiently serious check to some of the British exporting industries, especially the Lancashire cotton industry. On the other hand, American manufacturing industry was stimulated, and vested interests were created which were able to claim tariff protection against British competition when the war was over.

In general, it must be concluded that the wars between 1793 and 1815 had very mixed effects upon the welfare of the British industrial population. The manufacturers suffered not only from the uncertain fluctuations of demand and sale caused by changes in naval policy, but also from the uncertain supply of such raw materials as American cotton and merino wool. It is, however, important not to exaggerate the adverse effects of the wars upon industry. Different branches of industry suffered in different ways and in different degrees. Thus, the Yorkshire manufacturers of coarse cloth, suitable for army uniforms, suffered much less than the West Country manufacturers of fine broadcloth, or the East Anglian manufacturers of twills and bombazines for the Indian market. No doubt the cotton manufacture suffered more severely than most other industries, because its prosperity already depended entirely on the export market; yet even this industry expanded rapidly (though not steadily) during the wars.

To the iron industries the wars meant a greatly increased demand for cannon, firearms, shot, and other munitions. It is true that the financial disturbances of 1793 and 1797 produced embarrassment even among the ironmasters; but these temporary difficulties were soon forgotten in the abounding expansion and prosperity of wartime. Political friction with Sweden and Russia restricted the import of foreign iron and raised prices, while the appetite of the Government for ordnance of all kinds seemed insatiable. The exporting branches of the industry suffered, it is true, from the restriction of their continental markets, from the circuitous routes and the high freights of wartime, as well as from the confiscation of goods by the enemy. On the whole, however, the French wars were much more favourable to the metal industries than to the textile manufactures; and wartime technical advances, such as the general introduction of the improved puddling and rolling processes, gave the British iron industries a decided superiority over their continental rivals in the period after 1815. Even so, the post-war depression was more intense than that of other industries, and the process of readjustment to peace conditions was very painful. Prices fell, iron works were shut down and abandoned, thousands of workers were thrown out of employment. Wages rates declined from the abnormally high wartime level; though the

94

money wages of the iron workers (and possibly also their real wages) remained permanently at a higher level than before the war.

The wartime history of agriculture was in many respects parallel to that of the iron industry. In each case the wars brought a stimulation of the market and a corresponding expansion of the industry, with a period of high profits during the war and a subsequent period of intense depression. England was not as yet seriously dependent on foreign grain; the actual amount of grain imported into England before the French wars was relatively insignificant, and there were still many years in which the exports of grain exceeded the imports. Even during the war period the average deficiency was comparatively slight; Great Britain was dependent on foreign sources for only about five per cent. of her wheat supplies in average years. Nevertheless, the wars had a general tendency to cause high food prices, by dislocating transport arrangements, by causing the panic hoarding of foodstuffs, and by necessitating the feeding of people engaged in unproductive occupations. From whatever causes, there was at intervals during the wars a serious shortage of grain; this was the main motive for the feverish increase of enclosures during the war period. Much land hitherto waste was taken into cultivation, and the production of grain increased considerably in Scotland and Ireland as well as in England. From 1806 Irish wheat could be imported into Great Britain duty free. There were years, even during the wars, when the price of wheat was so low as to be unprofitable to the farmers, considering the increases which were taking place in rents, labourers' wages, and other farming expenses; but, on the other hand, there were years when the farmers could get almost any price for their produce, and when the Government welcomed the importation of foreign grain, whatever its origin.

Both in agriculture and in manufacturing industry, the inflationary effect of the wars tended to embitter industrial relations by widening the existing cleavage between employers and wage earners. The high wartime prices of agricultural produce brought profit to the farmers and landlords, but not to agricultural labourers. The farmers preferred to extend the existing system of outdoor allowances under the Poor Law, rather than to pay their labourers increased wages commensurate with the increased prices of foodstuffs.[1] On the other hand, it should be borne in mind that recruiting for the army and the navy stimulated the demand for labour in general during the war years, and it is noteworthy that the use of the threshing machine,[2] driven either by horses or steam, spread from Scotland to the North of England in this period, partly because farmers wished to economise in agricultural labour, which was becoming increasingly expensive there on account of the attractions of alternative employment in industry and mining.

In manufacturing industry, one evil effect of the wars was to exacerbate government policy towards the wage earners' organisations. All through the eighteenth century government action had been generally in favour of the employers and against any labour organisation which resulted in open disputes. But government policy towards labour combinations had not been uniformly repressive; some unions were apparently not interfered with, whilst others were troubled only occasionally. The economic dislocation of the war period increased the temptation to drastic and illegal action on the part of the wage earners, and at the same time strengthened the Government's hostility to the labour unions by adding an element of political suspicion which sometimes approximated to panic. It was in such an atmosphere of suspicion and re-

[1] The problem of agricultural pauperism during and after the wars is discussed in Chapter VIII, below.
[2] For the introduction of the threshing machine as a major cause of the 'Captain Swing' riots of 1830 in southern England, see N. Gash, 'Rural unemployment, 1815–34', *Economic History Review*, October 1935, pp. 90–93.

pression that the Combination Act of 1799 was hurried through Parliament at lightning speed and without effective discussion. This Combination Act comprehensively prohibited all organisations of industrial workmen for obtaining higher wages or more favourable conditions of work; and this prohibition was elaborated in the Combination Act of 1800, in spite of petitions from trade clubs and industrial benefit societies throughout the country. It is true that this second Combination Act forbade the combination of employers as well as of workmen; but the prohibition of employers' associations seems to have been a dead letter from the beginning. In fairness it must be added that even towards wage earners' organisations, and even after 1800, government policy was not uniformly repressive. Many strong unions remained in open activity without molestation, in many different trades and many different parts of the country. As concerns the old-established and well-organised skilled trades, the Acts seem to have been almost a dead letter in normal times. The chief use of the legislation was to prevent any widespread organisation for strikes, and to overcome labour combination in some of the new factory industries, such as cotton spinning, although it did not prevent an extensive strike of cotton spinners in the Manchester area in 1810.[1]

There were many instances of flagrant injustice during the period in the legal prosecution of combinations as conspiracies in restraint of trade; but the main burden of the Acts fell upon the new textile trades. The sporadic riots in the textile districts during the war period were often merely expressions of the vague unrest caused by the contemporary dislocation of economic life; they were, nevertheless, interpreted by the Government as evidence of widespread conspiracy against the existing social order, and were suppressed with military severity. The most notorious of these presumed

[1] M. D. George, 'The Combination Laws', *Economic History Review*, April 1936, pp. 172–78.

attempts at revolution was the series of Luddite riots in 1811 and 1812, when mobs of workmen went about the textile districts of the Midlands and the North of England, destroying machinery and burning factories. It was said that the rioters were organised with complete military discipline, and that the conspiracy extended from London to Carlisle. The combinations among the textile workers were held to be responsible for the disturbances, but this was never proved. Actually, the funds seem to have come from men in all trades, such as bricklayers, masons, weavers, colliers, and even from soldiers in provincial garrisons. It is, however, possible that the more elaborate details of the organisation were invented by the government spies and *agents provocateurs*, who were paid by results and seem in some cases to have fomented rebellion in order to get evidence about it.[1]

A more legitimate form of labour activity during the war period was the demand for the assessment of wages in the northern textile trades. This was an appeal to the principle of the Elizabethan Statute of Apprentices; it may, however, have been based on a misapprehension. The craftsmen in the old-established trades covered by the original Statute of 1563 were by this time unwilling to place any reliance upon wages assessments, and pinned their faith to collective bargaining; actually, the assessment of industrial wages had been almost entirely discontinued for several generations. In these older trades the struggle of the wage earners in the eighteenth century was not in defence of wages assessments but of the restrictions on apprenticeship; these also were being rapidly broken down as hindrances to the progress of industry. The textile workers, in petitioning to have the principle of the Statute of 1563 applied to their case, seem to have thought

[1] See J. L. and B. Hammond, *The Skilled Labourer, 1760–1832*, especially Chapter XII on 'The Adventures of Oliver the Spy'. F. O. Darvall, *Popular Disturbances and Public Order in Regency England* (1934), gives a more detailed and critical account.

that the Statute had been for the fixing of minimum wages; whereas the Statute had imposed penalties on any person paying *more* than the rates fixed, i.e. the wages assessments were for maximum rates.[1]

In 1800 the petitions of the weavers led to a special arbitration act for the cotton industry, in line with the arbitration provisions contained in the Combination Act of the same year. This cotton arbitration act was amended in 1804, but does not seem to have been of any effect. The cotton workers found it impossible to adapt the statute to the fixing of minimum wages; and the ultimate result of these attempts to apply the principle of wages assessment to the cotton trade was that the Government, in 1813–14, repealed both the assessment and the apprenticeship clauses of the Elizabethan Statute. Thus, the general tendency of labour legislation during the war period was to prevent the wage earners from combining to protect their common interests, while at the same time there was taken away even the shadow of the earlier system whereby industrial conditions were regulated by authority. It might be maintained, however, that a new system of industrial regulation, more directly concerned to promote the welfare of the workers, had already been foreshadowed in the Health and Morals of Apprentices Act of 1802.

The commercial and industrial difficulties of England during the French wars were greatly aggravated by frequent fluctuations in business credit, caused partly by the vicissitudes of warfare, but partly also by the financial policy of the Government and the peculiarities of the country's banking system. By one of its early charters the Bank of England had received a monopoly of the joint-stock issue of banknotes in England; this in effect (though not in law)

---

[1] There was a later Act of 1604, however, which provided for the fixing of *minimum* wages; see Bland, Brown and Tawney, *English Economic History: Select Documents* (1914), pp. 342–43.

amounted to a monopoly of joint-stock banking, because at this time the power to issue notes was considered to be an indispensable feature of large-scale banking operations. There were many private banks in England, and in London there were some important ones; these private banks could issue notes, but the scope of their business was restricted by the rule limiting the number of partners to six. In practice, the Bank of England was already the central gold reserve of the country; the stability of the banking system (and of public credit) depended in a crisis on the solvency of the Bank of England, though it had no direct control over the policy of the other banks.

In the original constitution of the Bank of England, the Bank had been forbidden to lend money to the Government without parliamentary sanction; this had been considered necessary in order to maintain parliamentary control over public finance. In practice, however, the custom had grown up of making temporary advances to the Government in anticipation of the collection of revenue. Such a system worked well in normal times, but it involved the danger that in times of financial stringency the Government was likely to use the "ways and means" advances as a cloak for large-scale unconstitutional borrowing from the Bank. On the outbreak of the French wars in 1793, Pitt went further than this by getting Parliament to cancel the original clause forbidding non-sanctioned advances. During the earlier years of the wars the Government borrowed largely from the Bank, in preference to raising adequate funds by the levy of increased taxation or by borrowing on the open market. The war expenses abroad between 1793 and 1797 were estimated at nearly £33,000,000; a considerable proportion of this was lent by the Bank of England, which was also lending money to the Emperor and the King of Prussia. There was, moreover, an internal drain of gold from the Bank's reserve, caused by wartime timidity and hoarding, the dislocation of communications, and the consequent necessity for giving extended commercial credit to customers.

By the end of 1794 the Bank's gold reserve was perilously low, but the Government refused to moderate its demands for loans, while the Bank's attempt to restrict ordinary commercial credit nearly caused a financial panic in the city. The Bank was still solvent, but it was not safe against a sudden "run" on its reserve, and its directors were becoming seriously alarmed. In 1796 they protested to the Government that "if any further loan or advance to the Emperor or any other foreign state should in the present state of things take place, it will, in all probability, prove fatal to the Bank". This spirited protest seems to have caused a temporary reduction in government borrowing, but other events were now combining to impair the solvency of the Bank. The action of the French Republic, in re-establishing its currency on a metallic basis after the depreciation of its paper *assignats*, caused a special external drain of gold; while the unsuccessful French attempt to invade Ireland in December, 1796, shook public confidence in England, and occasioned an internal drain. There was a run on the private bankers in Newcastle and they were forced to suspend cash payments. The effects of this local failure of credit soon spread throughout the country, causing the provincial bankers to make a general demand on the Bank of England for gold. Faced with this very serious threat to public credit the Government was forced, in February, 1797, to order the suspension of cash payments at the Bank of England. The Bank was then able to quieten the financial panic by a judicious expansion of its note issue, which thus became practically a system of inconvertible paper currency.

The general effect of such a suspension of cash payments was to remove the quasi-automatic check of a metallic standard upon the volume of credit currency, and so to encourage the progressive raising of the price level. Prices certainly were rising rapidly during the French wars; and it is equally certain that currency derangement was one main cause of the increased prices. This does not, however, imply that there were no other causes of high prices, or that the over-issue of Bank of England notes was the only cause of currency derangement. Actually, the Bank seems to have used its powers of note issue sparingly, and to have maintained a highly responsible policy in its discounting of commercial bills. Its notes depreciated only slightly before 1809; after that date the rate of depreciation was more rapid, but still moderate compared with that of the French *assignats* or the American "continentals" of the preceding generation. The main danger to the stability of the English banking system arose not from the policy of the Bank of England, but from the irresponsible over-issue of notes by the private country banks, which sprang up like mushrooms during the war period. The development of provincial banking earlier in the eighteenth century had been quite slow; and even so late as 1797 there were only 230 provincial banks in England. Thereafter the numbers rose rapidly to about 600 in 1808, to 721 in 1810, and no fewer than 940 in 1814. That this extraordinary increase of provincial banking was unsound, and dependent on the artificial situation created by the war, seems to be reflected in the fact that 240 country banks became insolvent between 1814 and 1816, while 104 others failed during the succeeding ten years.[1]

The increased seriousness of the currency situation after 1809 was recognised by most independent observers at the time. A special committee of inquiry into the question was formed in 1810, and issued a famous "Report on the Cause of the High Price of Gold Bullion, and the State of the Circulating Medium, and Exchanges between Great Britain and Foreign Parts". This Bullion Report of 1810 stated decidedly

[1] J. Sykes, *The Amalgamation Movement in English Banking*, 1926, pp. ix and x.

that there was an excess of paper currency circulating in the country, and that this was the cause of the high price of bullion and the adverse condition of the foreign exchanges; the Committee accordingly recommended a return to cash payments. The Bank of England refused to believe that its notes had depreciated in terms of goods, but asserted on the contrary that gold had appreciated in terms of both banknotes and goods. The Government, in its turn, declined to be guided by the Committee's report, and pointed out that there were many other causes of high prices besides currency policy, that the resumption of cash payments in the middle of a war was in any case impossible, and that the only alternative to an inconvertible currency was surrender to the French. The Government accordingly declared Bank of England notes to be legal tender at their face value, and considered that the controversy concerning depreciation was closed.

Another way in which the French wars reacted unfavourably upon economic welfare was by the rapid increase of the public debt, and a corresponding increase in the burden of taxation. During this generation of warfare the volume of public indebtedness swelled at a most alarming rate from a level of £228,000,000 in 1793 to a total in 1816 of £876,000,000. Even after allowing for the extreme financial strain of the French wars, which was accentuated by the financial exhaustion inherited from the previous wars of the later eighteenth century, this tremendous increase in the volume of indebtedness calls for some special explanation. The rate of accumulation was quicker in the earlier part of the wars (before the Peace of Amiens) than in the later part. This was partly because of the Government's tardiness in imposing increased taxation to meet the increased expenditure. After 1799 the revenue from taxation grew rapidly and nearly doubled between 1803 and 1815. This increase in the revenue from taxation was to some extent caused by Pitt's introduction of the income tax, which came into operation in 1799. During its first three years the income tax produced about £6,000,000 annually, and by the end of the wars, after it had been considerably remodelled by Addington in 1803, was bringing in over £14,000,000 each year. The benefit from Pitt's income tax was, however, to some small extent offset by the effect of his sinking fund of 1786, which continued in operation throughout the French wars, in spite of the accumulation of new debt on less advantageous terms. A more dangerous defect of wartime financial policy was the practice of borrowing at a discount to avoid raising the nominal rate of interest. This had the effect of increasing the country's capital commitment and making more difficult the conversion of the debt to a lower rate of interest after the war: though it may have secured the money at a slightly cheaper rate in the first instance.

The importance of Pitt's income tax as a financial precedent must not give rise to the idea that this tax was responsible for most of the increase in public revenue during the latter half of the war. Between 1803 and 1815 the annual public revenue increased by nearly £40,000,000; in the latter year the income tax yielded £14,600,000, and even this sum represented a considerable increase on previous years. It is therefore clear that alongside the growth of the income tax there had been a great increase in the yield of the indirect taxes during the later stages of the warfare, as well as in its earlier phase. Even at the end of the war the income tax was yielding less than the taxes on foodstuffs, manufactures, and raw materials, and considerably less than the taxes on drinks.[1] When every allowance has been made for the difficulties of the period, Pitt cannot be considered to have shone as a financial statesman in wartime; and the defects of his financial policy were reflected in the increased burdens imposed upon

[1] J. F. Rees, *Fiscal and Financial History of England*, 1921, p. 36: quoting Dowell, *History of Taxation and Taxes*, Vol. II, pp. 239–51.

the commercial and industrial classes of the nation, both during and after the wars. Nevertheless, even if Pitt had been an inspired financial genius, the burden of warfare would still have been a grievous affliction to the country, and one of the main causes of social distress.

PART II
THE AGE OF REFORMS
(1815–1860)

CHAPTER EIGHT

Agrarian Distress and Poor Law Reform

AT THE CLOSE of the French wars the British Government
had to face urgent economic problems on every side of
national life. When Parliament reassembled in 1816 the
speech from the throne declared that "the manufactures,
commerce and revenue of the United Kingdom were in a
flourishing condition". The omission to mention agriculture
was significant, however, and the prosperity of the nation in
other directions was not more than superficial. Less optimistic observers declared that there was "a very general depression in the prices of nearly all productions, and in the
value of all fixed property, entailing a convergence of losses
and failures among the agricultural, and commercial, and
manufacturing, and mining, and shipping, and building
interests".[1] It was the problem of agricultural distress that
Parliament, representing mainly the landed interest, considered most urgent. To the landlords and farmers, if not
to the labourers, the end of the war seemed to threaten
speedy ruin. The landlords, in quest of higher rents, had sunk
much capital in the improvement of inferior lands, beyond
the limit of economic safety on the basis of pre-war prices.
Farmers, relying on the continuance of higher prices, had
taken leases which could not be profitable to them if prices
were suddenly allowed to break. It was natural, therefore,
that the predominant interest in Parliament should seek to
maintain the price of wheat at a level approaching that experienced during the wars. There was no lack of plausible

[1] See H. Martineau, *History of the Thirty Years' Peace*, Bk. I, Chapter III.

109

grounds for deciding that agriculture ought to be protected from foreign competition. It was clearly dangerous, after a generation of warfare, to let the country become dependent on foreign sources for its food supplies; to prevent this by the adjustment of the Corn Laws to the needs of each particular generation was no innovation, but a matter of traditional policy. The landlords argued, moreover, that they had a special claim to protection since the burden of national and local taxation fell most heavily upon them, and their ruin would involve the dislocation of the revenue system of the country. The maintenance of arable cultivation was also demanded for the purpose of sustaining a vigorous rural population as a fighting stock in case of further warfare.

It was on such plausible grounds as these that Parliament hurriedly passed the Corn Law of 1815, by which the importation of foreign grain was prohibited except when the price of wheat in the English market was higher than eighty shillings a quarter. So far as this measure was effective in protecting agriculture from foreign competition it was necessarily against the interests of the manufacturing classes. It reduced the real wages of the workers by making them pay more for their food, while on the other hand it retarded industrial development by restricting the foreign outlets for English manufactured goods. It may, however, be questioned whether the protection given to the agricultural interest by the Corn Laws was as effectual as many contemporary observers supposed. The quantity of grain imported was certainly small in relation to the home production of cereals until after the repeal of the Corn Laws in the middle of the century; but in this there were many other factors involved, such as the state of transport. Certainly the prices of agricultural produce were higher, on the average, than they would have been if no Corn Laws had been in force. Nevertheless, there was a good deal of agrarian depression in the post-war generation; the price of corn fluctuated very wildly, and was often so low as to be ruinous to the farmers, in spite of the prohibition on foreign imports.

As to the reality of the agrarian depression there can hardly be any reasonable doubt, although spokesmen for the agricultural interest naturally did not present a balanced picture and gave undue prominence to the hardest cases. Richard Preston, M.P., said in 1816 that many small farmers were ceasing to be farmers from necessity, and becoming pensioners on the poor rate. In some places the lands were actually deserted, and growing no other crop than weeds. In Huntingdonshire, it was said, a circuit of three thousand acres was abandoned. C. C. Western gave particular details of the distressed condition of the agricultural population in Cambridgeshire, where the farmers were abandoning the cultivation of the land, and the labourers were finding it hard to get employment even at eightpence a day. "Whole parishes had been deserted, and the crowd of paupers increasing in numbers as they went from parish to parish spread wider and wider this awful desolation." [1] Reports of agrarian depression, and the consequent scarcity of agricultural employment, continued to be made at intervals for more than one generation, and were often supplemented by reports that the rural population was dwindling, and that land was falling out of arable cultivation. In the three years 1820–22 nearly seven hundred petitions complaining of agricultural distress were presented to Parliament, and the numbers presented in other years of the period were also considerable. The burden of pauperism was increasing ominously in most agricultural districts, especially in the South of England, and was becoming a most serious social problem.

The causes of this long depression of agriculture were complex and obscure: and they became especially difficult to analyse since the question developed into a bitter political

[1] *The Pamphleteer*, Vol. VII, No. XIII, pp. 81–124, 1816; Hansard, Vol. XXXIII (1816), p. 667 *et seq.*

controversy in which all sense of exact truth was lost by the contending parties. In the main, the agrarian depression was caused by reaction from the feverish activity of the war period, which had led to the extravagant sinking of capital in the improvement of inferior land. This source of trouble was accentuated by the currency derangements of the period, which inflated all values, and caused a readjustment of all incomes when the process of deflation began. The agrarian depression was not caused, or reflected, by any diminution in the amount of wheat grown. Between 1801 and 1811, under the stimulus of war conditions, home-grown wheat was estimated at an annual average of eleven million quarters. Between 1831 and 1841, which included a period of intense agrarian depression, the quantity grown was estimated at an average of about sixteen million quarters. This increased production was not enough to prevent high corn prices, for the population of the country was increasing in more than the proportion of eleven to sixteen. Such an increase in production does, however, imply that the depressed state of agriculture was not caused or accompanied by any general reversion from arable to pasture farming, in spite of the fact that many barren tracts which had been ploughed up during the wars could not possibly be kept under cultivation in time of peace.

It is extremely difficult, if not impossible, to discover the extent to which the agricultural distress of the post-war generation was aggravated by contemporary changes in agricultural methods and tenure. "Agricultural distress" is a vague and ambiguous phrase; it may mean low rents for landlords, low profits for farmers, low wages for labourers, or simply bad harvests. In 1816, for instance, bad harvests were followed by complaints of agricultural distress, and there were riots among the labourers in the southern and eastern counties. In 1822, on the other hand, there seems to have been an exceptionally good harvest of wheat; this caused low prices, and there were again complaints of agricultural distress. During the latter year, indeed, there were about two hundred and fifty petitions complaining of agricultural distress presented to Parliament. If the prosperity or distress of the agricultural labourers could be regarded as having some relationship to the increase or decrease of the rural population some approach to defining the problem might be made. Unfortunately, it cannot be assumed that any such relationship existed; for agrarian changes which diminished agricultural employment would not necessarily cause any acceleration of the normal drift from the countryside. The extent to which such changes caused serious distress among agricultural families might depend, indeed, on whether the decrease in employment were followed by migration or stagnation. Cobbett, in the 'twenties, believed that "the villages are regularly wasting away. . . . In all the real agricultural villages and parts of the kingdom there is a *shocking decay*. . . . One part of the nation has been depopulated to increase the population of another part".[1] On the other hand, there were innumerable reports from the agricultural counties that the unemployed labourers showed great obstinacy in refusing to leave their native villages, and that the rural population was increasing in a most unhealthy fashion. On this, as on many other questions, the census figures of population seem to contradict Cobbett's assertions.

Unlike Cobbett, the Government and the landlords felt that the main problem was, not to prevent the depopulation of the countryside but to cope with the stagnant and inert mass of unemployed labourers in the southern agricultural counties. This ominous growth of surplus labour was accompanied by an alarming increase in the burden of the poor rates, which had already been swollen by lax administration and financial inefficiency during the generation of warfare.

[1] See *Rural Rides*, October 31st and November 24th, 1822, and September 4th, 1826; *Political Register*, April 10th, 1823; *Political Works*, VI, pp. 337-38.

One village in Buckinghamshire complained in 1822 that it was spending on poor relief fully eight times as much as it had spent in 1795, and more than the total rental of the parish had amounted to at the earlier date. In the Sussex Weald, rent and poor rate had exactly changed places between 1792 and 1833.[1] Such instances were not uncommon in the southern agricultural counties between 1815 and 1834. The reality of the distress among the agricultural population cannot be doubted; but whether the increase of the burden of poor rates can be regarded as evidence of increased poverty is not so simple a question as might be supposed. It was, indeed, frequently asserted during the post-war period that a considerable part of the contemporary social distress was caused either by the poor-law system itself or by the inefficiency with which it was administered.

Throughout the history of the Poor Law the main questions have concerned the treatment of able-bodied persons who declare themselves to be willing to work but unable to find employment. There has been general agreement that the aged or otherwise helpless poor should be maintained, and that able-bodied persons who are unwilling to work should be punished rather than relieved. But there has been great disagreement concerning able-bodied unemployment, and the methods by which worthy though unfortunate persons should be distinguished from sturdy rogues and vagabonds. The treatment of the able-bodied unemployed poor turned during the seventeenth and eighteenth centuries upon the provision of work for them by the parish authorities, often in special workhouses or "houses of industry". It was for a long time commonly assumed that manufacturing industry might be carried on in such establishments with financial profit, if properly managed. This proved to be a fallacy; nor was the workhouse system particularly effective as a test of the applicants' willingness to work. There were many attempts to

[1] See Redford, *Labour Migration in England, 1800–1850*, p. 71.

stiffen the "workhouse test" by introducing new administrative devices, and such experiments often gave encouraging results in the first years of their operation; but in time they all reverted to inefficiency and squalor. The poor rates were reduced in the first instance, but soon began to rise again; the overseers found it easier to give the applicants tiny doles in aid of wages rather than to persist in a stern refusal of outdoor relief to all able-bodied persons.

During the later eighteenth century there developed a general tendency to disregard the workhouse test altogether, and to give outdoor relief to the able-bodied poor with a laxity which was in sharp contrast to the extreme stringency of earlier generations. Gilbert's Act of 1782 was primarily intended to facilitate the voluntary union of neighbouring parishes by incorporation, for the provision of more adequate "poor houses"; but it also provided that no person should be sent to such poorhouses except the aged, sick, or otherwise impotent poor. The decision not to admit able-bodied persons to the poorhouses implied that some form of outdoor relief was to be provided for them. According to the Act, poor persons "who shall be able and willing to work but who cannot get employment" were to be found employment by the guardians as near home as possible. The guardians were to arrange and pay for the maintenance of such poor persons and were to receive their wages as contributions towards the cost of their living, making up any deficit from the poor rate; but any surplus of wages over the cost of maintenance was to be returned to the labourer. This was, in theory, an extremely favourable arrangement from the labourer's point of view: he was guaranteed a minimum of subsistence and the possession of any extra earnings he might make. Needless to say, in practice there never were any surplus earnings.

The tendency of contemporary sentiment towards a more general provision of outdoor relief to the able-bodied in aid of wages found fuller expression in the Speenhamland decision of 1795; this was a ruling intended by the Berkshire justices to apply to their own county, but it was later adopted in most of the southern counties of England, and some of the northern. The French war was at that time causing food prices to rise rapidly, and agricultural wages were not yet rising to an equivalent extent. The Berkshire justices, in considering how this situation could best be met, decided that it would be inexpedient to assess wage rates according to the Elizabethan Statute of Apprentices. Instead, they "very earnestly recommend to the Farmers and others throughout the country to increase the pay of their labourers in proportion to the present price of provisions"; [1] and the justices further resolved to make allowances in aid of wages, in their respective districts, according to a sliding scale varying with the price of bread and the size of the family to be maintained. The same general principles were followed in parliamentary bills, promoted by Samuel Whitbread in 1795 and 1800; these parliamentary bills were rejected, but the system spread very rapidly without legislative aid.

The Speenhamland method of relieving distress combined a low but guaranteed minimum remuneration with some measure of family endowment. Many contemporary observers held that such a system had the incidental disadvantages of weakening individual responsibility and discouraging individual initiative. It must also have tended to keep wages low, thus subsidising the farmers (in a period of agricultural prosperity) at the expense of the other ratepayers. The contemporary trend towards the more general granting of outdoor relief received some legislative sanction from a statute of 1796 (36 Geo. III, cap. 23) which expressly permitted parish authorities to grant outdoor relief in cases of temporary illness or distress, and gave an even wider discretion to the justices. Thenceforward, outdoor relief, of one sort or another,

---

[1] *The Reading Mercury*, May 11th, 1795; reprinted in Bland, Brown and Tawney, *English Economic History, Select Documents*, 1919 edition, pp. 655–56.

became the rule rather than the exception, in many of the agricultural counties. Meanwhile, the settlement laws had been further relaxed by the Settlement and Poor Removal Amendment Act of 1795, which provided that in future no poor person was to be removed from any parish until he had actually become destitute and dependent on poor relief; the Act also made provision for the suspension of poor removal orders at the discretion of the justices in cases of sickness or other infirmity.

During the generation of warfare between 1793 and 1815 there was an ominous increase of pauperism in England, and it was alleged that the labouring classes were becoming de-moralised. Various causes contributed to produce this in-crease of pauperism. It arose partly from actual distress caused by the economic dislocation of wartime; partly from the fact that the families of militiamen were maintained out of the poor rates; partly from the Speenhamland system and other methods of granting outdoor allowances in aid of wages. The annual burden of the poor rates, which in the 1780s had been under two million pounds, increased to over four mil-lions by 1803, and to more than six millions after 1812. Sub-sequently the amount remained fairly constant down to 1834, fluctuating comparatively slightly in accordance with the movement of trade. In 1833 the money spent on poor relief was very little more than that spent in 1813. This was equivalent to a much greater real payment, however, since in the mean-time prices had been approximately halved. On the other hand, it has to be remembered that both the population and the wealth of the country had been growing rapidly during the interval; this would tend to counterbalance the increase in the real burden of the poor rate, though it is clear that the compensation was only partial. In the post-war period the disease of pauperism was felt to be gaining ground very quickly, and there was a growing conviction among the governing classes that radical changes were necessary either in the poor laws or in poor-law administration. Many remedies were proposed for particular abuses, and some miscellaneous amendments were adopted. But the problems involved were so complex, and politically so dangerous, that the responsible statesmen shrank from the task of reform.

Down to the famous Poor Law Amendment Act of 1834, the administration of relief was still based essentially upon the Elizabethan Poor Laws of 1597 and 1601. Even Lord Grey's reforming ministry felt that it would be safer to have the report of a special Royal Commission before framing any legislative measures. The Commission, which was appointed in 1832, issued its report in 1834, though some of the appendices of evidence were not ready until 1835; when completed, the report and appendices filled fifteen folio volumes, containing more than eight thousand pages. In general, the remedies recommended in the report were those suggested by Edwin Chadwick, a young barrister who had been a member of Jeremy Bentham's circle and was an enthusiastic Utilitarian. The central idea of Chadwick's social philosophy was the necessity of applying scientific principles to administrative routine, and of checking parochial inefficiency by centralised bureaucratic control. This tendency towards administrative centralisation is very evident in the Amendment Act of 1834.

The Commissioners' Report declared that most of the abuses, for which remedies must be sought, arose from the misapplication of funds which the Elizabethan Poor Law had directed to be employed in relieving the impotent poor and in setting to work the able-bodied unemployed poor. The greatest source of abuse, in the opinion of the Commissioners, was the outdoor relief given in aid of wages. The Commissioners condemned *all* outdoor relief on principle; their main practical proposal was to prohibit outdoor relief to the able-bodied poor, so as to make the workhouse test once more effective. This would necessarily entail the drastic reform of workhouse administration, together with the provision of workhouses in greater numbers and of larger size. As the general principle of their remedial measures, the Commissioners laid it down that the situation of the person relieved "shall not be made really or apparently so eligible as the situation of the independent labourer of the lowest class", because "in proportion as the condition of any pauper class is elevated above the condition of independent labourers, the condition of the independent class is depressed; their industry is impaired, their employment becomes unsteady, and its remuneration in wages is diminished". [1] If outdoor relief to the able-bodied were abolished, and the workhouse test made effective, the Commissioners considered that the most pressing evils of the existing system would be remedied.

They recognised, however, that such a drastic change could not be enforced merely by an Act of Parliament, but would require constant and continued pressure from some central controlling authority. The Commissioners therefore recommended the appointment of a board of commissioners to control the administration of the Poor Laws, with power to frame and enforce regulations for the government of workhouses; as far as might be practicable, such regulations were to be uniform throughout the country. As many parishes were too small and too poor to afford an adequate workhouse, the central board should be empowered to unite parishes for the purpose of workhouse management, and for the provision of new workhouses where necessary, each parish paying separately for the maintenance of its own paupers and making a proportionate contribution towards the expenses of the union workhouse establishment. It will be seen that the *legal* changes recommended by the Commissioners were very limited and cautious. No new principle was introduced; indeed, the reforms suggested were intended as a return to the original interpretation of the Elizabethan Poor Law. The

[1] *Report on the Poor Laws*, 1834, p. 228 (octavo edition).

practical success of the reformed system of poor-law administration would depend on whether the workhouse test was recognised as amounting to an absolute refusal of relief to the able-bodied poor; if it failed to exercise a strongly deterrent effect, the workhouses would be overcrowded and the new system would break down.

A Poor Law Amendment Bill based on the Commissioners' recommendations was drafted without delay, and passed quickly through Parliament in 1834, despite fierce opposition. A central board of three Poor Law Commissioners was appointed, with Edwin Chadwick as their secretary and a very energetic body of assistant commissioners as their local agents. Reformed methods of relief were introduced very rapidly throughout the agricultural counties; before the Commission's first term of office expired, in 1839, the new system of unions of parishes, under Boards of Guardians elected by the ratepayers, had been extended in some measure to about ninety-five per cent. of the parishes of England and Wales, including about eighty-five per cent. of the population. This represented an extraordinarily rapid rate of progress, considering the magnitude of the problems involved; in many districts, however, the changes had been introduced too recently for their success to be properly estimated at that date. Relief in aid of wages was still being given almost everywhere, except to able-bodied males, and in some places even to them. Non-resident relief was still an important problem, accounting for nearly 95,000 paupers, or about seventeen per cent. of the total number.

The Commissioners considered that the workhouse test had met with immediate and striking success; wherever workhouses were made efficient and used for the accommodation of able-bodied paupers, very few of the applicants persisted in their claims to relief. At Bradford (Wiltshire) over 250 persons relinquished relief rather than submit to separate inquiry into their poverty. At Bristol, out of 1400 persons who were offered relief in the workhouse, only about 85 accepted it. At Faring-don (Berks.) 87 labourers with families, who had been dependent on poor relief for years, were refused outdoor relief during two of the worst winter months. Yet the majority of these families refused to try the workhouse, and of the remainder only two stayed in the house more than four days. The others all found work, 78 of them in their own parish and two others in the immediate neighbourhood. Similar reports came from many other agricultural districts, leading the Commissioners to conclude that the much dreaded "surplus of labour" was largely a myth, created by former laxity in the granting of outdoor relief. In most cases the "redundant" labourers were said to have found employment without leaving home. To some extent this absorption of surplus labour was helped by favourable seasons and by unusual industrial activity during the first years of the Act's operation; but the Commissioners denied that these accidental circumstances had been important factors in the process.

Even in the agricultural counties there was, of course, a darker side to this picture of immediate and striking success; but the sporadic rioting which the new system caused in the rural districts was insignificant compared with the very determined opposition encountered in some of the industrial areas. Hitherto, the poor-law administration of the northern manufacturing districts had not had to face such grave problems as those encountered by the local authorities in the southern agricultural counties. Most classes of industrial workers were earning comparatively good wages during the industrial boom of the middle 'thirties, when the New Poor Law was first put into operation; but the necessity for a large-scale introduction of the new system into the manufacturing districts arose with the renewal of intense industrial depression towards the end of 1836. "Grievous reports of distress were being received in 1837 from all the manufacturing districts ... and well-informed observers feared that unless trade improved rapidly half a million workers at least would be idle in the manufacturing districts, in the very worst time of the year".[1] The workhouse test was clearly inapplicable to distress of this magnitude and urgency; moreover, the industrial population soon made it evident that they would not submit meekly to the dictates of the "three bashaws of Somerset House". In the West Riding of Yorkshire, especially at such places as Huddersfield, Bradford, and Todmorden, attempts to introduce the New Poor Law gave rise to serious popular disturbances, which finally merged into one of the more violent sections of the Chartist movement. In the end, the Poor Law Commissioners had to abandon the idea of prohibiting outdoor relief in the manufacturing districts, and to content themselves with the traditional expedient of task work, usually on the roads. In 1842 there were still 132 unions, out of 590, to which the general prohibitory order concerning outdoor relief had not been applied. In the quarter ending Lady Day, 1844, only 231,000 persons were relieved in workhouses in England and Wales, whereas 1,247,000 people received outdoor relief.

On the whole, it must be admitted that the New Poor Law proved quite inadequate as a remedy for industrial and urban distress. The Government had been more concerned, however, to reduce the burden of agrarian pauperism; and in this respect the Poor Law Commissioners had achieved their immediate objects. The amount spent on the relief of the poor dropped abruptly after 1834, and did not rise to its former level even during the distressed years between 1847 and 1850. Regarded from the financial point of view, the New Poor Law had certainly reduced the burden of pauperism; whether it had helped towards a solution of the problem of poverty is a more doubtful question.

[1] See Redford, *op. cit.*, Chapter VII, especially pp. 102–4.

CHAPTER NINE

Industrial and Commercial Progress

THERE WAS DURING the earlier nineteenth century a notable expansion in most of the manufacturing industries of England. Nevertheless, a good many transitional types of industrial organisation still persisted; down to the second quarter of the century, not a single English industry had been completely mechanised. The expansion was especially remarkable in the cotton industry, the workers in which increased more than tenfold in number during the half-century. Cotton spinning was already a factory industry at the beginning of the period; yet even in cotton spinning the changes in technique and organisation were by no means complete. Water power was still more important than steam power, even in this most progressive branch of manufactures; it was not until the second quarter of the century that the steam engine could be said to have ousted its rival, and in most other industries the change came later. The most important innovation in cotton-spinning machinery during the half-century was the self-actor mule which Roberts, a Manchester machine-maker, put on the market in 1825. The new machine was adopted more readily in the Lancashire cotton-spinning district than elsewhere, and this may have accelerated the process of localisation which was going on within the industry. In some other textile districts the old wooden hand jennies remained in use for at least another generation.

The woollen industries were in a still less completely mechanised stage than the cotton. Even in the middle of the nineteenth century some classes of woollen weavers had not yet adopted the fly shuttle. The spinning of wool for the worsted industries was in the second quarter of the century almost entirely done by power-driven machinery in factories; but wool combing was still mainly a handicraft process, in spite of the various wool-combing machines invented in the late eighteenth century. The slubbing of wool for the woollen manufacture proper was still done on the slubbing billy, which was a wooden hand machine. A special kind of carding machine was designed in 1834, to eliminate this slubbing process, which was intermediate between carding and spinning; but the new machine was not generally adopted until the second half of the century.

In both the cotton and the woollen industries the most important change of the earlier nineteenth century, from the social point of view, was the transition from domestic handloom weaving to power-loom weaving in factories using steam power. This transition necessarily involved the displacement of many thousands of hand-loom weavers, the majority of whom would not be able (even if they were willing) to find employment in the power-loom factories. Until the last decade of the eighteenth century this problem had not existed. Cartwright's power-loom, though patented in 1785, had not been commercially successful, and the hand-loom weavers enjoyed a brief period of exceptional prosperity between the American Revolution and the French wars. The vicissitudes of warfare dealt very harshly with the weavers, however, and their prosperity had vanished long before the close of hostilities in 1815, which brought new difficulties and deeper distress. During the post-war period the misery of the handloom weavers became deeper from year to year; but the industrial transition was by no means sudden. Even so late as 1830 it was estimated that there were in England and Scotland not more than 60,000 power-looms, while there were about 240,000 hand-looms. Power-loom weaving was by that time entering upon a period of rapid development after a generation of struggle; and by the middle of the century the victory of the power-driven machine was virtually complete.

The gradual transition in the manufacturing industries, from handicraft or water power to steam power and metal machinery, greatly increased the importance of the iron and coal industries, and both groups witnessed a remarkable expansion of production during the first half of the nineteenth century. The production of coal increased sixfold during the period, while the production of pig iron increased twelvefold. During the post-war period the iron industries painfully readjusted their organisation to peace-time needs, and found many new civil uses for iron in the manufacture of gas and water mains, pillars, railings, cables, and bridging materials: London even made experiments with iron for paving the roads. After 1830 the development of steam railways and steam shipping gave new scope for the expansion of the mining and metals industries, which was especially marked in Scotland. In the growth of the Scottish iron industry an important turning point seems to have been reached with Neilson's discovery of the hot-air blast in 1828–9. By means of the hot-air blast the Lanarkshire "splint" coal could be used in the smelting furnaces without the preliminary process of coking; and this reduced by more than sixty per cent. the amount of coal required to smelt each ton of iron. The hot-air blast was also introduced rapidly into the English and Welsh iron districts; but differences in the local coals prevented the effect of the change from being so far-reaching as in Scotland. Meanwhile, fuel was being still further economised by the gradual improvement of the puddling process; and Nasmyth's steam hammer, which was invented in 1839, soon proved its value in preparing the iron for the rolling mill.

The coal-mining industry was expanding fairly steadily throughout the earlier nineteenth century. The population of the country was increasing rapidly and the household use of coal was growing even more rapidly. More coal was being demanded for steam engines in industry, for locomotives and steamships, and for export. The demand of the blast furnaces for coal and coke was also increasing, in spite of the economies effected by the technical improvements already noticed. The progress of mining engineering during the period may be seen reflected in the greater depth of the pits, especially in Northumberland and Durham, which produced in the middle years of the century more than a quarter of the total English output. The development of the railroad in Durham led to an extraordinary activity in the sinking of deep pits, often at unprecedented cost; this deep sinking would have been impossible if considerable technical improvements had not been made in the winding apparatus. Deep pits called also for improved methods of ventilation; by the middle of the century furnace ventilation was becoming general in the Northumbrian pits, though the technique of the method was still crude.

Meanwhile, the new industry of mechanical engineering was coming nearer to maturity and was already beginning to rely in an increasing degree on machine tools; machinery was beginning to be made by machinery. This tendency was not only interesting as leading up to the modern method of standardisation, but was in itself essential to the spread of mechanical production in the other manufacturing industries. The early machines had been largely hand-made, and each machine had been constructed almost as a separate work of art. Even during the French wars, practically all the machine-making had been done with such simple tools as hammers, chisels, and files, with clumsy lathes and drills. In the next generation, however, many important machine-making appliances were introduced, such as planing machines, punching machines, wheel-cutting engines, Maudslay's slide rest, and Nasmyth's steam hammer: such were the inventions which transformed the engineering industry, and prepared the way for the more general introduction of iron bridges, railway locomotives, and steel steamships.

In the post-war period the steam engine was still comparatively little used outside a limited group of the leading industries; the introduction of steam power into the less progressive industries went on very gradually. After 1820, however, steam was being increasingly applied to coastal and river navigation; out of 328 steam engines in the Glasgow district in 1831, more than sixty were on steamboats. Nevertheless, in spite of some notable voyages across the Atlantic, the steamer remained essentially a river boat until the middle years of the century.[1] There was gradual transition from the low-pressure steam engine of the Watt type to the more economical high-pressure engine pioneered by Trevithick. Steam power increased very quickly in the textile industries during the 'thirties, especially round Manchester and Glasgow; by the middle of the century the cotton industry of Great Britain had at its disposal 71,000 h.p. of steam and 11,000 h.p. of water power. For all the other textile industries of the country there were available only 34,000 h.p. of steam and 13,000 h.p. of water power.[2] Even in the cotton industry the horse power used by the average firm must have been very low from the modern point of view; and the textile industries were at that time the main home of power-driven machinery. In agriculture the penetration of steam power was very slow indeed; even in corn milling, the steam engine had not been generally adopted by the middle of the century. For land drainage, however, steam made rapid progress after 1830; steam engines rapidly replaced the old windmills and proved much more efficient.

In all the main industries of the country expansion was accompanied by a process of localisation and specialisation; industry was being concentrated in those districts which became the great industrial areas of the next generation. Thus, in the cotton industry, Lancashire was gaining ground rapidly at the expense of the cotton-spinning districts round

[1] See Chapter XIV, below.   [2] Clapham, *op. cit.*, p. 442.

Belfast, Nottingham, and Glasgow. In the woollen and worsted industries, the West Riding of Yorkshire was out-stripping the older clothing districts of East Anglia and the West Country.[1] A similar though less drastic process of localisation was going on in the iron and coal trades, which was leading to the concentration of those industries in South Wales, in the Black Country, in Durham and Northumber-land, and on the coalfield of Lancashire and Yorkshire. Among the great national industries, distinguished by their localisation and concentration in densely populated urban areas, pre-eminence must be given to the textile manufac-tures, which in 1841 employed about 617,000 workers in Eng-land. Cotton was predominant among the textiles, and was already strongly concentrated in Lancashire. Next in im-portance among the national industries came the metal manu-factures, which employed about 100,000 workers. The largest group of metal workers were employed in the iron manu-factures; but there were so many special metal trades enumer-ated that the statistics do not lend themselves readily to analysis. Third in importance among the national industries was pottery, which employed about 23,000 workers. There were potters scattered over all the counties of England, and many of them doubtless supplied a merely local demand. But the majority of the pottery workers were concentrated in Staffordshire, and were producing for distant markets.[2]

Some branches of the textile, metal, and mining industries already contained many firms of modern size. Cotton spin-ning was almost completely dominated by firms which were

[1] For the decay of the Norfolk worsted industry, see M. F. Lloyd Prichard, 'The decline of Norwich', *Economic History Review*, 2nd series, III, No. 3, pp. 371–77. In some parts of the West Country, e.g. Trow-bridge, the cloth industry was reorganised under a factory system during the nineteenth century (K. G. Ponting, *The West of England Cloth Industry*, 1957, Chapter VII.).
[2] See Clive Day, 'The Distribution of Industrial Occupations in England, 1841–1861', in *Transactions of the Connecticut Academy of Arts and Sciences*, March 1927, Vol. 28, pp. 79–235, especially pp. 119–25.

gigantic, according to contemporary standards in other industries: the New Lanark spinning mills employed no fewer than 1600 workers in 1816. Where the spinning firms also controlled the organisation of weaving, they might have as many as 7,000 workers on their books; this was the number employed by Horrockses of Preston in 1816. Coal-mining, even so late as 1850, would not usually employ more than eighty workers to the mine, counting both underground and surface workers; but tin- and copper-mining, with some sections of the copper and brass industries, could show average figures comparable with the cotton industry. Iron-working was organised on the same large scale of operations, and the typical ironmaster controlled as much capital as the typical master cotton spinner.

Not all the industries of England were as progressive as those already mentioned. Among textiles, both linen and silk suffered from the competition of the conquering cotton industry, with its steam factories and its more efficient machinery. The silk industry, it is true, continued to expand by absorbing at starvation wages the most skilled among the handloom weavers displaced from the cotton industry; but such parasitic progress could be only temporary. There was an inevitable depression in lead mining when the wartime demand for munitions ceased; and the depression in this industry did not pass off so quickly as did the post-war depression in those branches of the iron industries which had been concentrating on the manufacture of ordnance. The progress of English manufacturing industry was certainly not uniform or continuous during the earlier nineteenth century. Not only were some industries unprogressive, but even within the most progressive there were districts which were stagnant or declining; and there were times during the half-century when business was almost at a standstill, and when all industrial districts suffered bitter distress.

The changes in industrial organisation and technique went

along with an unprecedented expansion in the volume and value of English commerce. The value of England's overseas trade approximately doubled during the first half of the nineteenth century, despite the persistent sag in the general level of prices after the close of the French wars. This rapid growth of England's overseas trade was, however, almost entirely confined to the period after 1822; during the post-war period commerce received a severe check and was, indeed, almost stagnant. There were severe checks to commerce in each of the later decades of the period; but these do not appear to have obscured the tendency towards the growth of overseas trade so markedly as did the trade depression between 1816 and 1822. Actually, the value of the exports appears to have been dwindling from the end of the wars until the early 'thirties; imports, on the other hand, increased fairly quickly during the post-war period, and by the middle of the century had already begun to exceed the exports in registered value.

To judge from the statistics of the import trade, England's most urgent demands were for raw cotton, raw wool, and timber. The import of cotton almost doubled itself during the 'thirties, and by 1849 had reached the very high figure of 346,000 tons, of which more than one-eighth was re-exported. In 1854 (after the repeal of the Corn Laws) the imports of raw cotton were practically equal in value to those of grain, and the two together made up more than a quarter of the total value of the imports. The trade in wool was on a much smaller scale, for the country had only comparatively recently become dependent on foreign wool to any marked degree. In the eighteenth century, the fine merino wool had come mainly from Spain; but after the French wars an increasing quantity came from Silesia and Saxony. Wool from the Australian colonies also began gradually to attract attention in England, though the quantities actually imported were as yet insignificant. Of the other textile materials, the flax imports grew rapidly during the half-century, partly because the linen industry was adopting machinery and increasing in scale, partly also because the home production of the fibre was dwindling. The trade in timber was more impressive in bulk than in monetary value; but the average value of the trade was probably not less than £3,000,000 a year during the later 'thirties. Altogether, the imports of cotton, wool and timber cost about £20,000,000 a year, at a time when the annual exports of British and Irish products did not amount to £50,000,000. There was very little import trade in metals or ores; while the trade in such "colonial produce" as tobacco, coffee and tea had been checked by the high commodity taxation which was one result of the wars. The trade in wine was stagnant, but there were tremendous imports of West Indian rum and French brandy. There was also a very large import of sugar, which was the basis of a profitable re-export trade.

British exports were composed almost entirely of manufactured goods, and of re-exported colonial produce. During the half-century there were some striking changes in the relative importance of different groups of exported commodities. The exports of woollen goods increased both in value and in quantity, but ceased to be the main staple of the export trade. Whereas in 1800 woollen goods had constituted more than a quarter of the exports in value, in 1850 they represented less than a seventh, and were now second in importance to cotton goods. The exports of cotton goods increased nearly sevenfold in value during the half-century, and their proportion of the value of the export trade rose from about a seventh to nearly a half. Altogether, the textile manufactures amounted to about seventy per cent. of the total value of British exports in the second quarter of the century; the trade in other kinds of manufactured goods was relatively insignificant. The declared value of the exports of British products increased from a yearly average of £35,600,000 during the period 1825–30 to a yearly average of £61,000,000 for the years 1845–50.

The United States were the largest single customer for British goods, taking £6,100,000 worth in 1830, out of a total of £38,200,000.

The expansion of the British export trade during the second quarter of the nineteenth century took place in spite of prohibitions and severe tariff restrictions in most of the main European countries. For the most part, British goods could reach such countries as France, Russia, and Austria only by a process of smuggling. It is true that the German Zollverein pursued a much more liberal policy, and Germany was easily the best customer for British textile goods, especially worsted "stuffs." Nevertheless, even the German tariffs had an upward tendency; and even when the duties remained at the same figure, their fixed rates (not being calculated *ad valorem*) became proportionally more burdensome as British manufactures were cheapened by technical progress. Fortunately England was not entirely dependent on the restricted markets of Europe, but had access to almost unlimited markets in tropical and subtropical countries. There was a steadily and rapidly increasing export trade in plain cotton goods from England to such countries as Turkey, India, China, the West Indies and the Brazils.

The commercial expansion which occurred during the earlier nineteenth century was far from being steady or continuous; there were serious shocks to business confidence and credit in every decade of the half-century. Immediately after the cessation of hostilities there was a feverish burst of speculative trading, which was ended by a severe commercial crisis in 1816. From this collapse the trade of the country did not completely recover until after the resumption of cash payments in 1821; indeed, the process of currency deflation was in itself enough to bring on a secondary crisis and a new crop of commercial bankruptcies. Fortunately the renewed depression soon passed off, and by 1823 trade was recovering so rapidly that Robinson (the Chancellor of the Exchequer) could talk optimistically about a "flood of prosperity". Business confidence was restored, the banks once more ventured to increase their advances of credit, prices began again to rise, commerce and industry became more profitable. Soon speculation became feverish in many departments of commerce, but especially in the trade with the new republics of South America, the former possessions of Spain. Large sums were subscribed to risky public loans for both South America and the weaker European states; this was accompanied by speculation in many grandiose industrial and commercial schemes, of which the most absurd was a company for draining the Red Sea to recover Pharaoh's chariots. In 1825 the threatened storm clouds burst, there was a fresh spate of bankruptcies, and the bank reserve fell dangerously low. In the end the Government was forced to order the Bank of England to increase its note issue, and then the financial stringency slowly passed away; but business confidence had received a rude shock, and trade remained stagnant for several years.

By 1833 there were various indications that trade had stabilised itself on a lower level. Trade and manufactures were being conducted with more prudence than in the earlier 'twenties; there had been some elimination of middlemen's profits, and a considerable reduction in trading expenses. Wages in most trades had fallen since 1825, but the general level of prices had fallen more than proportionately; real wages had probably increased, though it is true that the prices of foodstuffs had not fallen so markedly as the prices of other commodities. Commercial credit was plentiful; the provincial bankers were receiving large deposits and were therefore lending more confidently than they had done since 1825. The healthy condition of trade and industry was thought likely to continue, since there were signs that the foreign demand would increase, especially the demand from America for manufactured goods.

The improvement of trade was actually maintained in 1834.

and 1835, and remained healthy; there was as yet no wild speculation, though prices continued to rise. The prices of manufactured goods were rising more strongly than the prices of raw materials, and the industrial districts were therefore prospering. In the early part of 1836, however, it became known that the stocks of such commodities as cotton, silk, and sugar were reduced below the level required by the ordinary rate of consumption, and that there would probably be a temporary scarcity. Speculative interest was therefore aroused, with the result that prices began to rise very sharply. From this and other causes there ensued a serious financial crisis before the end of the year, and a calamitous depression of trade and manufacturing industry developed during 1837. Many business firms went bankrupt, especially among those connected with the American trade, and there was a substantial fall in the general price level. Many thousands of workers were suddenly thrown out of employment, and acute distress was reported from all the manufacturing districts.

Trade improved rather surprisingly in 1838, but a further crisis in 1839 showed that the recovery was premature; the expansion of foreign trade was again checked, and prices declined steadily. The troubles of the later 'thirties were followed by years of even deeper distress in the early 'forties. There were still frequent bankruptcies at Manchester in 1842, and mill fires seem to have been suspiciously numerous. By 1843, however, signs of a new recovery of trade were being reported, and the promise was fulfilled during the next two years. This short period of comparative prosperity led in its turn to the over-trading of 1846 and to the financial crisis of 1847.

From this bald summary of the commercial fluctuations which occurred during the earlier nineteenth century it appears that trade was at that time moving in almost regular cycles of eleven years' duration, culminating in the financial crises of 1825, 1836 and 1847. This apparent periodicity in the fluctuation of trade has naturally given rise to much speculation as to its nature and general causes. It may be remarked, however, that the fluctuation was not so regular as many writers have supposed; [1] nor is it easy to distinguish the general causes of fluctuation among the multitudinous special factors influencing the course of trade at any particular time. Each of the commercial crises of the period was the product of very complex forces; moreover, each crisis possessed peculiar features of its own, arising out of historical circumstances which from the business point of view must be considered accidental. The short burst of speculative activity at the end of the wars may be explained as a natural reaction from the wartime restrictions on trade; the speedy collapse of the boom followed inevitably from the exhausted financial condition of the continental countries and the normal persistence of economic dislocation into the post-war period. Political changes in South America have already been noticed as an important factor in the over-trading which led up to the crisis of 1825. Banking and currency changes in the United States, which encouraged the speculative purchase of public land, were prominent among the many special forces converging to cause the crisis of 1836–7; in England the speculative mania of the time found expression particularly in the promotion of new railway and joint-stock banking companies. A second "railway mania" was one of the first symptoms of the unhealthy financial activity which culminated in the crisis of 1847; but the most important and fundamental cause of that crisis appears to have been a general deficiency of the harvests throughout Europe. This general deficiency intensified the distress arising from the successive failures of the Irish potato

[1] For the statistical evidence see N. J. Silberling, 'British Prices and Business Cycles, 1779–1850', in *Review of Economic Statistics* (Harvard Economic Service), October 1923, Prel. Vol. V, Supplement 2. For a fuller, more recent, and more authoritative survey, see A. D. Gayer, W. W. Rostow and A. J. Schwartz, *The Growth and Fluctuation of the British Economy, 1790–1850*, 2 vols., 1953.

crop in 1845 and 1846; the Irish famine which ensued had most disastrous economic and social consequences upon all parts of the United Kingdom.

It is to be presumed that there was some general cause or group of causes underlying this tendency towards the regular alternation of financial laxity and stringency, commercial optimism and depression, industrial over-production and unemployment, social prosperity and distress. But to evolve a consistent theory, laying bare such general causes and at the same time giving due weight to all the special historical circumstances, would be an arduous and lengthy task which will not be attempted in this work.[1] Among the underlying causes of the recurrent crises, contemporary commercial opinion laid most emphasis on the influence of banking policy in relation to the supply of trading credit; on the other hand, the bankers retorted that fluctuations in banking policy merely reflected the varying demands of trade, and were therefore a symptom rather than a cause of commercial instability. This aspect of the problem must be reserved for fuller discussion.[2]

[1] See W. W. Rostow, *British Economy of the Nineteenth Century*, 1948, and R. C. O. Matthews, *A Study in Trade Cycle Theory: Economic Fluctuations in Great Britain, 1833–42*, 1954.
[2] See Chapter XII, below.

CHAPTER TEN

Labour Organisation and Co-operation

IN THE PERIOD of industrial depression after the French wars, employers in many manufacturing districts combined openly to enforce the reduction of wage rates. This policy produced such disastrous results that soon local movements in defence of the workers' standard of living attracted the support of many middle-class philanthropists, and even of some employers. Nevertheless, wage rates were reduced and strikes broke out all over the country. Francis Place, who now became the most effective champion of the workers' cause, had been an opponent of the combination laws for many years, especially the laws affecting the tailoring trades. In 1814 he "began to work seriously to procure a repeal of the laws against combinations"; [1] for this purpose he acquired control in 1818 of *The Gorgon*, a working-class newspaper which proved a useful instrument for propaganda during the next few years. Incidentally, this journalistic venture gained for Place two influential allies in J. R. McCulloch, the editor of *The Scotsman*, and Joseph Hume, a leader of the "Philosophic Radicals" in the House of Commons.

This alliance entered on a new phase in 1822, when Hume moved for a bill to repeal all laws against combinations and coaxed the Government into granting him a select committee. The prospects of the movement were for a time clouded by the discussion of more drastic proposals framed by George White and Gravener Henson; but in 1824 Hume at

[1] Place, quoted by Graham Wallas, *Life of Francis Place*, 1918 edition, p. 203.

last secured the appointment of his committee, which was given very wide terms of reference to inquire into the laws concerning the emigration of artisans, the exportation of machinery, and the combination of workmen. Place and Hume between them managed the committee's business, and secured a report in favour of allowing complete freedom of combination and emigration. Following upon this report, "a bill to repeal all the combination laws and to legalise trade societies was passed through both Houses, within less than a week, at the close of the session, without either debate or division . . . almost without the notice of members within or newspapers without".[1] Apparently the fortress had been evacuated without a shot fired.

Unfortunately, however, the repeal of the combination laws proved to be the signal for a wild outburst of strikes, accompanied by some violence, in many parts of the country. The employing classes realised with a shock that their legal remedies against insubordination had been weakened, and demanded a re-imposition of the restrictive statutes. In 1825 the ship-owning and shipbuilding interests, represented by Huskisson, moved for a committee of inquiry into the effect of the repeal, on the ground that the measure had been carried through without sufficient consideration. The committee appointed was composed mainly of supporters of the Government, and Place had to work very hard to prevent the entire reversal of the decisions arrived at in 1824. In the end, however, Parliament passed a statute which nominally re-established the common-law prohibition of industrial combinations, but specifically excepted from prosecution associations for the purpose of regulating wages or hours of labour. It is true that the Act imposed penalties for intimidation, molestation and obstruction. This made the preparation and conduct of strikes extremely hazardous for unionists. In the course of a strike acts might be committed which would render

[1] Webb, *History of Trade Unionism*, 1920 edition, p. 103.

the participants liable to prosecution on a charge of criminal conspiracy under the Common Law. This, broadly speaking, remained the legal position until the passing of the Conspiracy and Protection of Property Act in 1875. Place and Hume, however, were better pleased than were the employing classes with this compromise of 1825.

Place's work had thus been crowned with a considerable measure of success; but the results were very different from his expectations. He thought that freedom to combine would take away the desire to combine, and that combinations, being "for distant and doubtful experiments, for uncertain and precarious benefits", would soon cease to exist.[1] No conception could have been further from the truth. Trade societies sprang up all over the country, in all branches of manufacturing industry, and a vigorous attempt was made to promote common organisation among the various trades. This new movement was checked, however, by the financial crash of 1825; in the long trade depression which followed, industrial unemployment increased enormously, and the newly emancipated unions were powerless to prevent the general reduction of wage rates.

Hitherto, national trade unions in the modern sense had not come into existence. The experiences of the post-war period seemed, however, to have demonstrated the futility of all merely local and sectional combinations. In the first years after the repeal of the combination laws, therefore, the newly-won freedom of the industrial workers found expression in many ambitious attempts at labour organisation, sometimes aiming at national unions of the workers in particular trades, but sometimes at a general union of the workers in all the main trades of the country for the organisation of a general expropriatory strike. More than once, the establishment of a national *trade* union was a preliminary step towards the organisation of a general *trades* union. This was the case, for

[1] Place MSS. (B.M.) 27798–57: quoted Webb, *op. cit.*, p. 109.

instance, with the National Union of Cotton Spinners promoted in 1829 by John Doherty, the leader of the Manchester spinners. The cotton spinners' union was not a success; but Doherty had already formed more ambitious projects, and a meeting of delegates from twenty organised trades in 1830 led to the establishment of a National Association for the Protection of Labour. This organisation had soon enrolled as constituent members about a hundred and fifty separate trade societies, mainly among the textile workers of Lancashire, Cheshire, Derby and Nottingham.

In 1831 the National Association for the Protection of Labour was said to have a hundred thousand members; it had also its own weekly paper, *The Voice of the People*, which Doherty made a very influential organ of propaganda. In spite of this initial success, however, the movement soon showed many symptoms of internal weakness. A new secretary embezzled £100, and general financial weakness prevented effective action. The Lancashire branches refused to support a Nottinghamshire strike, and there was consequently some ill-feeling between the two main districts. The Manchester branch, in which the movement originated, soon died out, probably through a quarrel between Doherty and the executive committee of the association; the association itself died in 1832. Its place was then taken, however, by other national organisations, such as the Builders' Union, which was sometimes called the General Trades Union: this was a federal organisation of workers in all the building trades, including seven distinct crafts. By 1833 many other trade organisations were recovering from distress, or were being established for the first time, among such industrial workers as the Lancashire cotton spinners, the Leeds woollen workers, and the Staffordshire potters.

During 1833 there was more than one attempt to link these various trade unions into a more general organisation. The trend towards trades unionism was now supported and stimulated by Robert Owen, whose schemes of national labour organisation culminated in the Grand National Consolidated Trades Union during the winter of 1833-4. As applied to the reorganisation of manufacturing industry, Owen's ideas had much in common with the more recent ideals of the guild socialists. National companies were to be formed among the workers, to take over the various trades; and the activities of these national companies were to be co-ordinated through the Grand National Consolidated organisation, which was thus to become the central executive body of an industrial democracy. These ideals spread among all kinds of industrial workers with almost incredible rapidity. Within a few weeks of its formation the Grand National Consolidated Trades Union had recruited more than half a million members, of all industrial classes, including farm labourers and women workers. The declared policy of the union was to organise a general strike of all the wage earners throughout the country, to secure control of the means of production; to this end all merely local and sectional interests were to be subordinated. The organisation soon found itself burdened, however, with local and sectional strikes for the support of which its funds were quite inadequate. Many prosecutions of trade unionists took place, some for illegal conspiracy under the common law, some for molestation, intimidation, and obstruction. Most of the prosecutions, however, were under the laws relating to masters and servants; these laws for a long time to come prevented any real justice as between employers and workers. Most scandalous was the injustice done to six Dorsetshire labourers who had attempted to set up a local agricultural branch of the Grand National Consolidated. These "Dorchester Labourers" were convicted and transported under a little-known statute[1] (passed at the time of the naval mutiny in 1797), by which the administration of unlawful oaths was severely penalised. Persecuted on

[1] 37 Geo. III, c. 123.

all sides, and suffering also from internal dissensions, the trades-unionist movement soon collapsed like a house of cards. In August, 1834, the Grand National Consolidated was formally converted into Owen's British and Foreign Association of Industry, Humanity, and Knowledge; but neither this organisation, nor the Association of all Classes of all Nations which Owen founded in 1835, had any appreciable influence upon the progress of society.

Robert Owen's social ideals inspired most of the labour movements of the earlier 'thirties; his spiritual and intellectual leadership gave both strength and weakness to the attempts at industrial democracy. Since the end of the French wars, Owen's public significance had ceased to be bounded by his activities as a philanthropic industrial employer; he had become a social theorist and reformer of international importance. To escape from the defects of the existing organisation of industry Owen advocated (among other schemes) the formation of Villages of Unity and Co-operation, each consisting of (say) a thousand persons, with a thousand acres of land for agricultural and manufacturing purposes. The villagers were to live in blocks of houses built round large squares; in the squares would be erected public buildings, which would divide the squares into rectangles. Villages of this pattern could be built for about £100 a head, or a yearly rent of £5. The villagers would exchange the various products of their labour among themselves in an equitable fashion, and would thus be free from the degrading influences of modern commercialism and competition. Such ideas had a general likeness to the contemporary teachings of St.-Simon and Fourier in France, but had not hitherto attained any prominence in England. Villages of a somewhat similar character had been organised in America, though they had only been successful where religious fervour gripped a practical agricultural population, not afraid of hard living and hard work.

It seems likely that Owen borrowed the framework of his "rectangular paradises" from John Bellers' *Colledge of Industry* (1696), which had been brought to his notice by Francis Place. Owen also showed some affinity to Bellers in his currency theories. Bellers had declared that his community would have labour, and not money, as its standard of value. Owen developed this into the theory that an hour's labour should form the unit of currency. The labourer should receive a paper note certifying the number of hours he had worked in the production of useful articles; with this note he should be able to obtain goods representing an equal number of hours of labour. It was true that human labour was unequal in productive power; but the value of average unskilled labour could be estimated and its relation to the other grades of labour determined. All this amounted to the contention that the labourer ought to get a fair wage per hour. After much discussion Owen fixed this fair wage at sixpence an hour, and this was the basis of calculation adopted in his labour currency experiments; incidentally, it may be remarked that this was more than double the contemporary average rate of wages for unskilled labour.

Between 1820 and 1830 Owen had been occupied in making practical experiments with communities both in Great Britain and in America. A great deal of Owen's money was lost in America, and he returned to England in 1829 to lose the rest of his fortune in the labour exchanges and co-operative experiments of the early 'thirties. There were by 1830 nearly three hundred co-operative societies in Great Britain, and in the next few years the number increased to between four and five hundred. Many of these societies had the ultimate intention of forming themselves into complete and self-contained communities; but for the time being this ideal remained in the background. In actual practice, many of the co-operative societies of the time were little more than grocery stores; though the *typical* societies were associations of members of the same trade, who subscribed a small capital in order to purchase materials on which unemployed members could be set to work, with the hope of giving employment eventually to all the members.

As co-operative production grew in volume, it became necessary to organise wider markets for it, and "labour bazaars" were established to which the co-operative trade societies sent up their surplus produce. It was in such labour exchanges or bazaars that Owen's plan for a labour currency was given its trial in England. In 1832 Owen opened a National Equitable Labour Exchange in London, and was soon inundated with goods deposited in exchange for labour notes. His supporters were for a time in ecstasies about the coming millennium, and many other labour exchanges were opened by enthusiastic Owenites both in London and in provincial towns. Soon, however, it became evident that the managers of the exchanges were not sufficiently expert in valuing the goods deposited; some of the goods were priced too high and some too low. The methods of valuation employed proved far too rigid, and the commission charged by the exchanges for working expenses (1d. in the shilling) was too low. Many of the goods accepted were quite unsalable in the ordinary market, and these tended to accumulate in the exchange, while the better and cheaper goods were picked out by shrewd local tradesmen who had taken labour notes in their shops. In this way the goods left in the exchange gradually became such as were worth less than their price in labour notes; and therefore the labour notes themselves began to depreciate, until finally they had fallen to a commercial value below that which the average workman could earn in the ordinary labour market. In this fashion the Owenite labour exchanges gradually drifted towards insolvency, in spite of financial subsidies received from the profits of Owen's lecturing tours, and from other sources. By August, 1834, all the labour exchanges and bazaars in the country had been wound up and abandoned; of them all, the Birmingham exchange alone showed a final surplus.

Meanwhile, trade in general had become decidedly brisker, industrial employment was increasing, and industrial wages were rising. In these circumstances, the industrial workers showed little inclination to engage in ambitious and hazardous schemes for the economic reconstruction of society; and when, after 1836, the black cloud of trade depression once more descended upon the country, social unrest found expression in the political aspirations of the Chartist movement, rather than in any revival of the economic utopianism which had lain behind the trades-unionist and co-operative movements of the earlier 'thirties.

The aims of the Chartist movement were political, but the forces underlying it were largely economic. In its political aspect the movement carried on the traditions of the "Radical Reformers" who had been prominent in the history of the post-war generation. In its economic aspect Chartism was linked up with such diverse forces as the Owenite co-operative schemes, Attwood's currency heresies, the northern factory reform agitation and the opposition to the New Poor Law. From a political point of view the immediate cause of Chartism was the disillusionment of the working classes with the results of the Reform Act of 1832. From an economic point of view, however, a still more direct cause was the reaction from ideals of industrial democracy, following on the collapse of the trades-unionist movement and of the Owenite labour exchanges. The political aims of the Chartists focused the general social unrest of the time, and gave a temporary unity to economic forces which in origin and nature were widely divergent. It may be noted that the working-class leaders of local Chartism tended to come from the old handicrafts—hand-loom weavers, shoemakers, cabinet-makers, and stockingers, rather than from among workers in the new mechanised industries.

As a document, the People's Charter of 1838 was mainly the work of William Lovett, a cabinet-maker, acting as secretary of the London Working Men's Association. His programme of political reforms had an immediate success in concentrating the force of the working-class movements throughout the country; but the very magnitude of its success caused the control of the agitation to pass from such moderate reformers as Lovett, and gave greater prominence to irresponsible demagogues like Feargus O'Connor. O'Connor, who was a born mob orator, had already established his hold over the half-starved hand-loom weavers in the northern industrial districts; and his fiery eloquence was being reinforced by the journalistic claptrap of the *Northern Star*. Elaborate preparations were made during the closing months of 1838 for a great National Convention or People's Parliament, which was intended to demonstrate the solidarity of the working classes and scare the Government into granting the reforms demanded. At the various meetings, held throughout the country to elect delegates to the convention, local orators put forward the most varied aims, apparently in complete sincerity. At Sheffield, for instance, Ebenezer Elliott declared that the objects of the movement were "free trade, universal peace, freedom of religion, and national education".

When the fundamental disunity of the movement is appreciated, it is easy to understand the ludicrous feebleness of the National Convention of 1839. Nearly half the delegates were middle-class, middle-aged, and married, and were against any attempt at armed revolution. At the other extreme were simple-hearted fanatics who idolised O'Connor, and took literally his talk about the use of armed force. And the Convention could find nothing to do except to make futile speeches and issue futile manifestos. Small wonder was it that the middle-class delegates went home to mind their own businesses, and that the fanatics went home to foment rebellion.

The pathetic collapse of the movement in 1839 and 1840 needs no special explanation. It was already clear by the spring of 1839 that no general rising was to be expected; and the sporadic attempts at armed rebellion which took place in the following winter were suppressed with the greatest ease. Among other factors in the situation, the spreading network of railways and electric telegraphs was now placing greater power in the hands of the Government by enabling detachments of the army and the police to be moved about the country more swiftly.

By the summer of 1840 most of the more prominent Chartist leaders had been imprisoned on various charges; Chartism became dormant for the time being, and was never again so extensive or so threatening. A National Charter Association, which was to work for the Charter by peaceable and constitutional means, was founded at Manchester in 1840; but this new organisation grew only slowly, partly because of technical illegalities in its constitution, and a natural fear that the Government might make these irregularities the basis for further prosecutions. Another reason for tardiness in recovery was the surprisingly varied kinds of Chartism which were now competing for allegiance. There were Christian Chartists, who had churches at Birmingham, Bath, and Paisley. William Lovett was reviving his old schemes of national education even before he came out of prison. To these divergent tendencies within the Chartist movement there was added the competition of other movements with better financial backing. During the early 'forties the Anti-Corn-Law League was growing in strength rapidly, and caused a most serious conflict of opinion among the Chartists. O'Connor himself was a bitter enemy of the League; but many of his followers were attracted by the prospect of cheaper bread, and disregarded O'Connor's instruction to vote for Tory candidates. Joseph Sturge's Complete Suffrage Union of 1842 was (in O'Connor's opinion) merely a dodge of the Anti-Corn-Law Leaguers to cause still further dissension in the Chartist ranks; and for this view there may have been some shadow of justification. The Complete Suffrage Union was supported not only by an important section of the Free Traders, but also by many of the most prominent Chartists, including O'Brien, Lovett and the Christian Chartists. This was the most serious split that had occurred in the Chartist movement, and was especially dangerous since its supporters had abundant funds.

In these circumstances, and in time of bad trade, the task of preparing the Chartist National Petition of 1842 could not be easy. The new Chartist Convention met with the old difficulty of finding anything to do, and was drawn into the discussion of various irrelevant subjects, such as co-operation and teetotalism. The National Petition itself enumerated a very heterogeneous selection of grievances, ranging from protests against the existence of bribery in politics, the harshness of the New Poor Law, and the great inequalities of wealth, to complaints about the police force and the standing army, industrial and agricultural distress, and the established Church of England. For all these grievances the petition apparently suggested that the only remedy was the People's Charter. Needless to say, the National Petition was summarily rejected by the House of Commons, and Chartism was thenceforward a spent force. Even the European revolutions of 1848 failed to revive the martial ardour of either O'Connor or his followers, and the monster National Petition of that year was a pathetic fiasco. The Chartist movement survived in name for another decade; but Chartism as a politically influential force had been dead since 1842.

The political aspirations of the working classes had once more ended in disillusionment. For the next generation the main currents of the labour movement again took on a distinctly economic character, though the trade unions and co-operative societies which then arose were very different in both aims and methods from the organisations inspired by Owen in the early 'thirties. In the revival of trade unionism after 1840 the main emphasis was on the formation of separate national organisations for particular trades, such as the coal miners, engineers, iron founders, carpenters, and cotton spinners. It is true that in 1845 a National Association of United Trades was formed; but this body had hardly even a superficial resemblance to the Grand National Consolidated of eleven years before. The new association was an alliance of existing unions in particular trades, and was not intended to be more than a co-ordinating influence. Its policy of arbitration and conciliation, including a demand for the establishment of local "Boards of Trade", contrasted strongly with the earlier advocacy of a general expropriatory strike. In spite of its moderation, however, the National Association was distrusted by the larger trade unions as savouring of the tactics of 1834. The employers throughout the country naturally showed great hostility to the association, and after the middle of the century it ceased to exercise any significant influence upon the labour movement. Nevertheless, its moderate and conciliatory policy was conceived in much the same spirit as that of the new national trade unions within the separate industries.

The new unions were much milder and more "respectable" than their predecessors. Their policy was to avoid open conflict as much as possible, and to improve the circumstances of their members either by the method of mutual assurance on friendly society lines, or by limiting the supply of labour through the restriction of apprenticeship and the encouragement of emigration. The new spirit found expression not only in a more conciliatory policy, but in the development of a more substantial trade-union structure. Solid reserve funds were being built up under the care of permanent salaried officials chosen for administrative capacity rather than oratorical fervour. Loose confederations of local trade clubs were being moulded into consolidated national organisations. In the larger unions a nice balance was maintained between the almost absolute power of the central executive body over the reserve funds (from which strikes might be financed) and the local autonomy of the branches in the management of "friendly society" business.

Alongside this new growth of trade unionism there occurred a remarkably successful revival of working-class co-operation, which had failed so completely in the early 'thirties. The enterprise of the Rochdale Pioneers in 1844 reflected a genuine revival of the Owenite co-operative movement, though the final success of the venture was due to methods which Owen had not envisaged. Most of the original twenty-eight Pioneers were hand-loom weavers, who had recently gone through a disastrous strike and were disappointed with trade-union results. Some of the members were Chartists, and some were supporters of the movement in favour of factory legislation. All the leaders were enthusiastic Owenite socialists, and the original ideals of the society were practically identical with the objects of the earlier co-operators of the 'thirties.[1]

The success of the Rochdale Pioneers seems to have been due largely to their system of dividing the trading surplus in proportion to purchases. This was an indirect method of eliminating profit; the goods were sold at about the ordinary retail price, and the net surplus over cost was returned to the purchaser in the form of a bonus or rebate. The original rules of the Rochdale society, registered in 1845, provided that after paying the expenses of management and interest on capital the members should divide the remaining surplus quarterly among themselves in proportion to the amount of their respective purchases. The combination of this rule with others likely to appeal to the working classes, e.g., a single

[1] The original objects of the Rochdale Pioneers are set forth in Bland, Brown and Tawney, *op. cit.*, p. 643.

vote for each member, no matter how much share capital he held, open membership, and the sale of unadulterated goods, led to immediate success. Shortly after 1845 a rule was put into force providing that the dividend due to each member should be retained until he held five £1 shares in the society. On this capital the interest payable was fixed at 3½ per cent. in the first instance, and later increased to five per cent. This method of financing co-operative enterprise proved strikingly successful, and was taken up by other societies, founded in several Lancashire towns during the distressful times of 1847 and 1848. By 1851 there were about 130 co-operative stores trading in Scotland and the north of England. As yet, however, the societies were very small; Rochdale, with 670 members, was still the largest society, and most of the others had fewer than 100 members. The Scottish societies down to that time were dividing profits either upon capital or equally among the members; within the next few years, however, they adopted the Rochdale system, and thereafter expanded rapidly.[1]

[1] For a recent study of early co-operative history, see S. Pollard, 'Nineteenth-century co-operation: from community building to shop-keeping' (*Essays in Labour History*, ed. A. Briggs and J. Saville, 1960, pp. 74–112).

CHAPTER ELEVEN

Labour Legislation and Social Reform

MODERN FACTORY LEGISLATION has some features in common with the mediaeval labour regulations, which may be said to have culminated in the Elizabethan Statute of Apprentices. Its relationship to the Elizabethan Poor Law is less obvious, but equally real; for the factory legislation of modern England began with an attempt at safeguarding the health and morals of poor-law apprentices employed in manufacturing industry. The Elizabethan Poor Law had directed that pauper children should be apprenticed by the parish authorities to some trade; and in the seventeenth and eighteenth centuries the children were commonly employed in the parish "house of industry" along with the adult paupers. In typical cases of which details are known, pauper children were employed in the spinning rooms of these houses of industry from the age of five years, and worked for ten or twelve hours a day. This was no longer than many "free" children were worked at home by their parents; in the framework knitting trade of the eighteenth century the working hours were said to be sixteen or seventeen a day.

Parish apprenticeship was subject to grave abuses long before it became adopted on a larger scale as part of the early factory system. Nevertheless, the expansion of such apprenticeship into a wholesale method of supplying the factory master with cheap unskilled labour aroused widespread humanitarian opposition. Public attention was attracted to the abuse in 1784, and in that year the Lancashire justices resolved not to allow the apprenticeship of pauper children to cotton factories and other works in which the children would be employed during the night or for more than ten hours a day. The magistrates of other counties followed this example in later years; though it is clear that the evil was not peculiar to the cotton industry or to the factory system. Some of the worst cases of cruelty to parish apprentices were proved to be the work of small-scale domestic employers, in industries which had not yet been transformed by the introduction of power-driven machinery.

When the first Sir Robert Peel brought in his "Health and Morals of Apprentices" Bill in 1802, he found Parliament in a very sympathetic mood, and the measure passed into law without any serious opposition. The Act applied to all factories, and made various regulations which might justly be considered to err on the side of moderation. Apprentices were not to be employed more than twelve hours a day, and night work was to cease by a fixed date. Apprentices were to be instructed in reading, writing, and arithmetic, and were to attend church at least once a month as well as having religious instruction every Sunday. Each apprentice was to be given a new suit of clothing yearly; and there were other provisions concerning the sleeping accommodation, ventilation and whitewashing of the rooms. The justices of each county were to appoint visitors to supervise the administration of the Act; of these visitors one was to be a justice and the other a clergyman. Unfortunately the Act proved almost useless, partly because the visitors were very lax in their inspection, but mainly because the parish apprenticeship system was itself being superseded by the employment of "free" children, under contracts made with their parents.

In the post-war period the movement in favour of factory legislation received a new stimulus from the active propaganda carried on by Robert Owen, and the interest of the philanthropic public was roused by the striking success of his social and industrial experiments at New Lanark. In his mills

Owen employed no children under ten years of age; he worked the children for twelve hours a day, but allowed them to have an hour and a quarter off for meals. He considered, moreover, that the hours of labour could be still further reduced without financial loss, since if the children had more leisure they would be healthier and therefore more efficient. This was an incredible doctrine to Owen's fellow manufacturers in Scotland, and he had trouble with his business partners. Luckily, however, he managed to secure financial backing from a group of philanthropic Quakers and Utilitarians in London, and his earnestness gained him a small political following in favour of the legislative regulation of factory conditions. Sir Robert Peel (the elder) took charge of the movement, and secured the appointment of a committee of inquiry in 1815.

After long and tedious discussion the inquiry led in 1819 to a Factory Act which was a mere shadow of Owen's original recommendations. His draft Bill prohibited the employment of children under ten years old; the Act as passed allowed their employment at the age of nine years. The draft Bill provided that young persons under eighteen years old should not work more than ten and a half hours a day; the Act allowed young persons of sixteen years to work twelve hours a day. Owen asked for the appointment of paid and qualified inspectors; inspection under the Act was again left to the justices. The Act, moreover, applied only to cotton factories, although it was notorious that similar regulation was needed equally urgently in most other kinds of factories. The Factory Act of 1819, thus analysed from Owen's point of view, could not be considered a generous measure; nevertheless, it was distinctly in advance of contemporary practice. In some factories children were being employed at so early an age as three or four years; children of seven years old quite commonly worked thirteen or fourteen hours a day.

During the 'twenties the movement for industrial reform

turned on securing the repeal of the Combination Acts, rather than on any further interference with the hours of labour. In 1828, however, John Doherty, the Manchester trades-unionist leader, was active in the "Society for the Protection of Children employed in Cotton Factories", and in the following year he set up a small Short Time Committee in Lancashire. In 1830 the agitation in favour of restrictive factory legislation received a new stimulus when Richard Oastler began to write his letters to the *Leeds Mercury* on the subject of "Yorkshire Slavery". The movement for the abolition of slavery in the British Empire had at that time achieved great prominence, and Yorkshire was one of the strongest centres of the movement. Oastler contended that the condition of the factory children in the Yorkshire woollen and worsted mills (which were as yet not subject to regulation) was worse than that of the slaves in the West Indies; and, so far as concerned working hours, his view seems to have had justification. In the woollen mills it was usual to work the children for thirteen hours a day, and in the worsted mills for twelve and a half hours, exclusive of meals. In some smaller and remote establishments the conditions were even worse. The West Indian slaves often worked longer hours than these in time of crop; but "out of crop" the normal working day of the slaves was eleven and a half hours, while in practice it was often less.

Oastler's letters demanded a ten-hours day for all factory workers under twenty-one years old; and in this demand he soon found himself supported by men of all religious sects and all political parties. The first practical result of the renewed agitation was Hobhouse's Factory Act of 1831; though, as in the case of Peel's Factory Act of 1819, the measure actually passed cannot be regarded as embodying the ideas of the reforming party. The original proposal was to secure the ten-hours day for all factory workers under eighteen years old, and this was to apply to woollen and silk as well as **cotton** mills. Hobhouse's Act, as passed, provided that young persons under eighteen years of age should not have more than twelve hours' actual work a day, and that night work should be prohibited for all persons under twenty-one years. This was an advance on previous legislation and practice; but the measure applied only to cotton mills, and even so proved ineffective.

By this time, however, the ten-hours movement had grown in strength, not only in Lancashire and Yorkshire but also in London and in Parliament. In the last unreformed House of Commons Michael Sadler introduced a Ten Hours Bill and secured the appointment of a select committee, though it was well understood that no further progress would be possible until the Reform Act had been safely passed. Sadler's Bill proposed that no person under eighteen years old should be employed more than ten hours a day; no person under twenty-one years old should do any work between seven o'clock in the evening and six o'clock in the morning; and no child under nine years old should be employed at all in any factory. Sweeping as these proposals were, it may be remarked that the Bill had at least two defects, which were likely to reduce its effectiveness if it became law. In the first place, the Bill provided no proper machinery for factory inspection and for the enforcement of the law; in the second place, while the Bill provided for the restriction of the working hours of children and young persons, it promised no adequate safeguard against the continuance of excessively long hours for the grown-up workers. It is true that the ostensible object of the movement was to protect the children and young persons; but the working-class supporters of the ten-hours day had always had the ulterior object of restricting all factory hours, including those of the adult operatives. In Lancashire, indeed, the most prominent demand was for the restriction of the hours within which machinery could be worked in factories, since this would necessarily restrict the hours of all workers.

Sadler's Committee collected a great volume of evidence proving that factory children were being worked for over-long hours in unhealthy conditions, with disastrous consequences to their vitality and physique. No doubt the evidence was partisan and one-sided; but this made it all the more effective in arousing the public conscience to the necessity for reform. In the first reformed House of Commons the Ten Hours Bill was once more introduced, this time by Lord Ashley, since Sadler had failed to secure re-election. The Whig Government was ostensibly favourable to industrial reform, but insisted on appointing a new Royal Commission of Inquiry, on the ground that the evidence collected by Sadler's Committee was not sufficiently comprehensive or reliable. It was well understood, however, that the Government's motive in reopening the inquiry was not pure zeal for the truth, but an attempt to satisfy the nominal demands of the factory reformers without forfeiting the increasingly important support of the industrial employers. Naturally enough, the Royal Commission was "boycotted" by the Short Time Committees of the northern industrial districts, and protest meetings were held at various places. Nevertheless, to the surprise of the reformers, the Royal Commission reported in favour of further factory legislation: though its recommendations were not altogether favourable to the ultimate aims of the ten-hours movement.

The report of the Royal Commission was accepted by the Government as a basis for legislation; and in 1833 Lord Althorp introduced a Factory Bill which, after much discussion and some amendment, became a more nearly effective Factory Act than any of its predecessors. The Factory Act of 1833 prohibited night work (between 8.30 p.m. and 5.30 a.m.) for all persons under eighteen years of age, in all the main textile trades except lacemaking. No person under eighteen years old was to be employed for more than twelve hours a day or sixty-nine hours a week. No child under nine years old was to be employed at all, except in silk mills. In silk mills, children under thirteen years of age were not to work more than ten hours a day. In other kinds of textile factories no child under eleven years old was to be employed for more than nine hours a day or forty-eight hours a week; the age limit under this clause was to be raised to twelve years old after one year from the passing of the Act, and to thirteen years old a year later. The Act was to be enforced by four special factory inspectors, appointed to work definite circuits, with the powers of justices for the purpose of inspection.

Dissatisfaction with this comprehensive measure of reform turned mainly on two points. In the first place, it was clear that the Act would do little to shorten the working day of adult workers; nor did the Government intend that it should. The intention was that two relays of children should be employed for (say) seven and a half hours a day each; this could be done without infringing the regulations against night work, and would still allow the adult workers to be employed for fifteen hours a day. Such an arrangement (argued the Royal Commission and the Government) would be better for the children's health than having only one shift of children employed for ten hours a day: while it would be more acceptable to the employers through its economy in the use of machinery and of adult labour. The second main objection to the Act was that the government inspectors would be merely tools in the hands of the employing classes. In practice, however, this latter fear proved to be entirely without foundation; it was just this system of paid itinerant factory inspectors which made the Act of 1833 more nearly effective than any previous factory legislation.

During the later 'thirties and earlier 'forties the demand for industrial reform became part of the wider struggle between the agricultural and the manufacturing interest. The return of the Tories to power in 1841 aroused great hopes among the factory reformers; for in many of the manufacturing districts the election had been fought almost entirely on the factory question. It soon appeared, however, that many of the Tory leaders were less favourable to factory legislation, now that they were in office, than they had professed to be during the elections. Peel's opinions on the subject were decidedly hostile; he believed that salvation lay in emancipating the industrial system, rather than in controlling it. Early in 1842 Peel informed Ashley that the Government was not prepared to support the Ten Hours Bill, but would introduce factory legislation of its own. Gladstone was more friendly. He expressed his sympathy with proposals to fix a higher minimum age for "female infant" factory workers: to limit the number of women in proportion to the number of men in each factory: and to prohibit the employment of married women in factories during the lifetime of their husbands. This encouragement seems to have given a new emphasis to the question of female labour, and from this time down to the Ten Hours Act of 1847 the agitation turned mainly on the position of the women workers.

In the meantime, the question of industrial reform was being widened as the result of various investigations into working conditions. The Children's Employment Commission, which had been appointed in 1840, made its first report (dealing with mining conditions) in 1842. The Commissioners reported that children were ordinarily taken to work in the coal mines at eight or nine years of age, while in some exceptional instances they were employed even at four or five years old. The youngest children were employed down the pit as doorkeepers, opening and shutting the trap-doors on which the ventilation of the mine partly depended; they had a working day of twelve hours or more. Many of the children were employed as "hurriers", drawing the small trucks of coal along the passages, which were in some places not more than eighteen inches high. Pumping operations kept some of the children in the pit standing ankle-deep in water for twelve hours a day. In some districts, children were employed as engine tenters, with the responsibility of lowering and raising the cages in which the miners entered and left the pit. In Scotland, women and children were also employed to carry baskets of coal on their backs up steep ladders and along the passages to the pit bottom. Girls six years old were found carrying half a hundredweight of coal in this fashion. The worst victims of the mining system were the parish apprentices, who were still employed in considerable numbers in the coal mines of South Staffordshire, Lancashire, and the West Riding. Usually the hours of labour of the mining children varied from twelve to about sixteen a day; but in exceptional cases children had been known to remain in the pit for thirty-six hours at a stretch, working extra shifts. The employment of women in the mines aroused widespread public indignation, but was probably not so serious a problem as the employment of young children. Even before 1842 the employment of women underground was virtually confined to mines in the West Riding, Lancashire, Cheshire, Scotland and South Wales, and, according to the Census of 1841, the total number of women and girls employed in and around *all* the mines in Great Britain was only 6133, or less than 3 per cent. of the total mining labour force.[1]

This exposure of the scandalous abuse of child labour in the coal mines made a deep impression on the public conscience, and Ashley received promises of support from all sides; within a month after the publication of the Commission's report he introduced his very drastic Mines Bill, on June 7th, 1842. This measure proposed to exclude from the pits all women and girls, all boys under thirteen years old, and all parish apprentices; in addition, no man under twenty-one years old or over fifty was to be employed as a colliery engine tenter. The Bill passed safely through the House of Commons without serious opposition, and with only

[1] G. R. Porter, *The Progress of the Nation*, 1851 ed., p. 79.

two important amendments; but the House of Lords proved as hostile as the House of Commons had been friendly. Lord Londonderry led the opposition to the Bill, and received such strong support from the noble coal owners that there was a danger lest the Bill should be amended out of existence or consigned to a select committee. To prevent either of these calamities the reformers made several important concessions, and the Act, as finally allowed to pass, was a much more moderate measure of reform than Ashley had intended. Nevertheless, a substantial improvement of mining conditions was effected, and a valuable precedent set for further legislation.

The Mines Act of 1842 provided that boys under ten years old were not to be employed in the pits; parish apprentices were not to be employed under ten years old, or apprenticed beyond the age of eighteen years; boys were not to be employed as engine-men before the age of fifteen years; women and girls were not to be employed underground; government inspectors were to report on the state and condition of the persons working in the mines, but not on the state and condition of the mines, as one of the Commons' amendments had provided. No restriction was imposed on the hours of labour, though it was clear that children were working longer hours in the mines than in the factories.

Meanwhile the Government was preparing, somewhat tardily, to redeem its pledges to the factory reformers. In March, 1843, a government Factory Bill was introduced which proposed that the working day for children should be reduced to six and a half hours; though, on the other hand, the minimum age at which the children might begin work was to be reduced from nine years to eight years. "Young persons" were not to work more than twelve hours a day; for the purpose of this clause boys were to be young persons up to the age of eighteen and girls up to twenty-one years. There was also to be compulsory education for the factory children, under the direction of the Anglican clergyman, the churchwardens, and four other persons elected by the justices in petty sessions. Doubtless the Government regarded this educational clause as clearly desirable and very enlightened; but the idea of compulsory *Anglican* education actually wrecked the whole Bill, owing to vigorous Nonconformist opposition and agitation.

The new Factory Bill, which the Government introduced early in 1844, followed the same general lines as its predecessor, but made no provision for the improvement of factory children's education; it paid women workers a gallant compliment by proposing that they should all be accounted young persons; and it introduced various administrative improvements, suggested by the factory inspectors, including an attempt to abolish the relay system of employing children. Ashley made a determined effort to turn this government measure into a ten-hours bill; and after a prolonged debate his amendment was eventually carried against the Government. Four days later, however, another vote was taken on the question, with a contrary result. The House of Commons had thus rejected both the Government's twelve-hours day and Ashley's ten-hours day. The obvious solution of the problem was to compromise on a working day of eleven hours; but the Government preferred to withdraw the Bill and make yet another fresh start.

On the third reading of the new government Bill, Ashley moved that no young person should work more than eleven hours a day until 1847, and that afterwards the maximum should be reduced to ten hours. Peel called the amendment a proposal to put an income tax of $16\frac{1}{4}$ per cent. on the poor man, and emphasised the evils of leaving persons "in possession of time for which they had not a demand".[1] Both Peel and Graham (the Home Secretary) declared that the Government would resign if the amendment were carried, and in the

[1] Hansard, Third Series Vol. LXXIV, cols. 1081 and 1089.

end it was decisively rejected. After this, the government Bill passed rapidly through both Houses and became law. The Factory Act of 1844 provided that the working day for children in factories should not be longer than six and a half hours. Women and young persons were not to be employed for more than twelve hours a day, taken between the hours of 5.30 a.m. and 8.30 p.m. Moreover, by providing that the labour of all protected persons should begin at the same time, the Act attempted to abolish the system of employing children in relays, which facilitated the employment of grown-up persons for over-long hours. Unfortunately, the Act did not provide that all the protected persons should also *cease* work at the same time, or that their work should be continuous, and it was therefore possible to continue the relay system by the device of intermittent employment during the day.

During the next year or two the question of further factory legislation was rather overshadowed by the progress of fiscal reform and the Anti-Corn-Law agitation. Ashley secured the passing of an Act for the regulation of labouring conditions in calico-printing works in 1845, and early in 1846 he introduced a new Ten Hours Bill, just before resigning his seat on the question of the Corn Laws. The resignation of Peel shortly afterwards, and the formation of a Whig Government under Lord John Russell (who had supported Ashley's Bill) once more revived the hopes of the northern factory reformers. Early in 1847 the Ten Hours Bill was once more introduced, this time by Fielden, and had the support of the majority of the Cabinet as far as the committee stage. In the committee stage the government influence was used to substitute eleven hours for ten; but the followers of Peel abstained from voting on this issue, and the ten-hours provision was finally carried. The Factory Act of 1847 has always been recognised as an important landmark in the history of labour legislation; nevertheless, it was in some respects partially stultified by the ambiguity of the Factory Act of 1844, which still remained in force. Even under the later Act, the employers were still able to work the protected persons intermittently during the day, and the relay system could thus be maintained. In 1850 Ashley asked leave to bring in a Bill which "would carry into effect what had been the intention of Parliament in 1844". The Government preferred to bring forward its own measure, which fixed the hours of work for women and young persons within a twelve-hour limit, from 6 a.m. to 6 p.m., or alternatively from 7 a.m. to 7 p.m., allowing 1½ hours for meals, i.e. a ten and a half hours' working day. This Act of 1850 also stipulated that women and young persons should cease work on Saturdays at 2 p.m. The Act, which received a mixed welcome from the reformers, did not apply to children, so that it was still legal for their periods of employment to be taken at any time between 5.30 a.m. and 8.30 p.m. A relay system for children was still possible. In 1853, however, Palmerston decided to extend the 6 a.m. to 6 p.m. rule to children. It was not until 1874 that the factory workers secured the ten-hours day which Parliament had intended to give them in 1847.

The living conditions of the poorer classes needed improvement as urgently as their working conditions. The Municipal Reform Act of 1835, in spite of its importance in other respects, had done little to remedy the administrative chaos arising from the multiplicity of special authorities for such purposes as paving, lighting, sewerage, and police. Indeed, the sanitary condition of the towns remained deplorable down to and beyond the middle of the century. The towns were growing so rapidly that it would have needed extraordinary efforts on the part of the municipal authorities to keep pace with the increasing problems of sanitation. Special efforts were being made to raise the towns from their mediaeval condition; but the problems were too complex, and the conflicting factors too numerous, for the improvement to be immediately appreciable.

Most of the great towns of modern Britain reached their quickest rate of growth between 1821 and 1831, mainly by migration from the country districts; and this tremendous influx inevitably aggravated the sanitary evils inherited from previous centuries. Paving had in most towns not been extended beyond the main streets; scavenging was even more seriously neglected. London was in a particularly unfortunate condition, having about three hundred separate authorities for sanitary purposes, of various degrees of efficiency, and without any shadow of co-ordination. The whole of London was riddled with cesspools, many of them centuries old; the drinking water was largely got from pumps, and was contaminated not only from the cesspools but also from the town burial grounds. Evidently the cholera epidemic of 1831–2 had not been a sufficient warning.

The public interest in questions of urban sanitation was quickened by the investigations of Dr. Southwood Smith, who was physician to the London Fever Hospital, the Eastern Dispensary, and the London Jews' Hospital. From his firsthand contact with slum conditions, Southwood Smith was early impressed with the idea that the epidemics of the period were very largely the result of insanitary conditions which could be remedied. This idea, which was to be the main theme of an important agitation in favour of government intervention, received expression in reports which Southwood Smith made to the Poor Law Commissioners in 1838 and 1839, on the causes of sickness and mortality among the poorer classes of London.[1] The social conditions exposed in these reports were so disgusting as to make detailed description almost intolerable. Until that time very little improvement had been made in the sanitary condition of the poorer districts in London. In many localities there was an entire absence of drainage, and masses of decaying refuse of all sorts

[1] *Fourth Annual Report of the Poor Law Commissioners*, 1838. Appendix A, No. 1; *Fifth Annual Report*, 1839, Appendix C, No. 2.

were allowed to accumulate indefinitely. So filthy, close, and crowded were the houses, so poisonous was the air that in several parishes the relieving officers and physicians had lost their lives through sickness directly attributable to the conditions in which they worked. The fever, which constantly lurked in such districts, was mainly an adult disease, and constituted the main cause of urban pauperism. Of the people receiving poor relief in London, one-fifth were the victims of fever; in Bethnal Green the proportion was one-third, and in Whitechapel one-half. There was, evidently, a close connection between pauperism and insanitary living conditions; if money was spent on improving sanitary conditions, some of the expenditure might be recovered through a reduction in the burden of the poor rates.

In 1839 the Poor Law Commissioners extended the investigation of social conditions from London to the rest of the country. From the evidence collected in this inquiry, Edwin Chadwick in 1842 compiled his famous *Report on the Sanitary Condition of the Labouring Population of Great Britain*, which showed that the evils previously exposed in London were equally serious in most of the other great towns of the country. Schemes of drainage and cleansing were being adopted in many of the large towns by that time, but the schemes were often rendered futile by the lack of co-ordination amongst the special authorities created for particular purposes. Some of the main drains had been ignorantly constructed; others had been properly constructed, but did not work for lack of water; others, which did work properly, were not connected up with the houses. The water supply was very unsatisfactory in most of the great towns, and was worst in the poorer districts, where the need was most urgent. Chadwick's *Report* proved conclusively that various forms of disease, caused or aggravated by atmospheric impurities, damp, filth, and overcrowding, were prevalent more or less in every part of the country among the poorer classes. The greatest proportion of deaths among heads of families occurred from preventible causes, and it was estimated that the average loss of working ability through such causes was not less than eight or ten years of the working life.

Further evidence to the same effect was collected by several public inquiries in the early 'forties, notably by the Royal Commission on the State of Large Towns, which issued its first report in 1844. Out of fifty towns studied by the Commission, hardly one had satisfactory drainage, and in forty-two the drainage was definitely bad. It was therefore recommended that the Crown should have power to supervise and inspect the administration of sanitary laws in large towns and populous districts. The local authorities entrusted with the carrying out of these laws should receive wider administrative powers and control larger districts, but should be supervised by some central authority. In each district, moreover, the water supply and drainage, as well as the paving, lighting, and maintenance of the streets, should be concentrated in the hands of a single authority.

No legislation was passed to carry out the Commission's recommendations, but before the end of 1844 Dr. Southwood Smith had formed the "Health of Towns Association", with such influential supporters as Lord Normanby, Lord Ashley, and Lord Morpeth. During the next four years this Association maintained an active propaganda on the question of public health, and eventually forced Parliament to agree to legislation. Lord Morpeth's Public Health Act of 1848 established a General Board of Health, somewhat after the model of the Poor Law Board which had been set up in 1847. The Board might create a local health district and a local board of health, either on petition from not less than ten per cent. of the ratepayers or in any place where the annual mortality exceeded 23 per thousand. If the Act were adopted in a municipality, the town council would be the local sanitary authority; in other places a new authority would be set up as the local board of health, for the purpose of exercising such special functions as related to sewerage and drainage, the water supply, the lighting and maintenance of streets, the administration of burial grounds, the regulation of offensive trades, and the suppression of public nuisances.

The original General Board of Health consisted of Lord Morpeth, Lord Ashley, and Edwin Chadwick; Dr. Southwood Smith was added later as medical adviser. Neither Ashley nor Chadwick was likely to make the Board popular with the general public, and the controversy between centralised bureaucracy and local autonomy was revived in full force. After six years of hard and thankless work, carried out against persistent opposition, the original Board was able to report (before its dismissal in 1854) that 284 districts had requested to have the Act applied; the requests had been complied with in 182 cases, affecting a population of more than two millions. This result may be considered insignificant compared with the magnitude of the evils attacked; but the Board had set a precedent which was far more important than the work actually achieved. The Public Health Act of 1848 may most properly be regarded as foreshadowing the rapid evolution of urban sanitation which occurred during the second half of the nineteenth century.

CHAPTER TWELVE

Currency, Banking, and Joint-Stock Reforms

DURING THE EARLIER nineteenth century trading conditions were extraordinarily unsettled. The factors underlying this commercial instability were many and complex; but the business men of the time declared emphatically that the trouble was intensified, if not caused, by irresponsible banking policy which led to arbitrary fluctuations in the volume of credit currency. Throughout the post-war generation there was keen discussion about the proper relationship of the Bank of England to the other banks and to the currency. The paper currency of the country quickly recovered from the depreciation of the later years of the war, the foreign exchanges became more normal, and the price of gold bullion fell. In 1816 the Government decided to adopt the gold standard, and by the end of that year the Bank of England declared itself ready to resume cash payments. During the following year, however, the currency situation became worse again, partly through the heavy demands for gold on the part of continental countries which were strengthening their own currencies. This relapse led in 1819 to parliamentary inquiry into the currency question, and Peel secured the passing of an Act which provided for the resumption of cash payments at the Bank of England by 1823; the Bank was at the same time forbidden to make any advance to the Government without parliamentary authority, and the trade in bullion was declared free.

Peel's Act caused great anxiety among merchants both in

London and throughout the country, owing to the fear that the return to a gold basis would bring down prices too suddenly and cause renewed dislocation of commercial credit. The supporters of the resumption of cash payments argued that the degree of inflation was measured by the premium on gold, which was merely about five per cent., and that prices would only fall to that extent. Cash payments were eventually resumed in 1821, and in actual fact prices fell sharply: partly because in the post-war years there had been considerable over-production of goods and an accumulation of stock, which had to be liquidated now that the volume of commercial credit was reduced. The break in prices caused a severe financial crisis, accompanied by much commercial and industrial distress. Naturally Peel's opponents argued that this renewed trade depression was the result of the gold standard and currency deflation; though it was possible to maintain that the dislocation would have been avoided if the Bank had postponed the resumption of payments in gold *coin* until the latest date allowed by the Act.

Reference has already been made to the rapid recovery of trade from the crisis of 1821, and to the "flood of prosperity" which culminated in the commercial collapse of 1825.[1] This new shock to public and private credit inevitably called for searching inquiry into the organisation of the financial system. There had been many factors contributing to cause the widespread panic of 1825, but Peel had a strong body of opinion behind him when he maintained that a great part of the trouble could be traced to the Bank of England's monopoly of the joint-stock note issue. The privileged position of the Bank of England prevented the formation of other joint-stock banks, and left an undue degree of credit control in the hands of private bankers, many of whom had been issuing notes recklessly, without any adequate backing of gold. One

[1] See Chapter IX, p. 133, above.

possible remedy for such an unsatisfactory state of affairs was to encourage the establishment of larger and more responsible provincial banks; and this in turn involved a relaxation of the Bank of England's monopolistic privileges. Accordingly, the Bank Act of 1826 authorised the formation of joint-stock banks, with power to issue notes, provided that such banks were not less than sixty-five miles from London.

An opportunity for further progress in the same direction occurred in 1832, when there came up for discussion the question of renewing the Bank of England's charter. Much important evidence on the organisation of the banking system was reported by a Parliamentary Committee of 1832, and the Bank Charter Act of 1833 made several changes designed to prevent or mitigate any repetition of such a crisis as had occurred in 1825. With the idea of protecting the Bank against any unexpected drain of gold, caused by a sudden run on provincial banks, the notes issued by the Bank of England were declared to be legal tender, though convertible into gold at the Bank. On the other hand, the Bank's position might be considered weakened by the fact that the Act of 1833 declared legal the establishment of joint-stock banks even in London, provided they did not issue banknotes. This had hitherto been a debatable point in law; but after 1833 there could no longer be any uncertainty on the question, and many joint-stock banks sprang up in London during the next few years.

That these reforms did not remove the underlying causes of commercial instability was clearly shown by the recurrence of financial crises in the later 'thirties; contemporary opinion held, indeed, that irresponsible banking policy and defective banking organisation had been, in the 'thirties as in the 'twenties, among the main factors contributing to produce unsettled trading conditions. In particular, it seemed clear that the financial difficulties of the period were greatly increased by the uncertain and arbitrary policy of the Bank of England. Between 1833 and 1835 there was a great deal of speculation in foreign loans, in favour of such states as Russia, Portugal, Greece, Spain, Cuba, Belgium, and Florida; consequently there was a drain of bullion from England, which might normally have led the Bank of England to raise its discount rate and sell securities, so as to strengthen its gold reserve. Yet during this drain of bullion the Bank was increasing its liabilities and its holdings of securities; it was rediscounting country bills, and lending money in other ways at abnormally low rates. The principle upon which the Bank acted in regulating its note issue had been publicly stated by Horsley Palmer in 1832, and was restated by him in 1840; according to these statements the Bank aimed at keeping a reserve of bullion equal to one-third of its liabilities, in normal times. This proportion of bullion to securities was very high, and should have been amply sufficient to cope with any ordinary vicissitudes of trade; but in actual fact it is very difficult to believe that the Bank's policy was regulated in any close accordance with this principle. In the years between 1832 and 1840, there was only one year (1838) in which the reserve of bullion was equal to the proportion laid down by Horsley Palmer.

There was an evident need for some public control over the issue of credit currency, whether by the Bank of England or by other banks. Round this problem a fierce controversy raged throughout the second quarter of the nineteenth century. Many business men, who remembered the inconvertible paper currency of the French wars, considered that the Government had been unwise in adopting the gold standard and resuming cash payments during the post-war period. Some currency heretics even went so far as to assert that the commercial fluctuations of the period were "the necessary offspring of the monetary system we established on the return of peace, which rests the profits of trade and the wages of labour on the accidental variations in the supply of gold."[1] According to such critics, every attempt to put the gold standard into force had led to financial crisis and to trade depression, which had only been alleviated by the suspension of the standard. Thomas Attwood, the Birmingham leader, declared boldly that "it is the plenty of money that makes prosperity," and asked for "a depreciation of money equivalent to ten shillings to a bushel of wheat . . . not a wild increase of money, but such an increase of money as will be sufficient to raise the prices of property and labour above the level of the fixed charges which the law and the habits of the country impose upon production."[2]

The main currency controversy of the period, however, was among men who agreed that the gold standard was the best practicable regulating principle, but differed as to the form in which this regulating principle should be applied. From the prolonged discussion concerning the regulation of note issues, which went on throughout the second quarter of the nineteenth century, there emerged two conflicting theories, which became generally known as the banking principle and the currency principle. The supporters of the banking principle held that the banks ought to be left free to regulate the amount of notes issued, according to the state of trade, so long as the notes remained freely convertible into gold on demand. It could be assumed that the amount of notes in circulation would be quasi-automatically regulated, since if too many notes were issued they would be quickly presented for payment. Moreover, this reflux of notes did not necessarily or usually involve a demand for coin or any approach to panic conditions. There was a regular and normal reflux which, in the ordinary course, would give

[1] Cayley, draft resolutions in *First Report (Commons) on Commercial Distress*, 1848 (395), p. x.
[2] *Report on the Bank Charter*, 1832 (722): Evidence, pp. 457–59, qq. 5638, 5661–62; see also S. G. Checkland, 'The Birmingham economists, 1815–1850', *Economic History Review*, 2nd series, Vol. I, No. 1, 1948, pp. 1–19. ·

ample warning of any tendency to over-issue. This doctrine assumed, of course that bankers would take care to safeguard their own solvency; if this degree of prudence and responsibility could not be assumed it was obvious that convertible notes could be issued, in spite of a demand for gold for export, until the total bullion reserves were exhausted. Without going to this extreme, any over-issue would tend to cause the withdrawal of gold from circulation; this would weaken the gold reserve and prejudice the general financial situation. By the time the reflux of notes began to assume abnormal dimensions the mischief would have been done, and a financial crisis might have been caused.

According to the advocates of the currency principle, the primary duty of the banker, and especially of the Bank of England, was to maintain a sufficient reserve to safeguard the stability of public credit. The volume of the paper currency ought not to be regulated according to the demands of the business men, but should vary directly with the amount of gold in the country. S. J. Loyd (later Lord Overstone), one of the foremost bankers of the time, conceived "that the whole paper currency of the country should conform in its fluctuations to the fluctuations of the bullion. . . . There are no means of positively ascertaining that point, all that can be said is, that an efflux of gold requires a reduction in the aggregate paper circulation of the country, and in the absence of any specific proof at the time, with reference to any particular place, it is necessarily assumed that reduction ought to be rateable in its proportion."[1] To secure this correspondence between fluctuations in the gold reserve and fluctuations in the volume of credit currency, the note issue of the country should be unified in the hands of the Bank of England; but the Bank of England should itself be under public control, and should not have any large measure of discretionary

[1] S. J. Loyd, evidence before *Committee on Banks of Issue*, 1840, reprinted in Gregory's *British Banking Statutes*, 1929, Vol. I, p. 56.

authority. As a safeguard to this public control, the Bank of England should be compelled to publish full accounts regularly, and its note-issuing business should be kept distinct from its ordinary banking business. To such proposals opponents objected that a strict application of the currency principle would unduly limit the Bank's discretion in dealing with financial panics; while the limitation of the issue of banknotes would not prevent the inflation of credit, owing to the increasing use of cheques in the making of commercial advances.

The controversy between the banking and currency principles dragged on for many years, and parliamentary committees of inquiry asked more than fourteen thousand questions without coming to any conclusion. It was in these circumstances that Peel, in 1844, determined on decisive action in substantial agreement with the currency principle. The Bank Charter Act of 1844 accordingly provided that the note issues of the private and provincial joint-stock banks were not to be increased in the future, and that the right to issue notes was to be relinquished by any such bank in the event of its bankruptcy or amalgamation. The Bank of England was henceforth to be divided into two separate departments, one for banking business and the other for the issue of notes. The note-issue department was authorised to issue notes to the amount of its bullion reserve, and in addition to make a fiduciary issue of notes to the amount of £14,000,000, which was covered by the Bank's holding of gilt-edged stock. Provision was made for the publication of regular weekly Bank Returns; and the Bank of England was compelled to buy any gold offered to it at the fixed price of £3 17s. 9d. an ounce. The Government intended that the note issue of the Bank of England, as thus safeguarded, should ultimately absorb the note issue of all the other banks in the country; to this end it was provided that if any note-issuing bank ceased to issue notes, for any reason, the Bank of England might increase its own fiduciary issue by not more than two-thirds of the discontinued issue. This process of absorption went on all through the later nineteenth century, and is now complete; the last note-issuing bank, other than the Bank of England, went out of business in 1921.

Thomas Tooke considered the Bank Charter Act of 1844 to be "one of the most wanton, ill-advised, pedantic, and rash pieces of legislation" that had come within his knowledge, and described it as "a total, unmitigated, uncompensated, and in its consequences lamentable failure."[1] The experience of the next few years certainly fulfilled his prophecy that the separation of the banking and note-issuing business would accentuate the variations in the Bank's discount rate, and render the Bank's policy less elastic in time of emergency. If the Government imagined that the restriction and concentration of the country's note issue would prevent the recurrence of financial crises, their mistake was soon exposed. The financial crisis of 1847 was as alarming as the previous crises of 1836 and 1825 had been; and the Committee of the House of Lords which inquired into the causes of the commercial distress reported that the panic had been "materially aggravated" by the Act of 1844. The monetary crises of 1847, 1857 and 1866 each led to a suspension of the restrictive clauses of the Act of 1844; and this necessarily "called into question the wisdom of legislation which appeared to break down at the moment of greatest strain."[2] Nevertheless, the method of note issue established in 1844 proved remarkably durable, partly because the growing use of cheques made metallic currency and notes less important, and partly because the

[1] Tooke's *History of Prices*, Vol. IV, pp. 354 and 402.
[2] Gregory, Introduction to *British Banking Statutes*, p. xxv. See also the two centenary articles by P. B. Whale, 'A retrospective view of the Bank Charter Act of 1844', and J. K. Horsefield, 'The origins of the Bank Charter Act, 1844', reprinted in *Papers in English Monetary History*, edited by T. S. Ashton and R. S. Sayers, 1953, pp. 109-31.

banking department of the Bank of England was left free, after 1844-7, to manage the internal credit structure of the country. The Act of 1844 remained the basis of the English monetary system down to the outbreak of war in 1914.

Meanwhile, the character of the banking system of the country had been modified by many changes, and especially by the rapid rise of joint-stock banking. The modern growth of joint-stock banking in England may be dated from the Bank Act of 1826, which sanctioned the establishment of joint-stock banks, with note-issuing powers, provided that such banks were not less than sixty-five miles from London. The influence of the legal change was not at first very striking, and only thirty-nine joint-stock banks were formed during the following seven years; but after 1833 progress was more rapid. The Bank Charter Act of 1833 confirmed the legality of establishing joint-stock banks even in London, provided they did not issue banknotes; and in London the right to issue notes was by this time becoming a less indispensable part of the banker's function. The Act of 1833 gave a great stimulus to the joint-stock movement, and by 1841 there were 115 English joint-stock banks in operation. No fewer than 47 joint-stock banks were formed in 1836, and this speculative promotion of banking companies was a not inconsiderable factor in the financial crisis of that year. In 1836 a Parliamentary Committee was appointed to inquire into the operation of the Bank Act of 1826, on the ground that "a system of joint-stock banking has grown up already of great magnitude, which is daily extending its ramifications" without being subject to legal control in its operations. The Committee reported that "these Banks are rapidly extending in all directions; that new Companies are daily forming, and that an increased number of Branches and Agencies are spreading throughout England, even in small Towns and Villages . . . that a principle of competition exists which leads to the extinction of all Private Banks, and to their conversion into Banking Companies."[1]

The statistics of the movement confirm the impression that joint-stock banking was growing at the expense of private banking. In 1814 there had been 940 private banking firms in England; by 1842 there were only 311, as compared with 118 joint-stock banks. In the single year 1836 no fewer than 26 private banks were absorbed by joint-stock companies; over the period 1826–43 there were 122 banking amalgamations altogether, of which 93 were absorptions of private banks by joint-stock banks. During the same period about 170 private banks failed or suspended payment; and in many cases the absorption of the private banks by joint-stock companies was determined by the previous or imminent failure of the private firm. The relative merits of private and joint-stock banking were the subject of keen controversy during the 'thirties; but the working results seemed to demonstrate clearly the superiority of the joint-stock form, and the efficiency of the system of branch banks. The public confidence in the stability of private bankers had become thoroughly shaken, and this was frequently given as the reason for the conversion of private firms into joint-stock companies. There were, of course, cases in which the confidence in joint-stock banks was misplaced. Most of the instances in which joint-stock banks were absorbed by other joint-stock companies arose from the failure or weakness of the company absorbed; but, in general, the joint-stock banks certainly proved to be more stable and more reliable than the private banks.[2]

The first serious attempt to regulate the organisation of banking companies was made by the Joint Stock Banks Act

[1] Hansard, Third Series, vol. XXXIII, col. 840 *et seq.*; *Report on Joint Stock Banks*, 1836, reprinted in Gregory, *British Banking Statutes*, Vol. I, p. xli, Vol. II, pp. 221–22.

[2] See J. Sykes, *The Amalgamation Movement in English Banking*, 1926, Chapter I.

of 1844. This measure provided that no future banking company could operate without Letters Patent; no such bank was to have less than £100,000 of capital; no advances were to be made on the security of its own shares; the accounts were to be regularly published and audited; no share was to be of less value than £100; and there was to be no limitation of shareholders' liability. These provisions were evidently intended as a check on the formation of new banking companies; and the restrictive intention becomes even clearer if comparison is made with the other banking and company legislation of the same year. Since 1826 banking companies had been in a more favourable legal position than other joint-stock companies; joint-stock banks could be established by registration, whereas other joint-stock companies had to seek Letters Patent or a private Act of Parliament. Now the position was reversed; joint-stock companies in general were permitted to be established by registration, but banking companies must apply for Letters Patent. The same restrictive tendency is equally evident in the Bank Charter Act of 1844. Broadly regarded, the provisions of that Act restricting the issue of banknotes were designed to strengthen the Bank of England's control over the note issue of the country, and to prevent the growing joint-stock banks from increasing their note-issuing powers either directly or by amalgamation. Private banks were treated much more leniently than joint-stock banks in the event of amalgamation. One effect of the Bank Charter Act was therefore to encourage the amalgamation of private banks with each other for mutual defence against joint-stock aggression, and more generally to encourage private banking at the expense of the joint-stock organisations.

These restrictive measures may explain why the number of joint-stock banking amalgamations fell off markedly after 1844, and why only one new joint-stock bank was established between 1846 and 1860. Nevertheless, the victory of joint-stock over private banking was already assured, and there were various factors which tended to counteract the effect of the legislation of 1844. The extension of the principle of limited liability to banking companies in 1858 would certainly be a stimulating influence; though in actual fact a considerable proportion of the joint-stock banks remained on a basis of unlimited liability until the last quarter of the nineteenth century. Another stimulating influence was the admission of the joint-stock banks to the London Clearing House in 1854; but a more general factor was the growth of the cheque system, which reduced the importance of the note issue. For these and other reasons the expansion of joint-stock banking and the absorption of private banks continued, though at a slower pace. By the 1860s it was considered that "private banking has now ceased to be of any importance and the amalgamation of the still existing houses with great Joint Stock banks has become a mere question of time."[1]

The emergence of joint-stock companies in the nineteenth century calls for no special explanation; what requires to be explained is rather the tardiness of the movement in its earlier stages. The immediate reason for this slowness of development seems to have been the chaotic condition of the partnership laws; while the unsatisfactory state of the law was due, in its turn, partly to historical causes of long standing. Down to the second quarter of the nineteenth century the English law of partnership appears to have been without system, and could only be known from the judicial decisions on particular cases. Many of the rules thus established were not adapted to modern commercial organisation, especially to the development of large partnerships or joint-stock companies. The general rule applicable to all partnerships was that each partner was liable "for the whole debts and engagements of the partnership, not only to the extent of his share in the partnership stock, but to the whole amount of his separate

[1] F. Martin, *Banks and Bankers*, 1865, p. 186; quoted Sykes, *op. cit.*, p. 32.

property."[1] This rule could only be modified by a Crown Charter or an Act of Parliament, restricting creditors to claims on the corporate property. Any general limitation of the liability of shareholders in ordinary joint-stock companies was as yet not to be obtained; there was, indeed, an almost universal prejudice against joint-stock organisation, as being unsound even if not fraudulent.

This prejudice against joint-stock organisation had persisted for centuries, though the grounds for the prejudice had shifted from one generation to another. In the sixteenth and seventeenth centuries joint-stock companies had been regarded as obnoxious monopolies; in the early eighteenth century the abuse of the joint-stock form by speculative stock jobbers and company promoters led a large section of the investing public to believe that such companies were usually fraudulent. Moreover, the large number of worthless companies promoted at the time of the South Sea Bubble had led to the "Bubble Act" of 1720, by which persons concerned in joint-stock speculations (with the exception of two specified companies) were subjected to heavy penalties. The formation of companies with transferable shares was forbidden, unless they had obtained incorporation by Crown Charter or by Act of Parliament. Unincorporated companies had no legal existence, though a judicial decision handed down in 1811 ruled that an unincorporated company was not illegal if its objects were beneficial to the public (the case concerned a co-operative flour-milling company).[2] Unincorporated companies could not sue or be sued in their own names, though this obstacle was overcome to an increasing extent by the ingenious legal device of appointing a small body of trustees to act for the shareholders, and to control their property. In

---

[1] Bellenden Ker's *Report on the Law of Partnership*, 1837; printed as Appendix I of the *First Report on Joint Stock Companies*, 1844 (119), p. 245.
[2] H. A. Shannon, 'The coming of general limited liability', *Economic History*, supplement to *Economic Journal*, No. 6, January 1931, p. 269.

this way such unincorporated companies might be able to enforce contracts and recover debts. From 1801 onwards some unincorporated companies obtained private Acts of Parliament enabling them to sue and be sued in the name of an officer of the company.

After a time the Bubble Act became practically a dead letter; it must still have acted as a deterrent in some degree, but joint-stock partnerships began to be formed in various branches of enterprise. Then public interest in the question was stimulated by the great outburst of fraudulent company promoting during the "boom" of 1825; in that year the Bubble Act was finally repealed, on the ground that its effect had been mischievous, and unsuited to modern economic development. In the debate on the question, in the House of Commons, Hudson Gurney emphasised the necessity for introducing a system of registration for joint-stock companies, or of permitting the establishment of partnerships with limited liability, following a continental precedent. These proposed remedies were too far-reaching to be immediately adopted. In the succeeding years, however, there was legislation tending to help joint-stock companies in such matters as the power of suing and being sued; in particular, the Crown was empowered to grant to trading companies by Letters Patent any of the privileges which could be granted by a Charter of Incorporation.

After this there seemed no strong reason why such powers as that of suing and being sued should not be extended to all joint-stock companies, provided they were registered and had complied with certain regulations necessary as a safeguard against fraud; privileges of this nature had already been extended to banking partnerships in 1826. The desirability of some such reform became even clearer after the commercial dislocation of 1836-7, and careful inquiry was made into the effects of fraudulent company promotion upon the crisis. Finally, the Committee on Joint Stock Companies in 1844 recommended that all joint-stock companies (other than banking companies) should be registered in a special office. The registration of future companies should first be made provisionally, before the public announcement of the company, and should not be completed until after the company had actually been formed. On the complete registration of the company, it should have the power "to perform all acts for carrying into effect the purposes of such company, which a body corporate might do."[1] Any future company which failed to become registered was not to be recognised as lawful.

These recommendations were followed in the main by the Joint Stock Companies Acts of 1844, by which companies were able to register themselves and become legally recognised on comparatively simple terms, and with much less expense than by the earlier methods: but the individual shareholders did not obtain the privilege of limited liability. Under certain conditions limited liability was already recognised in France, Ireland, and the State of New York. In France and America the system had worked well; in Ireland the privilege had not been much used, though it had been legally established since 1781-2. There was a very long and violent conflict of opinion concerning the desirability of introducing the system into England. It was well understood that the limitation of shareholders' liability would increase the amount of capital available for commercial purposes, and would facilitate the co-operation of the capitalist with the business organiser; but it was still feared that the introduction of the system would lead to a great increase in the flotation of fraudulent companies.

The principle of limited liability was eventually adopted in the Limited Liability Act of 1855, under which the liability of shareholders was limited to the amount of the company's share capital held by them, including any portion of the

[1] *First Report on Joint Stock Companies*, 1844 (119), pp. xii–xv.

share capital not yet paid up. On the whole, the change was favourably received by the business community; but opposition to the principle if not widespread, was decidedly lively. The *Law Times* stigmatised the Act as the "Rogues' Charter," and declared that it engendered a mass of villainy.[1] Even the supporters of the change were often of opinion that joint-stock companies were inefficient in the actual conduct of business. Lord Stanley of Alderley, who was strongly in favour of the limitation of liability, considered "that mercantile operations would more successfully be carried on by one or a few individuals or by small partnerships than they could possibly be by a large number of men, who must delegate the management to a single individual or a few persons."[2]

In general, the attacks on the Limited Liability Act of 1855 were based on the well-worn ground that limited liability would encourage excessive and reckless enterprise, and would open the door to dishonesty and fraud. Part of the opposition arose, however, from the incompleteness and technical defects of the Act. These defects led to its repeal in the following year, and its replacement by the Joint Stock Companies Act of 1856, which was a much longer and more comprehensive measure. Two further Acts of 1857 and 1858 brought banking companies under subjection to modified forms of legislative regulation, and from that time it might be said that the foundations of modern company law had been laid.

[1] See R. R. Formoy, *Historical Foundations of Modern Company Law*, 1923, pp. 120–21.
[2] Hansard, Third Series, Vol. CXXXIX, col. 1919 (August 7th, 1855).

CHAPTER THIRTEEN

Fiscal Policy and Tariff Reform

ONE OF THE central features in the economic history of
England during the early nineteenth century was the an-
tagonism between the landlords and the manufacturers. The
manufacturers had an economic grievance arising from the
special protection given to agriculture by the Corn Laws;
though many manufacturing industries also were protected
by the heavy import duties on foreign goods. On the basis
of mercantilist theory, manufacturing industry had doubtless as good a claim as agriculture to protection against
foreign competition. In actual practice, however, no attempt
had been made, during the French wars, to frame a consistent tariff policy or to preserve a due balance of justice
between the divergent interests. The Government had been
hard pressed for money, and had taxed "everything on earth
and the waters under the earth". In the contemporary state
of financial theory and public opinion it was much easier (up
to a point) and decidedly less unpopular to raise revenue by
taxing commodities than by taxing income directly. That is
doubtless why, after the end of the wars, the first tax to be
taken off was Pitt's obnoxious income tax, which is nowadays
the mainstay of the public revenue. The income tax at that
time was still regarded as a special levy which most people denounced altogether as iniquitous and inquisitorial, while even
its friends could recommend it merely as a temporary
measure to meet a national emergency.

By the end of the eighteenth century the attempt at a
general regulation of overseas trade in the interests of the

185

home producer had already been recognised as a mistaken policy by many economic thinkers, notably by Adam Smith, whose *Inquiry into the Nature and Causes of the Wealth of Nations* (1776) became the gospel of a growing movement towards economic liberalism. The younger Pitt professed himself a disciple of Adam Smith, and brought forward several measures tending towards freer trade in the decade before the outbreak of the French wars; this nascent movement was checked, however, by the French Revolution, and was reversed during the generation of warfare which followed. Before the end of the wars the general economic situation had become profoundly changed. English industry was now technically far superior to its continental rivals, and was organised on a scale which could only be maintained by the development of extensive export markets; the need for greater freedom in international trade was accordingly more urgent.[1]

During the first years of peace the question could not be raised with any hope of immediate solution; for freer trade seemed to necessitate a great sacrifice of revenue, whereas the Government's imperative need was for more revenue, to make good the loss caused by its reluctant abolition of the income tax. Indirect taxation had already been exploited to the full; that is to say, increased rates of duty were not likely to increase the aggregate yield. Some attempts were made to retrench public expenditure; but the scope of this retrenchment was necessarily limited, since the main burden arose from the public debt charges. There were, no doubt, ways of reducing the debt charge slightly, even although the wartime practice of borrowing at a low nominal rate of interest (and at a heavy discount) had made conversion schemes difficult. In actual fact, however, the Government did not face its financial problems squarely; in the post-war period it was

[1] For dominant trends in economic opinion among leading British statesmen during the post-war years, see R. J. White, *Waterloo to Peterloo*, 1957, pp. 48–51.

not making both ends of the Budget meet, but was living on its capital, on the income "raided" from the sinking fund accumulated at wartime rates of interest, and on the proceeds of disguised borrowing. It was not until 1823 that revenue began to exceed expenditure, and even after that date there were various items on the national balance-sheet which called for a merciful auditor. By 1823, however, the most pressing financial problems inherited from the war period had been either solved or shelved; and the way was therefore open for the introduction of cautious tariff reforms, to which the Government had already shown itself moderately favourable.

A new stimulus to the movement for free trade was given by Thomas Tooke, who in 1820 drafted a petition to Parliament and circulated it for signature. He found, however, "that the Government were, at that time, far more sincere and resolute Free Traders than the Merchants of London". It was not until a director and an ex-governor of the Bank of England had led the way that other merchants could be persuaded to sign; yet there was undoubtedly a strong body of free-trade opinion in the city. Tooke's petition declared "that Freedom from Restraint is calculated to give the utmost extension to Foreign Trade, and the best direction to the Capital and Industry of the country"; and "that the maxim of buying in the cheapest market, and selling in the Dearest, which regulates every merchant in his individual dealings, is strictly applicable as the best rule for the trade of the whole Nation." [1] With these general principles the Government had some sympathy; but there were a great many obstacles to any rapid change in the existing tariff system. The change most urgently called for was the repeal of the Corn Laws; but this could not be expected from a Government which depended for its maintenance in power upon the support of the agricultural interest. Nevertheless, during the four years after

[1] Tooke op. cit., Vol. VI, Appendix I, pp. 331-44.

1823, Robinson as Chancellor of the Exchequer and Huskisson as President of the Board of Trade made a cautious beginning of fiscal reform, and laid down the general lines of advance which Peel and Gladstone were to follow later.

By 1825 Huskisson had revised the Navigation Laws, passed two Commercial Reciprocity Acts, and relaxed the monopolistic restrictions on colonial trade. In the European trade, the seventeenth-century barriers against Dutch shipping were removed, and the remaining restrictions upon European shipping were relatively unimportant. In the direct trade with other continents, British shipping was still protected against European competition; but the independent states in North and South America were now allowed to share in the trade. Commerce between different parts of the British Empire was still confined to British (including colonial) shipping; but the restrictions upon trade between British colonies and foreign countries were now relaxed in favour of such foreign countries as were willing to grant reciprocal privileges to Great Britain.[1] Meanwhile, a comprehensive scaling down of customs duties had been effected. Prohibitions and prohibitive duties were swept away, and protective duties on manufactured goods were reduced to moderate rates, with a maximum of thirty per cent. *ad valorem*. The import of silk goods, which had previously been prohibited, was now permitted at the maximum rate of duty; though this still left the silk industry in a privileged position as compared with the other textile trades. Cotton goods paid only ten per cent. duty, which merely counterbalanced the import duty on raw cotton. It was intended to round off this initial phase of commercial reform by a revision of the Corn Laws according to a sliding scale calculated to give protection without prohibition. Canning's untimely death in 1827 ended the sequence of reforms before the Corn Laws could be altered;

[1] For a fuller discussion of these complicated changes, see Clapham, *op. cit.*, 326–34.

but the sliding scale set up by the Wellington Ministry in
1828 was in essentials (though not in details) a reproduction
of the Canningite scheme, and remained the basis of agri-
cultural protection until the 'forties. The Whig Government of 1830 came in on a programme
of retrenchment and reform, and achieved some success in
both aspects during the following five years. They also set up
in 1833 the statistical department of the Board of Trade,
under G. R. Porter, in order to obtain from provincial
centres better and more regular economic information on
which to base government policy and actions.[1] In finance,
however, the Whigs were from the beginning less successful
than in administrative reforms. Detailed adjustments of commodity taxation went on throughout the 'thirties, with the
general intention of removing anomalies and sources of
injustice; but nothing like a clean sweep was attempted, and
it was a clean sweep that was needed if any radical improvement was to be made. In the later 'thirties the Whig Government under Melbourne displayed great financial ineptitude,
and the national finances went from bad to worse; after 1837
there were five successive financial years in which the Budgets
showed deficits necessitating renewed borrowing for general
purposes. "Baring's Levy" of 1840 made a desperate attempt
to check the shrinkage of revenue by imposing a uniform increase of five per cent. on almost every duty in the customs
and excise list; but the revenue did not respond to this special
effort, and indirect taxation had evidently reached its limit.
In 1841 the Whigs made a last-minute move to regain public
confidence by proposing a moderate reform of the customs
tariff, including an attempt to change the Corn Law sliding
scale into a fixed duty of eight shillings a quarter on foreign
wheat. Melbourne, however, was defeated in an attempt to
revise the sugar duties, and again on a direct vote of no

[1] L. Brown, *The Board of Trade and the Free-Trade Movement, 1830–42,*
1958, Chapter V.

confidence; Parliament was dissolved, and the Tories, under Peel, returned to power with an overwhelming majority.

When Peel entered upon office in 1841 the financial position of the country was deplorable. His administration had to face the accumulated deficiencies of five years: increased military and naval expenditure, with inherited war expenses in China, Persia and Afghanistan; a revenue system not responsive to increased rates of taxation; stagnation of trade, with exports dwindling in total value from year to year; deficient harvests, widespread unemployment, high prices, and increasing crime. Peel's first task was to find a practicable and moderate method of dealing with the Corn Law question, to give some temporary defence against the growing agitation led by Cobden and Bright. The Tory party which held power was certainly not ready for a complete abandonment of the Corn Laws, and to adopt the Whig proposal of a fixed duty was out of the question; Peel therefore contented himself in the first instance with a judicious revision of the existing sliding scale, without introducing any fundamental change of principle. He was then able to direct his attention to the more comprehensive tasks of balancing the national accounts and of simplifying the tariff in such a way as to give trade a better chance of recovery.

The effect of the existing tariff system in restricting foreign trade and hindering industrial recovery had been clearly demonstrated by many competent witnesses to the Committee on Import Duties in 1840. The Committee's report showed that 94·5 per cent. of the total customs revenue in 1838-9 had been produced by the duties on seventeen kinds of articles only, though there were nearly nine hundred kinds of articles on the customs lists. On 147 articles included in the list no net revenue was received, and 349 other kinds of articles produced only about £8,000 among them. The Committee therefore recommended that the burden of the customs duties should be concentrated on those articles which produced the most revenue. This simplification of the tariff would not only facilitate trade and benefit the revenue, "but would at the same time greatly diminish the cost of collection, remove multitudinous sources of complaint and vexation . . . and consolidate the great interests of peace and commerce by associating them intimately with the prosperity of the whole family of nations." [1]

This report was adopted by the Whigs as stating the required principle of policy; but Peel could not be so confident in his acceptance of the new gospel. He was now responsible for the government of the country, and he held office by the support of the landed interest, which would certainly oppose any comprehensive scheme of fiscal reform, if this seemed likely to involve the abolition of the Corn Laws. It was even doubtful whether the landlords would stand the reintroduction of the income tax, which would be necessary if any drastic alterations in the revenue system were to be made. The simplification of the tariff implied the abolition of the duties on exports and on the import of raw materials, as well as the abolition or reduction of the import duties on foodstuffs and manufactures. It was hoped that such a policy would stimulate demand and increase the aggregate yield of revenue. Even if this happened eventually, however, it was recognised that reduced rates of taxation would involve a loss of revenue in the first instance, until demand had had time to readjust itself. To tide over this initial period of revenue shrinkage, it was necessary to reimpose the income tax, as a temporary measure to meet the special emergency. Peel's first Budget, in 1842, reintroduced the income tax for three years certain, with the possibility of extension for two more years if necessary. The tax was to be levied on all incomes over £150, and at the rate of sevenpence in the pound. The proposed new tax was well received, as an emergency measure, by both Parliament and the City; the government funds rose in value

[1] *Report on Import Duties*, 1840 (601), pp. vi and vii.

on the Stock Exchange at once, and the Budget passed through Parliament with overwhelming majorities.

Protected by this financial expedient Peel proceeded to a comprehensive reform of the tariff. In his Budget of 1842 Peel's expressed principles were to remove all absolute prohibitions on the import of foreign goods: to reduce prohibitory duties to a moderate competitive level: to reduce the import duties on raw materials to not more than five per cent. of the value, on partly-manufactured goods to not more than twelve per cent., and on fully-manufactured goods to not more than twenty per cent. The actual work of revising the details of the tariff was done by the rising young Tory, W. E. Gladstone, who was then vice-president of the Board of Trade. It will be evident that Peel's tariff changes were largely a revival and extension of Huskisson's policy twenty years earlier, with its maximum rate of thirty per cent. on fully-manufactured goods; in its turn Peel's policy was to be the basis of Gladstone's commercial reforms in 1853 and 1860. The actual effect of the changes made in 1842 was to abolish, at a cost of £100,000, the remaining export duties on British manufactured goods, leaving only raw materials (coal, wool, and clay) subject to export duties: and to reduce, at a cost of only £270,000, the import duties on no fewer than 750 articles in the customs list, none of which was producing more than £10,000 a year. The duties on timber and coffee were considerably reduced, but remained preferential to colonial produce. Brandy and wines were reserved for future consideration, to serve as the basis of negotiation with France for a reciprocal relaxation of duties; and this was actually carried through by Cobden's commercial treaty with France in 1860.

Peel's bold policy seemed to be justified by results, for trade and industry began to recover almost at once, the customs revenue proved unexpectedly resilient, and the credit of the country was restored. In 1843 and 1844 only minor reductions in the tariff were made, for the Government wished to let the first reforms take effect before proceeding to more radical measures; but the large revenue surplus of 1844 was used to carry through an important conversion of public debt, which considerably reduced the interest charge. By that time the success of the tariff changes was obvious, and the income tax could have been dispensed with, if Peel had been content to forgo further reforms; but he was already planning a further revision of the customs list, and to that end secured a renewal of the income tax in 1845 for another three years. The Budget of 1845 swept away 520 customs duties, most of them unproductive and all of them vexatious (including duties on bulrushes, canaries, fossils and manna!). The remaining export duties were abolished, at a cost of £118,000. The excise duty on glass was taken off, at a cost of nearly £600,000; this led directly to a great expansion of the British glass industry, and indirectly to the building of the Crystal Palace in 1851. The duty on property sold by auction cost between £250,000 and £300,000 to repeal. Nearly all the remaining import duties on raw materials were now repealed, the only exceptions being the duties on tallow (repealed in 1860) and on timber (retained until 1866). The total nominal cost of these remissions of taxation in 1845 amounted to £3,340,000; but the stimulus to demand given by the reduction of duties had resulted in such a recovery of the aggregate tax revenue that a still further extension of the tariff reforms might be regarded as inevitable. Nevertheless, the free trade enthusiasts of the time were not likely to be satisfied with any tariff policy which did not abolish the Corn Laws; in the later months of 1845 it would have seemed mere frivolity to discuss the withdrawal of any other protective duties while leaving untouched the central question of agricultural protection.

The Corn Law of 1815 had not succeeded in maintaining the high grain prices of the war period, and had not even kept grain prices reasonably steady; indeed, the price level fluctuated more violently during the years immediately after the war than in almost any other period. The sliding scale of 1828 increased rather than diminished the uncertainty of the grain markets, and unduly encouraged speculative activity. When prices were rising, dealers were tempted to hold up the foreign supplies, so as to get higher prices and at the same time pay a lower rate of duty, thus aggravating the scarcity; on the other hand, when prices were falling, foreign grain was often rushed in hurriedly and increased the glut. In such circumstances corn dealing became almost a pure gamble. Nor could the farmer rely on steady prices for his home-grown grain. The price of wheat fell by more than fifty per cent. between 1831 and 1836, apart from the seasonal fluctuations within each year; during the years 1836–9 the highest prices recorded were more than double the lowest. It was therefore almost impossible to know how much land should be kept under grain crops; and the uncertain fluctuations in the price of wheat (and consequently of bread) were necessarily injurious to the working classes, since they implied continual changes in real wages.[1]

During the earlier 'thirties the question of reforming or repealing the Corn Laws had been shelved by the Whig Government on the ground that it was not urgent, since agriculture was in distress, while manufacturing industry was relatively prosperous. After the commercial collapse of 1837, however, this plea could no longer be sustained. Richard Cobden was already urging the Manchester Chamber of Commerce to press more insistently for the repeal of the Corn Laws, and many motions for committees of inquiry were being brought forward in Parliament. The really militant phase of the free trade movement began in 1838, when an informal meeting of seven men founded the Manchester Anti-Corn-Law Association, which soon enlarged itself into the more famous Anti-Corn-Law League headed by Cobden and Bright. Opposition was not slow to appear. The Central

---

[1] *Cf.* Sir John Clapham, 'Corn Laws Repeal, Free Trade and History', *Proc. Manchester Statistical Society*, 1945.

Agricultural Society undertook the organised defence of the Corn Laws, and the "physical force" Chartists showed their hostility to the industrial employers by breaking up free trade meetings. In Manchester they got more than they had bargained for, however, as the League encouraged those Manchester Irish who supported O'Connell against O'Connor to take reprisals against Chartist meetings. The Anti-Corn-Law League had substantial funds at its call, its paid agents and lecturers were very active, and its pamphlets (helped by the new Penny Post) were soon flooding the country. The League would accept no compromise from either the Whigs or the Tories. Russell's proposal of a fixed duty on corn was met by the League's more insistent demand for "Total and Immediate Repeal"; Peel's revised sliding scale of 1842 was denounced in Parliament by Cobden as "an insult to a suffering people".

Meanwhile, Peel was drifting steadily nearer to free trade principles, and the arguments with which he supported his other tariff reforms were almost equally applicable to the case of the Corn Laws. He had already, in 1842, openly agreed to the "general principle of free trade . . . that we should purchase in the cheapest market and sell in the dearest"; and his defensive position was still further weakened in 1843 by the admission of Canadian wheat at the nominal fixed duty of one shilling per quarter. The growth of wheat in Canada was as yet practically insignificant; but American wheat was counted as Canadian if it came through Canada. The Canadian import duty on American wheat was three shillings per quarter; thus American wheat could henceforth be imported into England at the fixed duty of four shillings per quarter, only one shilling of which reached the British Treasury. After this change the retention of the sliding scale for European grain could not be logically defended; its abolition was only a matter of time for Peel, and a question of educating his party to the change.

Peel's change of heart became increasingly evident, indeed, both to his own party and to his opponents. Disraeli, in 1845, declared openly that Peel would betray the agricultural interest at the first opportunity, as he had betrayed the Protestant interest in 1829. Cobden, from the opposite camp, asserted that the Government was only waiting for an excuse, such as a season of exceptional distress would give. The prophecies were fulfilled. The damp summer of 1845 developed into a soaking autumn. There were first fears that much foreign wheat would have to be imported to mix with the damp and unripened English grain; gradually it was realised that the English wheat crop would be an almost total failure, and that the yield would be deficient throughout Europe. While the corn was rotting in the ear, news came from Ireland that a blight had fallen on the potatoes, and that they were all rotten. By the middle of October it was evident that Ireland was on the verge of a famine more serious than any within living memory. The Anti-Corn-Law League raised the cry of "Open the ports", and there was general agreement in the country that some such action must be taken.

Peel clearly foresaw that, if the ports were once thrown open, it would be impossible to close them again; but he was unable to obtain the agreement of his colleagues to some such measure as would "secure the ultimate and not remote extinction of protective duties on corn". After long and futile discussions he resigned office, and Russell tried unsuccessfully to form a Whig administration. At the beginning of 1846, therefore, Peel returned to power pledged to a policy of free trade in corn, with practically the same cabinet, and with the very reluctant support of the Tories. He now proposed a comprehensive scheme of tariff reductions and remissions, which could be regarded as a culmination of his tariff policy of earlier years; among these miscellaneous measures he included the reform of the Corn Laws, and provided for their ultimate abandonment.

Peel's earlier Budgets had abolished the import duties on the raw materials of manufacturing industry, and there was therefore no longer the same justification for maintaining the duties on imported manufactured goods. Accordingly, the duties on some of the cheaper kinds of woollen, linen and cotton goods were now abolished, along with those on dressed hides; while the duties on the finer sorts of those textile fabrics were halved. The duty on silk goods was also halved, but even so was fifteen per cent. of the value. The duties on metal goods were reduced by one-third; while the general duty on fully manufactured foreign goods was reduced to a uniform ten per cent. There were other reductions or remissions of the duties on animals and animal products, seeds and vegetables, tallow, timber, soap, candles, starch, paper, brandy and spirits. Altogether, these various changes in the tariff entailed a nominal sacrifice of about £6,000,000 annually. Finally, Peel proposed that the existing sliding scale for corn should be abandoned. Instead, when the average price of wheat was 48s. the duty should be 10s. (i.e. half the existing rate); and the duty should fall by a shilling with every rise of a shilling in price, until at and above 53s. the duty should be fixed at 4s. This reduced scale was to last for three years, and should cease definitely in 1849, leaving only a nominal registration duty of a shilling a quarter for the future.[1] All British colonial wheat and flour would be forthwith admitted at this nominal rate. As a partial compensation for this great change, the agricultural interest would be relieved of some special burdens, and agricultural development would be encouraged by public loans for such purposes as drainage. Attacks on this arrangement were staved off, from both the protectionist and abolitionist camps; but with the successful

---

[1] Owing to harvest failures and consequent scarcity of food, the sliding scale of 1846 was suspended between the 1st January 1847 and the 1st March 1848, and was actually in operation only between the latter date and the 1st February 1849. The shilling registration duty was not taken off until 1869.

passage of the Bill, Peel's political career ended. His own party voted against him on the night that the Corn Law measure passed safely through the House of Lords, and Peel resigned office for ever. With his fall the Conservative party went into the political wilderness, and never regained real power until after the election of 1874.

Peel had good reason to be proud of the results achieved by his ministry. The ordinary public expenditure had increased by about £1,000,000 between 1842 and 1846; but the public debt had been reduced in capital amount by about £14,000,000, and the interest on a large portion of the remainder had been reduced, making altogether a reduction in the annual debt charge of nearly £1,500,000. Meanwhile, 605 customs duties had been totally abolished, and 1,035 reductions of duties had been made. On the average, nearly £2,500,000 (nominal) of taxation had been remitted annually over the five years; yet the tax revenue had risen from about £50,250,000 in 1841 to £55,000,000 in 1846. The domestic policy of the Government had been equally successful. Important measures had been passed for the regulation of banking, joint-stock companies, railways, factories, and mines. Trade and industry had taken an upward turn in 1843, and by 1846 had even become excessively active. The recovery of trade after 1843 should not too readily be ascribed, however, to the beneficial effects of Peel's tariff changes; an unsympathetic survey of the period might suggest that Peel had, in effect, caught the upward trend of the decennial trade cycle, and that part of his success was due to good luck as well as good management. Certainly his commercial, financial and administrative reforms did not prevent the recurrence of financial dislocation in 1847, and of social distress as severe as any that had troubled the preceding generation.

The free trade policy followed by Peel in the 'forties reached its full maturity in the reforms carried out by Gladstone a decade later. Like Peel, Gladstone carried out his reduction of indirect taxation under the protection of the income tax; his Budget of 1853 placed as much reliance upon this financial expedient as had Peel's Budget of 1842. Like Peel, Gladstone still regarded the income tax as an emergency measure; he declared that it was neither intended nor suited to be a permanent feature of the fiscal system. In 1853 the income tax was renewed, as a strictly temporary measure, for another seven years; within that period the tax was to sink by stages from sevenpence to fivepence in the pound, and at the end of the period it was to be abolished. In the meantime, the fiscal system was to be adjusted to meet the changing situation. The temporary extension of the income tax was to be used to facilitate the further remission of duties "in order to bring to completion the noble work of commercial reform."

The general principle of Gladstone's fiscal policy, in the Budget of 1853, was to abolish the duties which were unproductive, together with most of the duties on semi-manufactured goods: and to reduce the duties on fully manufactured goods to a general level not exceeding ten per cent. of the value. For the rest, his intention was to substitute rated duties for duties *ad valorem*; to eliminate colonial preferences; and to lower the import duties on foreign foodstuffs, such as tea, cocoa, fruit, eggs and butter. Besides these foodstuffs, there were 123 articles which his Budget proposed to set altogether free from duty, and 133 other articles on which the duties were to be reduced. The general effect of these changes was to produce a great simplification of the customs system, which was accompanied by important administrative reforms and a consolidation of the customs code. On the whole, this Budget of 1853 must be considered a meritorious attempt at financial reform, though the outbreak of the Crimean War completely upset the Government's calculations. The Budget of 1854 aimed at paying for the impending war by taxation, and as far as possible by direct taxation. In point of fact, however, Gladstone went out of office in 1855, and his successor found that large-scale borrowing for military purposes was inevitable. The war added over £32,000,000 to the national debt, and also extra taxation to the amount of about £38,000,000, of which sixty-five per cent. was accounted for by direct taxation. A more serious result of the war was the persistence of disturbed political conditions in Europe, which resulted in a general increase of armaments; national finance was still struggling with the legacy of the war throughout the later 'fifties.

In 1859 Gladstone again became Chancellor of the Exchequer and could resume his interrupted programme of commercial reform. His Budget of 1860 involved an open confession that the calculations of 1853 had been falsified, in particular by the persistent increase of public expenditure caused by warfare and increased armaments. For this general growth of public expenditure Gladstone's remedy was a commercial treaty with France, which might dispel the mutual suspicions of the two countries. He described this measure as a counter-irritant, arousing the sense of commercial interest to counteract military passion. Under cover of such a treaty it would be possible to take up again the task of commercial reform; and such a revival of his earlier free trade policy would justify the continuance of the income tax, which could still be defended as necessary for a special purpose. Accordingly, the Budget of 1860 carried through the policy of free trade by abolishing the duties on a variety of articles, including butter, eggs, cheese, nuts and tallow. Only forty-eight articles remained subject to customs duties, and henceforth the tariff was not in any real sense protective.

By the Cobden-Chevalier Treaty of 1860 Great Britain agreed to abolish all duties on manufactured goods, to bring down the duty on brandy to the colonial level, and to reduce the import duties on wines. These concessions were offered to all countries alike, but would in fact be most beneficial to France. On the other hand, France made concessions only to Great Britain. There were reductions of the duties on British coal and coke, bar and pig iron, steel, tools and machinery, yarns, and manufactured goods of hemp and flax. All prohibitions were to be removed; and high duties were to be reduced to a maximum of thirty per cent. of the value, a maximum which was to drop to twenty-five per cent. after 1864. The treaty also included a most-favoured-nation clause which proved to be more important than was originally intended; for France began to conclude commercial treaties with other countries for the reciprocal relaxation of tariffs, and Great Britain benefited from many consequent reductions of the obstacles to international trade. Gladstone himself thought of 1860 as "the last of the cardinal and organic years of emancipatory fiscal legislation. . . . With the French Treaty, he used to say, the movement in favour of free trade reached its zenith." [1] From a wider point of view the Treaty might be regarded also as inaugurating a new age of economic liberalism in Europe.

[1] Morley's *Gladstone*, Book V, Chapter II. On all aspects of the treaty, and its consequences, see A. L. Dunham *The Anglo-French Treaty of Commerce of 1860* (1930).

CHAPTER FOURTEEN

The Development of Transport

AT THE END of the French wars the English transport system was still based on canals, rivers, and roads, with some help from rudimentary railroads; nevertheless, foreign observers considered it to be the best transport system in the world. The canals had been particularly important in the carriage of coal, on which the industrial developments of the later eighteenth century had largely depended; but there was also a great volume of traffic in general merchandise and there were active passenger services on all the main inland waterways. The financial results of the canal enterprises varied enormously; but the canals which served the industrial districts were making very high profits and had practically a monopoly of the heavy industrial traffic. This was one of the main incentives to the construction of railways. Taking the unsuccessful enterprises along with the successful, the average canal dividends did not exceed six per cent.; but the ten most successful canals declared dividends averaging nearly twenty-eight per cent. in 1825.

Since 1790 railroads had been making more technical progress than canals, especially in the colliery districts. The coalfields of the Tyne and of South Wales had as yet much greater lengths of railroad than such districts as South Lancashire and the district round Birmingham, where canals were plentiful. Generally speaking, railroads were being built where the nature of the ground made the cutting of canals too expensive to be profitable. Until the steam locomotive established itself as a commercially efficient machine, railroads were regarded mainly as feeders of the river and canal system. This point of view was strengthened by the imperfection of the rails used. Even in the immediate post-war period most of the rails were still made of cast iron, which was brittle and therefore required more frequent replacement; this quickly became more costly when locomotive traction developed rapidly on colliery lines between 1804 and 1815.[1] In 1820, however, a method of making improved rails by rolling wrought iron was patented by J. Birkinshaw, a foreman at Bedlington ironworks, in Northumberland. Rails made by this method were adopted in 1824 by the promoters of the Liverpool and Manchester Railway, and eventually became the standard rails for steam railways.

The main roads of the country had been greatly improved in the preceding generation by the efforts of such men as McAdam and Telford, working for various turnpike trusts and other public authorities. In general, however, the turnpike authorities were narrowly local and not very efficient; and the great majority of English roads were not under turnpike trusts at all. The resultant neglect of road maintenance and improvement was particularly serious since the roads were bearing a much heavier volume of traffic than in previous centuries. The best days of the coaching era were between 1820 and 1836. At the latter date there were more than three thousand coaches on the road, giving employment to about thirty thousand men; the "fast" coaches were by that time running at ten miles an hour, though they were killing the horses to do it.

The slow evolution of English railroads, from their obscure origins in the sixteenth century, received a powerful stimulus from the introduction of steam locomotive engines in the early years of the nineteenth century; and the modern phase of

[1] The locomotive replaced the labour of horses, and the incentive to do this was considerable during the French Wars, when horses and fodder rose in price as the result of military demands.

railway development may be regarded as beginning either in 1825, with the completion of the Stockton and Darlington Railway, or with the opening of the Liverpool and Manchester line in 1830. Down to 1829 it was still uncertain whether the steam locomotive would displace horse traction in railway work. The results obtained on the Stockton and Darlington line were not regarded as conclusive, especially as there was strong opposition to the introduction of locomotives on the part of wealthy landowners through whose estates the steam monsters were to run. The triumph of the Stephensons' "Rocket," at the Rainhill locomotive trials in 1829,[1] clearly demonstrated the superiority of steam locomotion, and by 1835 the technical victory was complete; but even then there was still little experience of the actual working of steam locomotives on finished railroads, apart from the two lines already mentioned. By that time many important railways were in the course of construction, but their financial solidity was as yet uncertain. The average profits of the early railways were not large, though there were striking exceptions. As late as 1850, the gross receipts of all the existing railways never reached eight per cent. of the capital expenditure; but this figure includes many entirely unsuccessful lines.

Between 1825 and the end of 1835, Parliament passed fifty-four Railway Acts. Of the new lines sanctioned, by far the most important was the London and Birmingham Railway, with a length of 112½ miles, and a capital of £5,500,000. Down to 1838, when the London and Birmingham line was opened, about 490 miles of railroad had been constructed in England and Wales. Of this total nearly half belonged to the London and Birmingham, with its continuations northwards as far as Preston by the Grand Junction and the North Union lines. In 1836 and 1837, out of more than eighty railway companies projected, thirty-nine new lines were actually sanctioned for Great Britain, with others for Ireland. Altogether,

[1] George and Robert Stephenson shared the Rainhill prize.

the railway "mania" of 1836–7 added about a thousand miles to the railway system, when the various schemes had been completed. After those years there was a pause in the movement. In 1838 and 1839 only five Railway Acts were passed; in 1840 there was none, and in 1841 only one. By the summer of 1843 there were about 1900 miles of railroad open in Great Britain, and not much was in process of construction.

Down to 1840 the canal companies had not suffered severely from the competition of the railways. The Leeds and Liverpool Canal, which had paid sixteen per cent. in 1825, paid twenty per cent. in 1838–9; the Grand Junction Canal for the same two years paid thirteen per cent. and twelve per cent. respectively, and many other canals showed similar results. In 1840 it was reported that "carriers using waggons or vans on roads cannot successfully compete with a railway. . . . The canals, however, still retain their business; and having reduced their charges continue to be used for the carriage of goods, in cases especially where the weight gives them some advantage over the railway. As far as regards the heavy merchandise, it appears probable that the canals will always secure the public against any unreasonable demands on the part of the railway companies." [1] But the danger that the railways would gain a monopoly of inland transport was to prove more serious and more urgent than the committee expected. The railways were already taking over the passenger and parcels traffic from both the canals and the turnpike roads; and the stage coaches were already dwindling in numbers.

There was, moreover, already a movement towards the amalgamation of railways, which tended to make for monopolistic control within the railway system itself. In 1834 the North Union Railway had been formed by the amalgamation of the Preston and Wigan Railway with the Wigan Branch Railway, and there was thus opened a continuous line from

[1] *Third Report on Railway Communication*, 1840 (299), pp. 8 and 9.

Preston to Newton-le-Willows, near Warrington. There a connection was made with the Liverpool and Manchester line, and with the projected Grand Junction Railway from Warrington to Birmingham,[1] which would in its turn link up with the London and Birmingham Railway to form the first trunk line of the English railway system. The promotion of new railway companies and the amalgamation of existing lines were severely checked by the financial crisis of 1836–7; but speculative activity revived with the general recovery of trade after 1843, and the main lines of communication throughout the country had been sanctioned before the movement again came to a halt in 1846. The middle 'forties constituted a most significant period in railway history, not merely because of the great number of new lines sanctioned, but also because of the important amalgamations which were then accomplished. Between 1844 and 1847 English railways were, in effect, transformed from a large number of disconnected lines to a relatively small number of main lines forming the framework of the English railway system as it exists at the present time.

In the railroad amalgamations of the middle 'forties the outstanding figure was that of George Hudson, the "Railway King", who for a time became one of the most important financial magnates in the country.[2] Hudson was already a wealthy man when, in 1833, he started the York Banking Company. During the railway boom of the next few years he promoted the York and North Midland Railway, and became its chairman; it was in this capacity that he engineered the consolidations by which the Midland Railway was created in 1843–4. The Midland Railway was formed by the amalgamation of three separate lines with a common terminus at Derby. Of these three lines, the Midland Coun-

---

[1] The Grand Junction Railway Company absorbed a short line from Warrington to Newton-le-Willows in 1835.
[2] See R. S. Lambert, *The Railway King*, 1934.

ties Railway (from Derby to Rugby by Leicester) competed directly with the Birmingham and Derby Railway; both were suffering from the effects of their "cut-throat" competition, of which the main benefit was accruing to the North Midland Railway, which took on the traffic from Derby to the north. The North Midland Railway linked up at Leeds with Hudson's line, the York and North Midland, which had connections as far as Darlington by the Great North of England Railway. Beyond Darlington, a scheme to run through Durham and Newcastle had been sanctioned, with the possibility of an extension into Scotland by the east coast route. Hudson was a director of the North Midland, as well as chairman of the York and North Midland; he now worked for the amalgamation of all the three lines which met at Derby. Parliamentary opinion was favourable to the union of the two competing lines, but hostile to the inclusion of the "end-on" line; the two competing lines, however, showed no disposition to come to an agreement, and wasted both time and money in futile bargaining. Finally Hudson intervened forcibly in the negotiations, and carried through the triple amalgamation by a mixture of will power, bullying and financial skill. The united company controlled 179 miles of line, and had a capital of £6,000,000; economies in operation were made almost immediately after the union, a dividend of six per cent. was paid in the first financial year, and the stock went rapidly to a high premium.

The early success of the Midland amalgamation accelerated the negotiations which led in 1846 to the formation of the London and North Western Railway. In the middle 'forties the London and Birmingham Railway and the Great Western were engaged in a crucial struggle, which involved among other issues a conflict between Brunel's broad gauge and Stephenson's narrow gauge. The struggle turned mainly upon a fight for the control of the Grand Junction Railway, which had already absorbed the Liverpool and Manchester line, and had made traffic agreements with the Manchester and Birmingham Railway (as far as Crewe). The danger was that the Grand Junction would amalgamate with the Great Western, which would thus be able to compete with the London and Birmingham for the traffic of the north-western counties. During 1845 the issue of the negotiations often hung in a delicate balance; but in the end the London and Birmingham succeeded in buying over the Grand Junction, together with the Manchester and Birmingham line. After that the negotiations went more smoothly, and in the summer of 1846 the London and North Western Railway received parliamentary sanction; it had a capital of £17,000,000, its length amounted to 379 miles, and its estimated revenue was about £2,000,000 a year.

The Midland and the North Western amalgamations were the two outstanding consolidations of the middle 'forties; but there was a whole host of less famous railway consolidations, which all had the same tendency towards the knitting together of short, disconnected lines into a compact railway network under semi-monopolistic control. Not only were the railways amalgamating with each other in the middle 'forties, but they were also absorbing the canals at an ominous rate. Between 1845 and 1847 canals with an aggregate length of nearly a thousand miles were taken over by railway companies. Meanwhile, the introduction of steamships in the coasting trade was still further restricting the volume of canal traffic; from that time there was a progressive decline in the importance of the English canal system. It was obvious that the railways were rapidly acquiring a monopolistic control over the internal transport and communications of the country. Railroad amalgamations and consolidations increased the danger that this monopolistic position might be abused for the exploitation of the public. In these circumstances, there was an evident necessity for some public control over railway development and railway policy.

The movement for public control of the railways began during the railway fever of 1836. Lord Londonderry declared that there ought to be some provision for the reversion of railways to the State after a fixed period of operation; and James Morrison, M.P. for Ipswich, urged that there was danger of a transport monopoly which would make state control inevitable.[1] In 1839 a Select Committee on Railway Communication was appointed, following a petition against the monopolistic policy of the London and Birmingham line. This committee dimly envisaged the danger of a future monopoly of inland transport by the railways, and recommended the creation of a Railway Board under the Board of Trade; practically the same committee was reappointed in the following year, and made the same proposal. As a result of the reports of these committees, Lord Seymour's Railway Act of 1840 established a Railway Department of the Board of Trade, which was authorised to call for accounts, with power to enforce all the Acts referring to railways and to send an inspector to any railway to approve the safety of the line. All railway bye-laws were to be submitted for the Board's approval.

Seymour's Act was amended and supplemented by Gladstone's Railway Act of 1842. The Board was now authorised, on the application of either party, to decide disputes between inter-connecting railways, on questions concerning joint traffic and from the point of view of the public safety; and the Board was also empowered to postpone the opening of lines which did not meet with the approval of its inspectors. These two Acts of 1840 and 1842 did not result in any effective control of railway policy; and the arbitration clauses were never used. Nevertheless, the power to call for information was an important precedent, and the system of inspection did useful work in watching over the public safety.

[1] *Journals of the House of Commons*, Vol. 91, p. 378; Hansard, Third Series, Vol. XXXIII, col. 977 *et seq.*

The railroad and canal amalgamations of the middle 'forties revived the fear that a monopoly of inland transport was being organised, and determined efforts were made to avert the danger. Early in 1844, Gladstone moved for a committee of inquiry, on the ground that railway speculation was reviving, and that inquiry would be too late if it were not prompt: the Midland Railway amalgamation was already being considered. The committee interpreted its functions very widely, and its six reports dealt with such varied topics as private bill procedure, railway rates, governmental supervision, and the question of amalgamations. The third report of the committee was especially important through its emphasis on the *national* importance of the railways, and its strong plea for parliamentary control. Among other reforms, the committee recommended that if at the end of fifteen years' operation the annual divisible profits on the paid-up share capital of any railway equalled or exceeded ten per cent., the Government should have the option of revising the fares and charges, against a guarantee to make the profits up to ten per cent. if the revision reduced them below this rate. After the same period of operation the Government should have the option of purchasing any new line (*i.e.* any line sanctioned after 1844) on payment of twenty-five times the amount of the annual profits, calculated on the average of the three preceding years.

Gladstone, as President of the Board of Trade, introduced a Railway Bill which followed the committee's recommendations closely, except that the *maximum* rate of profit on which the terms of purchase were to be calculated was fixed at ten per cent. This proposal met with strong opposition from the railway interests in Parliament, and the Act as passed made ten per cent. the *minimum* rate of profit on which the terms of purchase were to be calculated; if the annual profits exceeded ten per cent., the terms should be twenty-five years' purchase of the profits, however high. These provisions for purchase and revision of rates were ineffective, for various reasons. All the lines sanctioned before 1844 escaped the Act; they included the main trunk lines, with an aggregate length of 2300 miles. If the railways were to be "nationalised," it was clearly desirable that they should all be purchased, and at the same time; whereas the Act of 1844 would allow only partial and piecemeal purchase. Moreover, even in 1844 there were only four railway companies paying as much as ten per cent., and the rate of profits decreased steadily in later years. Thus both the purchasing clauses and the revising clauses of the Act of 1844 were totally useless, or worse than useless. Gladstone's interest in railway problems was checked, and the possibility of railway nationalisation dropped out of practical politics for several generations.

Another recommendation of the committee of 1844 was that all railway bills should be submitted to a department of the Board of Trade before being considered by the House of Commons; such a preliminary examination would allow questions of public safety and public policy to receive more careful attention and more competent technical criticism. Accordingly, a special railway department of the Board of Trade was established, and became commonly known as "Dalhousie's Board". This Board might have done useful work in sifting out the unsound and fraudulent schemes from the genuine projects for new lines and improvements; but the operations of the Board were strongly resisted by the railway interests in the House of Commons, on the ostensible grounds that the constitutional rights of Parliament were being infringed, and that parliamentary functions were being taken over by the civil service. In general, Dalhousie's Board wished Parliament to exercise greater caution in sanctioning new lines or amalgamations; whereas Parliament was in favour of pushing the railway bills through as rapidly as possible, and could afford to disregard the decisions of the Board, which had merely advisory functions. In such circumstances the Board could hardly continue to function; it was dissolved in the summer of 1845.

The abandonment of Dalhousie's Board led in 1846 to renewed recommendations in favour of a separate government department for the supervision of railways. Parliament was being flooded with railway bills of all kinds, which could not be adequately investigated in the House of Commons. Some of the projects were summarily rejected as not complying with standing orders and other regulations; but 435 Bills out of 800 were left for parliamentary consideration. Of these, 83 were withdrawn, 91 were lost in committee, 15 were rejected by the House of Lords, and 246 were successful. Preliminary inspection by a strong Board would obviously have sifted out many of the weaker schemes and saved Parliament much time, which could have been spent in giving more adequate consideration to the remaining schemes. During the session Wilson-Patten had secured the appointment of a committee on railway amalgamations, which quickly issued two short reports, without taking any evidence from railway representatives. The committee's first main recommendation was that the rates and tolls of amalgamated companies should be subject to revision. Moreover, since private arrangements between companies might effect the same purpose as legal amalgamation, the committee further recommended "that some department of the executive Government, so constituted as to command general respect and confidence, should be charged with the supervision of railways and canals." This recommendation was reinforced, in almost identical terms, by the report of a contemporary committee of the House of Lords, and by the resolutions of Morrison's Committee on Railway Acts Enactments, which was sitting at the same time with more general powers of inquiry.[1]

---

[1] *Second Report on Railways and Canals Amalgamations*, 1846 (275), p. v.; *Lords Report on Railways*, 1846 (H.C. 489), p. 7; *First Report on Railway Acts Enactments*, 1846 (590).

In August, 1846, a Government Bill for the establishment of a Railway Board was introduced, and passed into law without opposition. There were to be five members of the Board, including a paid president and two paid commissioners; the president and the two unpaid commissioners might sit in Parliament. The commissioners were to take over the railway business of the Board of Trade, and to report on railway schemes, "if so directed by Parliament". But the parliamentary session ended on the day when the Bill passed, and by the time the commissioners came into office the "railway mania" of 1846 was over. After the collapse of that bubble there was for some years no considerable volume of new railway business. The Railway Board had therefore very little to do; it was soon reabsorbed into the Board of Trade, and was finally abolished in 1851.

By the middle of the century the railways had become more important than the roads and the canals in the carriage of both passengers and goods. The main railway companies had already acquired a semi-monopolistic control over the inland transport system, and all attempts at effective public control had been successfully resisted. There was a steadily growing body of opinion in favour of creating a separate jurisdiction for the supervision of railways, to replace or supplement the inefficient control exercised by Parliament; but it was evident that Parliament was not yet ready for any drastic change of system.

The ill success of the early attempts at the public control of the railways is not altogether surprising, when it is remembered that the contemporary trend of maritime policy was towards the *abolition* of public control. Huskisson had done important work by his relaxation of the Navigation Laws in the 'twenties; and the shipping difficulties experienced in combating the Irish potato famine demonstrated the necessity of repealing all the surviving restrictions on maritime intercourse. Between 1846 and 1849 the English

Navigation Laws had to sustain diplomatic onslaughts from Holland, the United States, and the German Zollverein. Petitions in favour of repeal came also from the British colonies in North America and the West Indies, which considered that freer trade with the United States might be some partial compensation for the withdrawal of colonial preferences. After a fierce parliamentary struggle, the surviving Navigation Laws were repealed in 1849, except that the British coasting trade was still restricted to British ships manned by British crews.

The reservation of the coasting trade arose from the unwillingness of the United States to throw open the American coasting trade, which was of immeasurably greater potential importance. Even after the British coasting trade was set free, in 1853, the American coasting trade remained a close preserve, and a most valuable training ground for the growing mercantile marine of the United States. During the preceding generation, American shipping had been making extraordinarily rapid progress, helped by the special advantage of cheap timber from the great American forests. By the middle of the century the American "clippers" were decidedly superior to comparable English ships in sailing efficiency and speed; American tonnage was already almost equal to British tonnage, and the two combined amounted to more than a half of the world's total shipping. Greater freedom in ocean transport was regarded by the Americans as likely to give them the maritime leadership of the world in the near future. The failure of this ambition was caused partly by the dislocating effect of the American Civil War, which drove American shipping from the ocean; but a more fundamental reason for the continued leadership of British shipping was the gradual transition from wooden ships to iron, and from sailing ships to steamers.[1]

[1] See H. Moyse-Bartlett, *From Sail to Steam* (Historical Association, 1946), and the books there recommended.

The steamer and the iron boat had both been invented in the 1780s; yet eighty years later the wooden sailing ship was still holding its own (though with increasing difficulty) in ocean transport. Small steamers had been creeping into use as river boats in England, Scotland, and America during the later stages of the Napoleonic wars. In the post-war period steamboat services were organised from Great Britain to Ireland and France; and from that time their use on European waterways steadily extended. Oceanic steamship services still seemed a very remote possibility, however, owing to the difficulty of carrying enough coal to feed the engines throughout a long voyage. Even in the later 'thirties many "experts" maintained that this difficulty in itself would always prevent the establishment of regular steamship services across the Atlantic.

The American steamer *Savannah* had crossed the Atlantic to Liverpool in 1819, but she had used steam only as an occasional auxiliary to sails. Apparently it was the *Sirius*, in 1838, which first crossed the Atlantic using steam all the way, though the credit for this feat has commonly been given to the Canadian *Royal William*. In 1838 at least three English steamers crossed the Atlantic to New York, from London, Bristol, and Liverpool. During the next few years several famous steamship lines established themselves in Great Britain, with the help of government subsidies included in contracts for the conveyance of the mails. By successive stages the mail services to India and the Far East were taken over by the Peninsular and Oriental Steam Navigation Company. The grant of the North Atlantic contract to Samuel Cunard in 1839 led to the growth of the Cunard Line. The Royal Mail Steam Packet Company received the contract for the West Indian mails in 1840; and in the same year the Pacific Steam Navigation Company was established. By that time there were steamboat services on all the main European rivers; but oceanic steam shipping had still a hard battle to fight with iron-hulled "tramp" sailing ships. On the longer oceanic voyages (e.g. to Australia) steamship lines did not establish themselves until well into the second half of the century.[1]

The progress of iron shipping was even slower than that of steam shipping. The first iron steamer was built in England in 1822, and was navigated across the Channel to the Seine; but the immediate results of the new development were small. In 1847 iron ships were still so rare that Lloyd's had no regular rating arrangements for them, though they had been accepted for registration as early as 1837. One daring prophet maintained in 1844 that "eventually almost all steam vessels would be built of iron"; [2] but four years later, when parliamentary committees investigated the prospects of British shipping in connection with the proposal to repeal the Navigation Laws, not a single iron shipbuilder or marine engine maker was called to give evidence. Yet the main hope for the future supremacy of British shipping over its American and European rivals lay in the superiority of the British iron and engineering industries.

[1] See G. S. Graham, 'The ascendancy of the sailing ship, 1850–85', *Economic History Review*, August 1956, pp. 74–88.
[2] B. G. Willcox, before the *Committee on British Shipping*, 1844; quoted by Clapham, *op. cit.*, p. 441.

CHAPTER FIFTEEN

The Age of New Gold

IN THE MIDDLE years of the nineteenth century the economic troubles of the preceding generation seemed to vanish as if by magic. There was a notably increased demand for manufactured goods, for export to America and elsewhere. The abnormal demand persisted for several years, and by 1853 it was so pronounced as to counterbalance the large imports of grain which had become possible through the repeal of the Corn Laws. The vast expansion of the foreign trade of the country caused such an extraordinary demand for shipping that freight rates rose enormously, and higher wages were at once conceded in the ship-building trades. Subsequently, other trades demanded higher wages, and obtained rises of from twelve to fifty per cent. Furnace keepers in some Scottish iron works received increases of sixty per cent., and unskilled labourers in the building trades received forty-eight per cent. Farmers found great difficulty in getting sufficient labourers for harvest work, and had to bid against railway and public works contractors; navvies were earning as much as 4s. 6d. a day. The wages of cotton spinners increased by only twenty-five per cent., and the wages of power-loom weavers by only fifteen per cent.; but these moderately increased wages in the cotton trade were earned in a curtailed working week.

The abnormal prosperity of industry and trade was not achieved at the expense of agriculture, as had been feared by many opponents of the free trade movement; on the contrary, English agriculture had never been more prosperous

217

than it was in the generation which followed the repeal of the Corn Laws. There was no serious fall in the price of wheat; and, at the slightly reduced prices which were obtained, wheat growing was more profitable than in the earlier period, because the costs of production were being more than proportionately reduced by technical improvements. The population of the country was still increasing rapidly, the national standard of living was rising, and transport charges still gave the native agriculturists a considerable protection against foreign competition. Both wheat growers and stock feeders prospered, farming profits increased and rents rose. The enlargement of farms continued, especially since the technical progress of the period demanded the sinking of much capital in drainage, artificial manures, special cattle foods, and agricultural machinery, which gave a considerable advantage to the large-scale farmers.

This new rhythm in economic life was the resultant of many interrelated forces. "The rapid increase of railways in every part of the world; the improvements in the navigation and speed of ships; the rapid spread of population into new and fertile regions; the quick succession of important discoveries in practical science . . . the adoption more or less completely of principles of free trade," were all factors considered by well-informed contemporary writers to have accelerated the rate of progress and increased the material prosperity of the world.[1] The extension of railway transport had an especially important effect upon employment, prices, and social welfare in England. During the later 'forties, railroad construction gave employment to between half a million and a million workers during a period of dear food and extreme commercial difficulty. To pay for this constructional work, railway "calls" put heavy financial pressure upon the investing classes for some years; but after 1850 the railways began to be more profitable to the shareholders, and con-

[1] Tooke and Newmarch, *History of Prices*, Vol. VI, p. 136.

tributed to the general prosperity of the country by tending to reduce the cost of transport.

While due consideration must be given to the complexity of the forces influencing the course of trade during the 'fifties, it seems clear that the strongest single factor modifying the economic history of the period was the influx of new gold which resulted from the mining discoveries in California and Australia. The first decided effects of the Californian gold discoveries of 1848 made themselves felt in England in 1849. It was this influx of bullion which occasioned the sudden increase in the American demand for manufactured goods; and during the immediately succeeding years the abnormal British exports to America were balanced by imports of American bullion. In 1852 the effects of the Australian gold discoveries began to show themselves in a great wave of emigration and an expansion of the export trade to Australia. The influx of new gold was hailed as "The Currency Extension Act of Nature", and the Banking School gloated over the quasi-miraculous defeat of their opponents. The regular monthly consignments of new gold arriving in England were declared to have "operated at once as the solvents of actual or prospective financial difficulties and straits which could not have been cured so effectually, or so speedily, by any other means." [1] It is true that the intervention of Nature in the currency controversy did not prevent the punctual arrival of the decennial financial crisis in 1857, when the Bank Charter Act of 1844 had to be suspended for the second time; but in the early and middle 'fifties the new gold had certainly exerted a very positive influence upon all branches of economic activity.

The total stock of gold in Europe and America at the end of 1848 was about £560,000,000. During the next eight years the aggregate addition from California, Australia, and Russia amounted to about £174,000,000, representing nearly

[1] Tooke and Newmarch, *History of Prices*, Vol. VI. p. 203.

a quarter of the total stock in 1856. Practically all the new gold went into additional coinage for various countries. France and the United States accounted for £60,000,000 and £50,000,000 respectively. In France this additional gold coinage was mainly in substitution for silver coinage withdrawn by English purchases for export to the East, and by exports to Germany and Northern Europe. In the United States the new gold coinage was in substitution partly for paper currency and partly for foreign coins. The United Kingdom *added* about £20,000,000 to her gold coinage; and increases were also made in the gold coinage of various other countries, including Brazil, Egypt, and Portugal. In the aggregate, the metallic currency of the leading countries seems to have been increased by about thirty per cent. as a result of the influx of new gold during the eight years after 1848. Moreover, the increase in the gold reserves of the banks made possible a substantial expansion of credit currency.

One effect of this increase of money was reflected in the general tendency towards higher prices in most classes of goods. In foodstuffs the rise in prices was almost continuous after 1850; and the same tendency was traceable in most of the raw materials of manufacturing industry. The tendency was not so strong, it is true, in the market for colonial and tropical produce such as tea, sugar, tobacco, and cotton. The low price of raw cotton went along with low prices for cotton manufactured goods; yet the cotton industry was quite prosperous. The demand for manufactured goods remained strong even in trades where the increased cost of the raw material necessitated increases in the prices of finished goods; and manufacturers derived an additional advantage from the fact that costs of production were being reduced by continued mechanical progress.

Apart from their reverberation upon the volume of credit, the discoveries of gold became linked with economic changes throughout the world in a way which may be readily imagined. The gold miners had more money, and spent it; therefore prices rose in the gold-bearing regions and stimulated imports, especially imports of manufactured goods from centres like Birmingham and Lancashire. The prices of such manufactured goods rose, and this tended to increase the production of them; therefore more raw material was required, the prices of raw materials rose, and their production increased. A similar process of reverberation can be traced to account for the increased wages of labour throughout the world. The exceptionally large increases of wages among the metal workers and general labourers may have a special significance; for from both these occupations there would be an especially serious drain of labour by emigration to the new gold fields. It may be argued that higher prices would tend to neutralise higher wages, and so reduce the stimulus to productive activity: and similarly, that higher wages would reduce the stimulus given to business enterprise by higher prices. But what has to be considered is the effect upon commercial and industrial activity of *rising* (and not merely *higher*) prices and wages. The influence of the new gold was decidedly important during the interval which elapsed before the additions to the quantity of money were neutralised by a corresponding rise in the general price level. All things considered, the increased supplies of money must be regarded as having given a stupendous impetus to the production of material goods during the 'fifties; and capital investments made during this period, with a view to increasing production, continued to affect industry long after the initial stimulus had faded.

England in 1860 was prosperous and somewhat complacent. The customs, the excise, the assessed taxes, and the post office were yielding more revenue than at any earlier time. The foreign trade of the country had never been so active. Industrial employment was plentiful, and wages were high; consequently the problem of pauperism had become less urgent. The financial credit of the country was unchallenged, the rate of discount was low, and there was an abundance of capital seeking investment. The Government had concluded a most advantageous commercial treaty with the traditional enemy, France; and there were signs that this treaty was to inaugurate an age of international economic liberalism of which England, as the "workshop of the world", would reap the fullest benefit. It is true that many of the social problems inherited from an earlier generation still called urgently for treatment. Housing and sanitary conditions were still scandalous both in towns and in country districts; while the poor-law workhouses were still said to be less comfortable than the prisons. In both industry and agriculture the labour of young children continued to be recklessly exploited. "Climbing boys" were still being suffocated in narrow chimneys; the agricultural gang system had not yet been restricted by law; the public conscience was not yet fully roused to the evils of sweated labour in the tailoring, dressmaking, and millinery trades, though Hood's "Song of the Shirt" was nearly twenty years old. Such social and economic problems were, however, regarded as relics of a less happy age. The lines along which their remedy was to be sought had already been laid down; the disappearance of the evils was thought to be mainly a matter of time and perseverance.

Arnold Toynbee, who grew up from childhood to manhood during the 'sixties, was amazed at the improvement which had taken place in the material condition of the English working classes since 1846. This improvement he attributed mainly to four causes: free trade, factory legislation, trade unions, and co-operative societies. Free trade (he said) "has enormously increased the aggregate wealth of the country, and therefore increased the demand for labour . . . it has created greater steadiness in trade. . . . Since 1846 workmen have been more regularly employed than in the preceding half-century. . . . Factory legislation has raised the condition of women and children by imposing a limit on the hours of work, and especially the sanitary environment of the labourer. . . . Trades-Unions, again, have done much to avert social and industrial disorder." The co-operative societies, like the trade unions, "have taught the power and merit of voluntary association and self-help." Since 1860, he considered, the relations between employers and workmen had decidedly improved. Employers were beginning to recognise the necessity for labour organisations, "and the advantages of being able to treat with a whole body of workmen through their most intelligent members." [1]

Toynbee was, perhaps, somewhat optimistic in his account of the economic progress which England had made during his lifetime. The tranquillity of 1860 was a breathing space between two periods of struggle, rather than a transition from an age of distress to an age of unbroken prosperity. Before the end of 1861 the Civil War in America had begun to cast the ominous shadow of a cotton famine across the industry of Lancashire. In 1865 Jevons's book on *The Coal Question* warned England that the national prosperity was based on a dwindling raw material. In the later 'sixties, respectable trade unionism had to bear the odium aroused by the "Sheffield Outrages", while the risings and riots of the Fenians recalled uneasy memories of the Chartist disturbances. In the 'seventies English agriculture had for the first time to meet the full force of trans-oceanic competition, made possible by the transport developments of the preceding generation; after the 'seventies, too, the industrial future of England never seemed so secure as it had done during the middle years of the century. Nevertheless, the Victorians of 1860 had some justification for their complacency. They had struggled painfully out of the distress of the 'forties to a position of unprecedented prosperity; and their material achievements enabled England to bear the economic changes of the

[1] Toynbee, *The Industrial Revolution*, 3rd ed., 1890, pp. 144–49.

succeeding generation with far less distress than had accompanied earlier periods of social reconstruction.

The "Industrial Revolution" of the eighteenth century had not been a social catastrophe; but it had accentuated many existing social and economic problems, though at the same time it made possible an increase of material wealth adequate to remedy most of those evils, if properly administered. The difficulties of town life had been enormously increased by the rapid growth of population and by an acceleration of the normal townward drift from the countryside. The cleavage between capital and labour had been widened by the rise of new classes of wage earners under the factory system. The organisation of agriculture had been profoundly disturbed by the necessity for feeding the growing population of the industrial towns. The old system of commercial regulation, which had been tolerable while England remained a land of domestic industry and peasant agriculture, no longer fitted a country whose mechanised industries needed ever-widening foreign markets in order to reap the maximum benefits of large-scale production.

The readjustment of social organisation to the changed economic conditions would doubtless have caused considerable temporary distress, even if the transition had been allowed to proceed without distortion; but in actual fact the readjustment was hindered, and for a time prevented, by the frequent recurrence of warfare during the later eighteenth century, and especially by the long wars against France between 1793 and 1815. The strain of the French wars caused the postponement of many philanthropic schemes for social reform. Relations between employers and workers were embittered in both agriculture and manufacturing industry. Technical progress was diverted from its peacetime line of development, even if it was not seriously checked. Foreign trade was hampered by the vicissitudes of warfare, as well as by the deliberate blockades and embargoes imposed by both belligerent and neutral nations; the nascent economic liberalism of the 1780s was stifled in the wartime reversion to a narrow mercantilist system which the world had outgrown.

Even after the return of peace, the exhaustion of all the belligerent countries and the reactionary tradition persisting from the war period still retarded the process of social and economic reconstruction. It was not until the second quarter of the nineteenth century that the direct effects of the French wars had been shaken off; thereafter the forces of reform gathered strength rapidly, and achieved notable success. Parliamentary and municipal reforms foreshadowed a closer approach to political democracy. Searching investigation into the sanitary conditions of the large towns led to a tentative beginning of public health legislation. Factory legislation ameliorated some of the worst consequences of the new industrial system. The scarcity of business capital, which may have been responsible for some of the ruthlessness of industrial employers during the earlier decades of the century, was eased by reforms in banking and company organisation, as well as by the gradual growth of prosperity in the country. The long struggle for commercial freedom bore fruit in the repeal of the Corn Laws, the breakdown of the protective tariff, the abolition of the Navigation Laws, and the approach to economic liberalism in some foreign countries. Meanwhile the emergence of a more responsible trade unionism and a more business-like co-operative movement, together with the progress of such organisations as mechanics' institutes, friendly societies, and trustee savings banks, showed that the industrial working classes were fully alive to the advantages of self-help and mutual improvement. The governing classes were brought to realise that the typical working man was neither a brutalised sot nor a dangerous revolutionary. The working classes discovered that collective bargaining, backed by strong reserve funds, usually paid better than strikes. Disraeli's "Two Nations" still existed side by side in the

England of 1860; but they were learning to respect each other. "Civilisation had begun slowly to raise its head above the smoke." [1] The struggle for private wealth was becoming more compatible with the pursuit of the social welfare.

[1] Hammond, *The Rise of Modern Industry*, 1925, p. 256.

LIST OF WORKS
FOR FURTHER READING AND REFERENCE

In making this list special preference has been given to the works which have been found most useful in writing the present book; thus the list may partially atone for the paucity of footnotes in the preceding pages. The items are arranged, in each section, according to their dates of publication.

It should be remembered that much information on particular aspects of the subject has appeared in the form of articles in such periodicals as *Economica* (1921 onwards); the *Economic History Review* (1927 onwards); *Economic History*, a supplement to the *Economic Journal* (Nos. 1–15, January 1926 to February 1940); the *Journal of Economic and Business History* (Harvard, 4 vols., 1928–31); and the *Journal of Economic History* (Chicago, 1941 onwards). The files of the *Agricultural History Review* (1953 onwards), the *Journal of Transport History* (1953 onwards), and *Business History* (from 1958), should also be consulted.

A. BIBLIOGRAPHIES

J. B. WILLIAMS, *A Guide to the Printed Materials for English Social and Economic History, 1750–1850* (2 vols., 1926).

H. L. BEALES and G. D. H. COLE, *A Select List of Books on Economic and Social History, 1700–1850* (1927).

E. POWER, *The Industrial Revolution, 1750–1850: A Select Bibliography* (1927).

T. S. ASHTON, *The Industrial Revolution: A Study in Bibliography* (1937).

B. GENERAL WORKS

A. TOYNBEE, *The Industrial Revolution of the Eighteenth Century in England* (1884).

A. E. BLAND, P. A. BROWN and R. H. TAWNEY, *English Economic History: Select Documents*, Part III (1914).

L. W. MOFFIT, *England on the Eve of the Industrial Revolution: A Study of Economic and Social Conditions from 1740 to 1760* (1925).

SIR JOHN CLAPHAM, *An Economic History of Modern Britain*: Vol. I, *The Early Railway Age, 1820–1850* (1926).

PAUL MANTOUX, *The Industrial Revolution in the Eighteenth Century* (Eng. trans., 1928, revised ed. 1961).

H. L. BEALES, *The Industrial Revolution, 1750–1850: an introductory essay* (first ed., 1928, reissue with new introd., 1958).

C. R. FAY, *Great Britain from Adam Smith to the Present Day* (1928).

A. H. DODD, *The Industrial Revolution in North Wales* (1933).

G. P. JONES and A. G. POOL, *A Hundred Years of Economic Development in Great Britain* (1939), covers the period 1837–1939.

C. R. FAY, *English Economic History, mainly since 1700* (1940).

SIR GEORGE CLARK, *The Wealth of England from 1496 to 1760* (1946).

T. S. ASHTON, *The Industrial Revolution, 1760–1830* (1948).

A. H. JOHN, *The Industrial Development of South Wales, 1750–1850* (1950).

W. SCHLOTE, *British Overseas Trade from 1700 to the 1930s* (1952).

W. H. B. COURT, *A Concise Economic History of Britain from 1750 to Recent Times* (1954).

T. S. ASHTON, *An Economic History of England: the Eighteenth Century* (1955).

W. HOFFMANN, *British Industry, 1700–1950* (1955).

D. MARSHALL, *English People in the Eighteenth Century* (1956).

C. BOOKS ON SPECIAL SUBJECTS

CHAPTER I THE BIRTH OF THE MODERN INDUSTRIAL ECONOMY

E. A. PRATT, *History of Inland Transportation and Communication in England* (1909).

R. B. WESTERFIELD, 'Middlemen in English Business, particularly between 1660 and 1760' (*Trans. Connecticut Academy of Arts and Sciences*, Vol. XIX, 1915, pp. 111–445).

H. HEATON, *The Yorkshire Woollen and Worsted Industries from the Earliest Times up to the Industrial Revolution* (1920).

W. BOWDEN, *Industrial Society in England towards the End of the Eighteenth Century* (1925).

R. D. RICHARDS, *The Early History of Banking in England* (1929).

T. S. WILLAN, *River Navigation in England, 1600–1750* (1936).

T. S. WILLAN, *The English Coasting Trade* (1938).

L. A. HARPER, *The English Navigation Laws* (1939).

CHAPTER II CHANGES IN THE TEXTILE INDUSTRIES

J. L. and B. HAMMOND, *The Skilled Labourer, 1760–1832* (1920), especially Chapter VI, on the woollen and worsted industries.

G. W. DANIELS, *The Early English Cotton Industry* (1920).

G. UNWIN (and others), *Samuel Oldknow and the Arkwrights* (1924).

W. B. CRUMP (ed.), *The Leeds Woollen Industry, 1780–1820* (1931).

A. P. WADSWORTH and J. DE L. MANN, *The Cotton Trade and Industrial Lancashire, 1600–1780* (1931).

W. B. CRUMP and G. GHORBAL, *History of the Huddersfield Woollen Industry* (1935).

K. G. PONTING, *The West of England Cloth Industry* (1957).

R. S. FITTON and A. P. WADSWORTH, *The Strutts and the Arkwrights, 1758–1830* (1958).

E. M. SIGSWORTH, *Black Dyke Mills: a history* (1958).

CHAPTER III CHANGES IN THE IRON, COAL AND ENGINEERING INDUSTRIES

G. I. H. LLOYD, *The Cutlery Trades* (1913).

J. LORD, *Capital and Steam Power, 1750–1800* (1923).

T. S. ASHTON, *Iron and Steel in the Industrial Revolution* (1924, 2nd rev. ed., 1951).

H. W. DICKINSON and R. JENKINS, *James Watt and the Steam Engine* (1927).

T. S. ASHTON and J. SYKES, *The Coal Industry of the Eighteenth Century* (1929).

E. ROLL, *An Early Experiment in Industrial Organisation: being a History of the Firm of Boulton and Watt, 1775–1805* (1930).

H. W. DICKINSON, *James Watt* (1936); *Matthew Boulton* (1937).

W. H. B. COURT, *The Rise of the Midland Industries, 1600–1838* (1938).

H. W. DICKINSON, *A Short History of the Steam Engine* (1939).

A. RAISTRICK, *Dynasty of Ironfounders: the Darbys and Coalbrookdale* (1953).

J. D. MARSHALL, *Furness and the Industrial Revolution* (1958).

CHAPTER IV THE INDUSTRIAL CAPITALISTS

S. SMILES, *Lives of the Engineers* (3 vols., 1861–62); *Industrial Biography* (1863); *Lives of Boulton and Watt* (1865).

E. METEYARD, *Life of Josiah Wedgwood* (1865).

G. H. WRIGHT, *Chronicles of the Birmingham Chamber of Commerce* (1913).

H. HAMILTON, *The English Brass and Copper Industries to 1800* (1926), especially Chapters VI–VIII.

I. GRUBB, *Quakerism and Industry before 1800* (1930).

L. D. BEBB, *Nonconformity and Social and Economic Life, 1660–1800* (1934).

A. REDFORD, *Manchester Merchants and Foreign Trade:* Vol. I, *1794–1858* (1934); Vol. II, *1850–1939* (1956).

R. V. HOLT, *The Unitarian Contribution to Social Progress in England* (1938, 2nd rev. ed. 1952).

A. RAISTRICK, *Quakers in Science and Industry* (1950).

M. W. BERESFORD, *The Leeds Chambers of Commerce* (1951).

J. ROWE, *Cornwall in the Age of the Industrial Revolution* (1953).

J. P. ADDIS, *The Crawshay Dynasty* (1957).

See also the works mentioned under Chapters II and III above.

Chapter V The Industrial Wage Earners

S. and B. WEBB, *History of Trade Unionism* (1894: rev. ed., 1920).

M. D. GEORGE, *London Life in the Eighteenth Century* (1925).

M. C. BUER, *Health, Wealth, and Population in the Early Days of the Industrial Revolution* (1926).

G. T. GRIFFITH, *Population Problems of the Age of Malthus* (1926).

A. REDFORD, *Labour Migration in England, 1800–1850* (1926).

I. PINCHBECK, *Women Workers and the Industrial Revolution, 1750–1850* (1930).

E. W. GILBOY, *Wages in Eighteenth Century England* (1934).

R. F. WEARMOUTH, *Methodism and the Common People of the Eighteenth Century* (1945).

G. D. H. COLE and R. POSTGATE, *The Common People, 1746–1946* (1946).

Chapter VI Changes in Agriculture

G. SLATER, *The English Peasantry and the Enclosure of the Common Fields* (1909).

A. H. JOHNSON, *The Disappearance of the Small Landowner* (1909).

W. H. R. CURTLER, *A Short History of English Agriculture* (1909).

J. L. and B. HAMMOND, *The Village Labourer, 1760–1832* (1911, new ed. in two vols., 1947).

LORD ERNLE, *English Farming, Past and Present* (1912: 5th ed., 1936).

W. H. R. CURTLER, *The Enclosure and Redistribution of our Land* (1920).

W. G. HOSKINS, *The Midland Peasant* (1957).

J. THIRSK, *English Peasant Farming* (1957).

R. TROW-SMITH, *A History of British Livestock Husbandry, 1700–1900* (1959).

W. H. CHALONER, 'Bibliography of recent work on enclosure, the open fields, and related topics' (*Agricultural History Review*, Vol. II, 1954).

Chapter VII The Economic Effects of the French Wars

T. TOOKE, *History of Prices*: Vol. I (1838).

S. DOWELL, *History of Taxation and Taxes in England* (4 vols., 1884).

A. CUNNINGHAM, *British Credit in the last Napoleonic War* (1910).

E. CANNAN, *The Paper Pound of 1797–1821* (1919).

E. F. HECKSCHER, *The Continental System* (1922).

W. F. GALPIN, *The Grain Supply of England during the Napoleonic Period* (1925).

F. O. DARVALL, *Popular Disturbances and Public Order in Regency England* (1934).

F. A. WELLS, *The British Hosiery Trade* (1935).

A. HOPE-JONES, *Income Tax in the Napoleonic Wars* (1939).

A. FARNSWORTH, *Addington, Author of the Modern Income Tax* (1951).

L. S. PRESSNELL, *Country Banking in the Industrial Revolution* (1956).

F. CROUZET, *L'Economie Britannique et le Blocus Continental, 1806–1813* (2 vols., 1958).

Chapter VIII Agrarian Distress and Poor Law Reform

W. COBBETT, *Rural Rides* (1830)—cheap edition in Everyman's Library, 2 vols., from the edition of 1853.

Poor Law Commissioners' Report, 1834 (reprinted 1905, Cd. 2728).

SIR GEORGE NICHOLLS, *History of the English Poor Law*: Vol. II (1854).

T. MACKAY, *History of the English Poor Law*: Vol. III (1899).

D. MARSHALL, *The English Poor in the Eighteenth Century* (1926).

S. and B. WEBB, *English Local Government: English Poor Law History*: Part I: *The Old Poor Law* (1927). Part II: *The Last Hundred Years* (2 vols., 1929).

L. P. ADAMS, *Agricultural Depression and Farm Relief in England, 1813–1852* (1932).

See also the works mentioned under Chapter VI.

Chapter IX Industrial and Commercial Progress

G. R. PORTER, *The Progress of the Nation* (3 vols., 1836–43).

N. J. SILBERLING, 'British Prices and Business Cycles, 1779–1850' (*Review of Economic Statistics*, prelim. Vol. V, Supplement 2, 1923).

C. DAY, 'The distribution of industrial occupations in England, 1841–1861' (*Trans. Connecticut Academy of Arts and Sciences*, Vol. XXVIII, March 1927, pp. 79–235).

G. C. ALLEN, *The Industrial Development of Birmingham and the Black Country* (1929).

H. D. FONG, *Triumph of Factory System in England* (1930).

W. W. ROSTOW, *British Economy of the Nineteenth Century* (1948).

A. D. GAYER, W. W. ROSTOW and A. J. SCHWARTZ, *Growth and Fluctuation of the British Economy, 1790–1850* (2 vols., 1953).

See especially Sir John Clapham, *op. cit.*, Chapters V, VI, X and XII.

CHAPTER X LABOUR ORGANISATION AND CO-OPERATION

S. and B. WEBB, *History of Trade Unionism* (1894, 2nd ed. 1920).

G. WALLAS, *Life of Francis Place* (1898, 2nd ed., 1918).

F. PODMORE, *Life of Robert Owen* (2 vols., 1906).

M. HOVELL, *The Chartist Movement* (1918, reimpression 1950).

M. BEER, *A History of British Socialism* (2 vols., 1919–20).

C. R. FAY, *Life and Labour in the Nineteenth Century* (1920).

R. F. WEARMOUTH, *Methodism and the Working Class Movements of England, 1800–1850* (1937).

D. WILLIAMS, *John Frost* (1939).

G. D. H. COLE, *Chartist Portraits* (1941).

G. D. H. COLE, *A Century of Co-operation* (1945).

M. I. COLE, *Robert Owen of New Lanark* (1953).

A. R. SCHOYEN, *The Chartist Challenge: A Portrait of George Julian Harney* (1958).

A. BRIGGS (ed.), *Chartist Studies* (1959).

CHAPTER XI LABOUR LEGISLATION AND SOCIAL REFORM

E. HODDER, *Life and Work of the Seventh Earl of Shaftesbury* (3 vols., 1886).

B. L. HUTCHINS, *The Public Health Agitation, 1833–1848* (1909).

B. L. HUTCHINS and A. HARRISON, *History of Factory Legislation* (1911).

J. L. and B. HAMMOND, *The Town Labourer, 1760–1832* (1917), especially Chapters VIII and IX; *Lord Shaftesbury* (1923); *The Age of the Chartists, 1832–1854* (1930).

J. W. BREADY, *Lord Shaftesbury and Social-Industrial Progress* (1926).

C. DRIVER, *Tory Radical: The Life of Richard Oastler* (1946).

M. W. THOMAS, *The Early Factory Legislation* (1948).

S. E. FINER, *The Life and Times of Sir Edwin Chadwick* (1952).

R. A. LEWIS, *Edwin Chadwick and the Public Health Movement, 1832–1854* (1952).

W. H. HUTT, 'The factory system of the early nineteenth century' (*Capitalism and the Historians*, ed. F. A. Hayek, 1954, pp. 160–88).

F. ENGELS, *The Condition of the Working Class in England* (trans. and ed. W. O. Henderson and W. H. Chaloner, 1958).

CHAPTER XII CURRENCY, BANKING AND JOINT-STOCK REFORMS

R. R. FORMOY, *Historical Foundations of Modern Company Law* (1923).

J. SYKES, *The Amalgamation Movement in English Banking* (1926).

T. E. GREGORY, *Introduction to Tooke and Newmarch's History of Prices* (1928); *Select Statutes, Documents, and Reports relating to British Banking* (1929), especially the introduction.

A. E. FEAVEARYEAR, *The Pound Sterling* (1931).

G. H. EVANS, *British Corporation Finance, 1775–1850* (1936).

B. C. HUNT, *Development of the Business Corporation in England, 1800–1867* (1936)

A. B. DUBOIS, *The English Business Company after the Bubble Act, 1720–1800* (1938).

E. WOOD, *English Theories of Central Banking Control, 1819–1858* (1939).

SIR JOHN CLAPHAM, *The Bank of England: A History* (2 vols., 1944).

C. A. COOKE, *Corporation, Trust and Company* (1950).

T. S. ASHTON and R. S. SAYERS, *Papers in English Monetary History* (1953).

CHAPTER XIII FISCAL POLICY AND TARIFF REFORM

S. BUXTON, *Finance and Politics, 1783–1885* (2 vols., 1888).

C. S. PARKER, *Sir Robert Peel* (3 vols., 1892–99).

J. MORLEY, *Life of Gladstone* (3 vols., 1903).

A. W. ACWORTH, *Financial Reconstruction in England, 1815–1822* (1925).

D. G. BARNES, *A History of the English Corn Laws from 1660–1846* (1930).

A. L. DUNHAM, *The Anglo-French Treaty of Commerce of 1860* (1930).

C. R. FAY, *The Corn Laws and Social England* (1932).

R. L. SCHUYLER, *The Fall of the Old Colonial System: a Study in British Free Trade, 1770–1870* (1945).

R. PROUTY, *The Transformation of the Board of Trade, 1830–1855* (1957).

L. BROWN, *The Board of Trade and the Free Trade Movement, 1830–42* (1958).

N. MCCORD, *The Anti-Corn Law League, 1838–1846* (1958).

A. H. IMLAH, *Economic Elements in the Pax Britannica: Studies in British Foreign Trade in the Nineteenth Century* (1958).

CHAPTER XIV THE DEVELOPMENT OF TRANSPORT

E. CLEVELAND STEVENS, *English Railways: their Development and their Relation to the State* (1915).

W. T. JACKMAN, *Development of Transportation in Modern England* (2 vols., 1916).

H. G. LEWIN, *Early British Railways* (1925); *The Railway Mania and its Aftermath* (1936).

R. S. LAMBERT, *The Railway King, 1800–1871* (1934).

C. E. LEE, *The Evolution of Railways* (1937, 2nd rev. ed., 1942).

C. F. D. MARSHALL, *A History of British Railways down to the year 1830* (1938).

D. B. TYLER, *Steam Conquers the Atlantic* (1939).

C. H. ELLIS, *British Railway History . . . 1830–1876* (1954).

L. T. C. ROLT, *Isambard Kingdom Brunel* (1957).

L. T. C. ROLT, *Thomas Telford* (1958).

H. P. SPRATT, *The Birth of the Steamboat* (1958).

L. T. C. ROLT, *George and Robert Stephenson* (1960).

See also SIR JOHN CLAPHAM, *Economic History of Modern Britain*, Vol. I, Chapters III, IX and XII.

CHAPTER XV THE AGE OF NEW GOLD

See especially TOOKE and NEWMARCH, *History of Prices*, Vol. VI (1857), and SIR WALTER LAYTON and G. CROWTHER, *Introduction to the Study of Prices* (ed. of 1938). With J. S. MILL, *Principles of Political Economy* (1848), Book IV, Chapter VII, 'On the probable futurity of the labouring classes', compare A. TOYNBEE, *op. cit.*, Chapter XIV, on 'The future of the working classes'. Among more recent books to be consulted are L. H. JENKS, *The Migration of British Capital to 1875* (1927), and J. R. T. HUGHES, *Fluctuations in Trade, Industry and Finance: a study of British Economic Development, 1850–1860* (1960).

INDEX

INDEX

Cranage, George and Thomas, 35
Crawshays of Cyfarthfa, 48; Richard, 51
Credit system, 12, 49-50, 52, 99-103, 132-6, 169-80, 192, 220-1
Crewe, 208
Cromford, 22, 47
Crompton, Samuel, 23-4, 50, 53
Crowley, Sir Ambrose, 6, 51
Cuba, 172
Cunard, Samuel, 215
Currency, 64, 66, 70 n, 99-103, 112, 132, 135, 143-5, 169-77, 180, 219-21
Cutlery, 32, 36, 55

Dale, David, 24, 51, 64
Dalhousie, Lord, 211-12
Darbys of Coalbrookdale, 7, 33, 35-6, 40-1, 48-9, 51, 54
Darlington, 203-4, 207
Davy, Sir Humphry, 39
Deanston, 64
Debt, National, 100-4, 186-7, 193, 198, 200
Denmark, 90
Derby and Derbyshire, 13, 18, 47, 54, 64, 76, 140, 206-7
Derwent, River, 13, 22
Disraeli, Benjamin, 196, 225-6
Dissenters, see Nonconformity
Distress, social, 63-4, 66, 70, 88, 96-7, 105; chap. 8, passim; 124, 134-5, 148, 198, 223
Dockyards, 5
Doherty, John, 139-40, 155
Domestic industry, 9-11, 17, 20-1, 24, 32, 47, 50-2, 63-4, 68-70, 85, 124-5, 152-3, 224
Domestic servants, 17
"Dorchester labourers", 141
Douglas, River, 12
Drainage, land, 67, 76, 86, 127, 197, 218; mines, 37-8; towns, 67, 165-6; see also Sanitation
Dublin, 13
Dudley Castle, 7

Durham, 72, 126, 128, 207
Dyeing, 27-8, 55

East Anglia, 27, 128 and n
East India Company, 4, 56
Eden, William (later Lord Auckland), 57
Education, 146-7, 153, 161-2
Eggs, 199-200
Egypt, 220
Elliott, Ebenezer, 146
Emigration, 4, 138, 149, 219, 221
Employers' organisations, 46, 53-9, 97, 137-8
Enclosure, 14, 76-81, 83-7, 95; see also Agriculture
Engineering, chap. 3, passim; 49-53, 126, 149, 216
Excise duties, 57-8, 189, 193, 221
Export trade, 4, 8, 12, 17, 19, 24, 55-6, 70-1, 75, 80, 88-93, 110, 126, 128-32, 186, 190-3, 200-1, 217, 219, 224

Factories and factory system, 5-6, 10-11, 17-27, 29, 32, 47-50, 52-3, 63-7, 68-9, 85, 97, 123-4, 128-9, 134, 152-9, 162-4, 224
Factory legislation, 66-7, 99, 145, 150, 153-9, 161-4, 198, 222-3, 225
Fairs and markets, 12
Faringdon, 121
Fenians, 223
Fielden of Todmorden, Joshua, 46, 51; John, 163
Finance, 12, 46, 94, 99-105, 117, 122, 132-6, 139, 154, 169-80, 198-9, 206-7, 218-19; see also Banking
Finance, public, 57, 99-105, 117, 122, 163; chap. 13, passim; see also Debt, National, and Taxation
Flax, 131, 201
Florida, 172

237

Ireland and Irish, 57, 66, 68, 95, 101, 131, 135-6, 183, 195-6, 204, 213, 215
Iron and steel industries, 6, 7, 8, 11; chap. 3, *passim*; 48-9, 53-4, 55, 57-8, 94, 125-9, 149, 201, 203, 214-17
Irwell, River, 12
Italy, 19, 90

Jenny (spinning), 21-3, 26, 51, 123
Jevons, W. S., 223
Joint stock organisation, 99-100, 135, 170-1, 175-84, 198, 225

Kay, John, 7, 19-20, 25
Kay, Robert, 20
Kelly, William, 24
Kent, 85
King, Gregory, 75-6

Labour exchanges (Owenite), 144-5
Labour organisation, 11, 46, 52, 55, 59; chap. 5, *passim*; 95-9; chap. 10, *passim*; 222-3, 225
Lancashire, 10, 12, 13, 14, 19-28, 40, 44-5, 55, 72, 76, 85, 93, 123, 127-8, 140, 151, 152-3, 155-6, 160, 202, 221, 223
Law Times, 184
Lead-mining, 49, 129
Leeds, 140, 205, 207
Leicestershire and Leicester, 78-9, 86-7, 207
Liability, limited, 180-4
Lincolnshire, 76
Linen industry, 10, 20, 25, 27, 51, 55, 129, 131, 197, 201
Liverpool, 4, 13-15, 19, 203-7, 215
Living conditions, 66-9, 153, 164; *see also* Housing
Lloyd's, 216
Localisation of industries, 30-2, 123, 127-8
Lombe, Sir Thomas, 18, 22, 47, 64

London, 4, 6, 7, 12-14, 18, 28, 49, 57-8, 61, 63, 67, 76, 82, 98, 125, 144, 146, 154, 156, 165-6, 170, 177, 180, 187, 191-2, 204-8, 215
London Working Men's Association, 146
Londonderry, Lord, 161, 209
Lovett, William, 146-8
Loyd, S. J. (Lord Overstone), 175
Luddism and machine breaking, 63-6, 71, 97-8

McAdam, J. L., 203
Macclesfield, 18
McCulloch, J. R., 137
Machinery, 5, 9-10, 17-27, 29-30, 32, 35-6, 47-9, 63-6, 70, 80-1, 96, 98, 123-31, 153, 158, 218; export of machinery, 55, 138, 201
Manchester, 13-15, 18, 19, 24, 26, 28, 55, 57, 59, 62, 66-8, 97, 123, 126, 134, 140, 147, 194-5, 203-4, 206-8
Manures, 218
Maudslay, Henry, 126
Mechanics' institutes, 225
Medical knowledge, advances in, 72-3
Melbourne, Lord, 189
Merchants, 4, 10, 12, 14, 47, 55, 58-9, 90, 133, 169-70, 187
Mersey, River, 12, 15
Metal industries, 5-8, 11, 18; chap. 3, *passim*; 47-56, 94-5, 125, 128, 131, 197, 221; *see also* Iron and steel, Copper and brass
Middlesex, 45
Migration, labour, 52, 64 n, 66, 86, 87 n, 111, 113, 164-5, 224
Mines Royal Company, 6
Mining industries, 5, 6, 11, 15, 18; chap. 3, *passim*; 58, 96, 98, 109, 125-9, 159-61, 198, 219-21; *see also* Coal industry, Lead-mining
Monopolistic combinations, 53-6, 177-80, 205-13
Morpeth, Lord, 167-8

Morrison, James, 209, 212
Mule (spinning), 23-4, 27, 123
Muller, Anton, of Danzig, 25
Municipal reform, 164, 167, 225

Nail-making, 32, 34-6, 51, 55
Napoleon Bonaparte, 53, 58, 90-3
Nasmyth, James, 126
National Association for the Protection of Labour (1830-1), 140
National Association of United Trades (1845), 149
National Union of Cotton Spinners (1829), 140
Navigation Laws, 4, 188, 213-14, 216, 225
Need, Samuel, 47
Neilson, J. B., 125
New Lanark, 24, 46, 64, 129, 153-4
New York (City), 215
New York (State), 183
Newcastle-upon-Tyne, 6, 13, 33, 101, 207
Newcomen, Thomas ("fire" engine), 7, 33, 37-8, 40-2, 44, 48
Newspapers, 62
Newton-le-Willows, 206
Nicholls, Sir George, 65
Nonconformity, 46
Norfolk and Norwich, 55, 78 n, 81-2, 128 n
Normanby, Lord, 167
North America, 4, 19, 188, 214-15; see also America (U.S.A.)
Northamptonshire and Northampton, 22, 86
Northumberland, 126, 128, 203
Northern Star, 146
Nottingham and Notts., 10, 13, 22, 27, 44, 47, 76, 128, 140
Nuts, 200

Oastler, Richard, 155
O'Brien, J. Bronterre, 148
O'Connell, Daniel, 195
O'Connor, Feargus, 146-8, 195

Oldham, 62
Oldknow, Samuel (of Mellor), 46, 62 n, 64
Onions, Peter, 35
Open-field system, 68, 76-8, 81, 83-7; see also Agriculture
Ordnance and munitions, 5-6, 34-5, 48, 58, 94, 129, 200
Overseas trade, 4, 8, 11, 56-7, 88-93, 130-2, 185-6, 217, 219-21
Owen, Robert, 46, 51, 141-5, 150, 153-4

Paisley, 147
Palmer, Horsley, 172
Palmerston, Viscount, 164
Paper industry, 7-8, 57, 197
Parliamentary reform and representation, 54, 145-8, 156, 225
Partnership, law of, 180-2
Patten, Wilson, 212
Paul, Lewis, 19, 20-21
Pedlars, 12
Peel, Robert, 28, 46, 51
Peel, Sir Robert (the elder), 46, 153-5
Peel, Sir Robert (the younger), 159, 162-3, 169-70, 175, 188, 190-9
Percival, Dr. Thomas, 66-7
Persia, 190
Philosophic Radicals (Utilitarians), 118, 137-8, 154
Pitt the Younger, 57-8, 100, 103-4, 185-6
Place, Francis, 137-9, 143
Poor laws and pauperism, 52, 65, 67, 68 n, 72, 75, 96, and n, 111, 113-22, 145, 148, 152-3, 165, 221-2
Poor Law Amendment Act (1834), 118-22
Population and depopulation, 3, 70-3, 75, 77, 81, 86-7, 112-13, 218, 224
Postal services, 195, 215, 221
Porter, G. R., 160 n, 189

Portugal, 172, 220
Potatoes, 77, 82, 135, 196, 213
Pottery industry, 11, 57, 128, 140
Power loom, 25-7, 124-5, 217
Preston, 129, 204-6
Preston, Richard, M.P., 111
Prestonpans, 28
Prices, 54, 56, 64, 66, 69-73, 75, 78, 88, 94-5, 101-2, 109-17, 129-30, 132-4, 144, 169-70, 173, 190, 193-4, 218-21

Quakers, 46, 154

Railway Boards, 211-13
Railways, 16, 36, 39-40, 126, 135, 147, 198, 202-13, 217-19; railway companies: Birmingham & Derby, 207; Grand Junction, 204, 206-8; Great North of England, 207; Great Western, 207-8; Liverpool & Manchester, 203, 207; London & Birmingham, 204, 207; London & North Western, 207-8; Manchester & Birmingham, 208; Midland, 206-7, 210; Midland Counties, 206-7; North Midland, 207; North Union, 204-6; Preston & Wigan, 205; Stockton & Darlington, 204; Warrington & Newton-le-Willows, 206; Wigan Branch, 205; York & North Midland, 206-7
Rainhill trials (1829), 204
Reciprocity Acts, 188
Rents, 75, 81-2, 95, 109, 112-13, 218
Riots and social disturbances, 26, 63-6, 71, 95-8, 112-13, 121, 138, 147, 223
Rivers and river transport, 12-13, 22, 27, 127, 202-3, 215-16
Roads and road transports, 13-14, 45, 79, 86, 122, 125, 202-3, 213
Roberts, Richard, 24, 123

Robinson, F. J., 132-3, 187-8
Rochdale Pioneers, 150-1
Rocket locomotive, 204
Roebuck, John, 28, 43, 51
Rotherhithe, 49
Royal William steamship, 215
Royal Society of London, 7
Runcorn, 15
Russell, Lord John, 163, 195-6
Russia, 31, 53, 92, 94, 132, 172, 219

Sadler, M. T., 156-7
St.-Simon, 142
Sanitation, 66-8, 164-8, 222, 225
Sankey Navigation, 15
Salt industry, 12
Savannah steamship, 215
Savings banks, 225
Savery, Thomas ("fire" engine), 40
Saxony, 9, 20, 80, 130
Science, 7, 81, 218
Scotland, 5, 24, 31, 46, 47, 51, 53, 58, 82, 95-6, 124-5, 127, 151, 154, 160, 207, 215, 217
Scotsman, The, 137
Seine, River, 216
Settlement and Removal, Act of (1662), 52
Settlement and Removal, Act of (1795), 117
Seymour, Lord, 209
Sheep, 9, 78-80, 84, 197
Sheffield, 32, 51, 59, 146, 223
Shipping and shipbuilding, 4-6, 35, 49, 56, 89-93, 109, 125-7, 138, 188, 208, 213-17
Shoemaking, 145
Short Time Committees, 155, 157
Shropshire, 34, 44-5, 54
Silesia, 130
Silk industry, 8, 10, 18-19, 22, 47, 55, 57, 129, 134, 155, 158, 188, 197
Silver, 221

Working conditions, 64–9, 96–9, 152–64
Worsley, 15, 37
Wright, I. and J., bankers, of Nottingham, 47
Wright, William, of Manchester, 24

Yorkshire and York, 9, 13, 26–7, 44–5, 54–5, 68, 72, 76, 94, 128, 155–6, 160, 206–7
Young, Arthur, 81–2

Zollverein, 132, 214